"It does not matter how much education a black man has, where he went to college, or how much fame and fortune he has attained; he can expect to suffer some injustices in his life based entirely on the color of his skin. This situation, regardless of how it manifests, cannot help but cause him to be angry. For many different reasons, however, black men choose not to share the pain, anguish, and hurt they experience. Instead, they choose to be 'cool' and the chances are quite good that many of the black men that have experienced hurts to their pride and self-respect feel very angry about being treated unfairly. . . .

"Much has been written about what people can do to cope with anger in the short run, but the more significant question is whether a man, over time, can use his anger as an incentive and fuel to achieve greater clarity and discover new and more self-empowering ways to deal with old problems and new ones when they arise."

—Ernest H. Johnson, Ph.D.

BROTHERS
ON THE MEND

Understanding and Healing
Anger for African-American Men
and Women

ERNEST H. JOHNSON, Ph.D.

POCKET BOOKS
New York   London   Toronto   Sydney   Singapore

POCKET BOOKS, a division of Simon & Schuster Inc.
1230 Avenue of the Americas, New York, NY 10020

Copyright © 1998 by Dr. Ernest Johnson

Originally published in 1998 in hardcover by Pocket Books

Library of Congress Cataloging-in-Publication Data

Johnson, Ernest H.
    Brothers on the mend : understanding and healing male anger for African-American men and women / Ernest H. Johnson.
        p.   cm.
    Includes index.
    ISBN 0-671-51146-7
    1. Anger.   2. Afro-American men—Psychology.   3. Masculinity.
    I. Title.
    BF575.A5J63   1998   97-43194
    152.4'7'081—dc21   CIP

First Pocket Books trade paperback printing January 1999

10 9 8 7 6 5 4 3 2

POCKET and colophon are registered trademarks of Simon & Schuster Inc.

Cover design by Tom McKeveny
Front cover photo © Erica Lansner/Black Star

Printed in the U.S.A.

For every man, woman, and child touched by the African-American men who gathered on the Mall in Washington, D.C., on October 16, 1995. May this book serve the purpose of reminding each of us that every day we wake up is a Day of Atonement and Reconciliation and a day to be proud of the Million Man March.

Acknowledgments

I must acknowledge that I was helped immensely in the overall organization of this book by Mr. Vern Smith, who is the managing editor for *Newsweek* in Atlanta, Georgia. I am thankful for his commitment and help in nurturing this book from conception to completion.

I wish to acknowledge Paul McCarthy, my editor during the initial stages of this book, whose encouragement, insightful criticism, and endless patience enabled me to make this a better book. No writer could ask for a more sensitive and understanding editor. I am also very grateful to each person at Pocket Books who succeeded Paul for their thoughtful editorial assistance. Finally, I thank my agent, Denise Stinson, for consistently sound advice and for believing in my work. I am forever thankful for her inspiring, awesome, and life-transforming suggestions about how to turn a good project into a great masterpiece.

I offer a special thanks to all the individuals who shared their stories with me. I have presented the information in a way that guarantees the confidentiality of our conversations. May this book be a source of guidance and inspiration in your search for a peaceful existence.

Contents

Contents

PART 2
OTHER STRATEGIES FOR
MANAGING ANGER AND STRESS

Introduction

This book is for African-American men who are concerned about the negativity that anger has caused in their lives.

It's for those brothers who want less conflict in their relationships and those who seek better ways of expressing their needs and addressing challenges constructively. For those black men who were inspired by the spiritual significance of the Million Man March, this book will provide some specific guidelines for enhancing their personal development and for strengthening family relations.

It is also for black women, some of whom may be single mothers concerned about preventing anger in their sons. For sisters who yearn to understand the rage that can sometimes consume their man, ultimately destroying the relationship, this book will provide some clues and suggest techniques for coping.

It is time to deal with the cancerous effect of unchecked anger. Like an inexorable tidal wave, the health and emotional problems of African-American men reached an acute state over the past decade. AIDS and violence threaten to wipe out large segments of the young black male population before they can even consider a future. Perhaps saddest of all, we continue to lose many black men because of their inability to come to terms with the role of anger, hostility, and rage in their lives. Whereas the life expectancy for most Americans has remained at record high levels, the life span of African-American males has actually declined, and the trend continues even today.

Even though a large part of the discrepancy in health between black and white males can be attributed to well-established lifestyle risk factors (e.g., excessive smoking, alcohol intake, hypertension), it is possible that the stress associated with economic and psychological impoverishment may be the major cause of excessive use of alcohol and cigarettes as well as poor dietary habits and engagement in risky sexual behaviors. It is also possible that the health and emotional problems of black American males are directly related to the style used to cope with stress. The bulk of the evidence suggests a strong association between having conflicts in the expression of anger when provoked and homicide as well as major health problems such as hypertension, heart disease, and cancer. Recent studies also show that anger and rage are also related to risky sexual behavioral practices that increase the chance of being exposed to HIV.

Black men are two and one-half times as likely to be unemployed as whites, and African-American men earn substantially lower incomes even if they have reached the middle class. If the primary means for male identity in our society is the "job" you have and the "work" that you do, then the inability of African-American men to gain meaningful employment, a decent education, and a good income means that they are nothing—"invisible" men as the black writer Ralph Ellison put it. Ultimately, the lack of meaningful employment results in a "downward spiral" ending with a loss of self-respect, intense and often overwhelming feelings of hopelessness, anger and fear, and further interpersonal and economic problems for black men and their families.

What I intend to accomplish with this book is to identify problems associated with the experience and expression of anger and suggest solutions. This book is important because other books dealing with the management of anger don't offer prescriptions for coping with frustrations that are specific to black men. Although the problems of black men are not new, they have been discussed without any hint at offering solutions. Black psychologists have been reluctant to openly discuss the problems of black men because of the fear that any admission of problems can be used to further divide our people.

My interest in the deadly role that anger has on the livelihood of black men emerged from my commitment to help empower black men to live their dreams. My training in clinical and medical psychology has provided me the opportunity to understand the role that anger plays in the lives of black men. The information for this book was assembled from interviews with black men, research I've conducted over the past decade, and my personal experiences with anger. Like many of the brothers who are described throughout the book, I've had my difficulties handling anger and I've seen how this perfectly normal emotion affects relationships and how it contributes to poor health.

Many of the brothers who are unable to recognize anger in their lives do sense that they have been under immense stress and that much of this stress is still present. If you are one of those brothers who usually feels stressed-out rather than actual anger, perhaps it would be helpful for you to substitute the word *stressed-out* every time the word *anger* appears in this book to make it more applicable to you.

Take every story that is told very seriously and as an example of the situations that African-American men encounter. If you are a woman reading this book, it is important that you consider the possibility that the men in your life (e.g., father, husband, son, brother, lover, cousin, friend, etc.) have had encounters that are similar to those that are described, and yet you are unaware of the hurt and emotional anguish that they have experienced. In fact, it is very possible that you are not even aware that they had the encounter in the first place. Sure, you may have noticed that the brother looked depressed, seemed angry, and was generally acting a little strange, but in many situations black men don't talk to their women about the frequent assaults on their pride and dignity.

To constructively use anger as a tool for change and healing, we will be learning to develop skills in six areas:

1. How to identify situations where black men are angry, and yet are either unaware of the anger or are suppressing it. We will focus on learning how to ask ourselves and others the kind of questions that allow the fullest reasons and solutions to the challenge. Some examples:

- What really is going on in this situation?
- What do I think about the situation?
- What about the situation makes me angry?
- What do I feel?
- What am I responsible for in this situation?
- What should I do?
- How do I want the situation changed?
- What are the things that I will not do?
- What can I learn from this situation?

When most of us encounter frustrating situations that cause angry feelings to flare up, we tend to ask "Why me?" questions that presuppose limitations on how we can deal with the challenge. Some examples:

- Why am I angry?
- Why is this person angry at me?
- Why can't we just get along?
- Why am I always the person who gets into trouble?
- Why do I allow myself to always act this way?

Not surprisingly, "Why me?" questions generate mostly negative answers that offer few solutions for managing the current challenge or preventing the situation from repeating itself. Managing anger effectively goes hand in hand with developing a more powerful way of asking questions that help us gain access to the resources that we need to make happen whatever we want.

2. How to identify core beliefs, values, assumptions, and attitudes underlying problems with anger. Essentially, the way a man feels and what he experiences and internalizes as anger comes from what he is focusing his attention on. The problem is that men delete most of what else is going on around them beyond their beliefs. Most of us are consciously aware of only a few bits and pieces of the situations that we are challenged by. As a consequence, we seldom gain a full perspective on the cause of our anger and rage. While each of us has the power to focus on the positive and negative aspects in our lives, too many black men are conditioned to overlook the positives and get trapped in the negatives. If a man focuses on being angry and violent, he is sure to react in precisely that manner. As you learn to restructure anger-triggering thoughts, you'll find that you are less likely to become upset by challenges.

3. How to identify and interrupt your habitual ways of looking at the world and how inner dialogue and body language can trigger anger and rage. Each of us has a well-established set of rituals that lead to buildups of anger. Learning how to observe and change these habitual ways of behavior can ultimately increase our ability to respond to familiar situations in new ways.

4. You will learn how to condition yourself so that you associate things in ways that make you feel and behave the way that you want. It is my belief that most black men desire to deal with the challenges of life in a peaceful, stress-free manner. However, they have developed so many negative neuro-associations about being black men that they act like robots with but one choice in dealing with adversity. But, a man who is free perceives every challenge from the perspective that he has an unlimited number of ways to deal with them. While the physical bonds of slavery are gone, many black men continue to be imprisoned by their own minds and the rage they harbored about the past.

5. You will also increase your ability to cope effectively with stress. Instead of exploding when stress exceeds your tolerance threshold, you can use specific relaxation and meditation procedures to gain a better perspective about the

challenges. You will also learn how to identify stresses and needs that lie below your anger so that you can better understand and move past the real problem.

6. You will also learn how to expose some of the common obstacles to self-development that African-American men encounter. The major aim of these sections is to address the question of whether black men perceive that the obstacles to success are blocked by internal factors such as emotional maturity or external factors such as racism.

In the chapters that follow, we will take a close look at the anatomy of anger and how this basic emotion can affect every relationship, including the one that we have with ourselves. This book explores the beliefs and values that comprise the foundation for why black men suppress their feelings.

The first part of the book will provide you with a better understanding of the reasons black men have problems with anger. The areas evaluated include family relationships, black women, work-related stress, and how men deal with their own health challenges. There will be a discussion of the circumstances that trigger anger in these situations. At the end of each chapter is a section entitled "Prescriptions for Change," which describes several ways to deal with the challenges. Strategies and exercises for increasing self-awareness are also offered to help you create your own destiny. As a rule, the more time you spend using the specific prescriptions and self-awareness strategies, the more likely you are to reduce and eliminate anger problems from your life.

The second part of the book describes methods for coping with anger, frustration, and stress. The coping techniques focus on strategies for stopping anger before it escalates, overcoming obstacles to healing and managing anger, and the management of stress using relaxation and meditation techniques. While these techniques apply to all men, they are presented here to augment the specific techniques that are offered in the first section of the book. Finally, we will address the psychology of staying cool and preventing anger, focusing on the role of spirituality in managing stress.

If you are concerned about the problems of anger in your life or a health problem, it is always best to seek out professional help. The exercises offered throughout the book can help you cope with your feelings, but the prescriptions that are offered are no substitute for professional psychological or medical advice about your health. *If you have a health problem, it is always important to have yourself examined by a physician and follow the medical regime that you are provided. Stress associated with anger and frustration can contribute to the onset of health problems, aggravate existing health problems, and interfere with the care provided by a physician. Because of these possibilities it would also be a good idea for you to consider practicing the stress managing techniques that are described throughout the book and particularly those in chapter 11, "The Psychology of Staying Cool."*

Coping with angry and hurt feelings is difficult, but it can be done. Read on!

PART I

UNDERSTANDING ANGER AND LIFE STRESS

1

Why Are
Black Men Angry?

Tony, a thirty-nine-year-old black business executive, had just returned home after dropping his wife and kids off at the airport to visit his mother-in-law. He was carrying grocery bags into his new home in a predominantly white neighborhood when a police car pulled up. Two white officers got out, eyeing Tony suspiciously. A burglary had recently occurred in the area, they explained. Despite Tony's protest that he owned the home, one of the officers demanded to see some identification. Tony discovered he had left his wallet on the kitchen counter, but his explanations seemed only to further convince the officers that something was amiss. Saying that they were being cautious and checking out all strangers, they immediately handcuffed Tony. He felt his muscles start to tighten. His breathing became shallow as he started to perspire and feel both nervous and angry about what was taking place.

Inside the house, the officers made Tony accompany them as they walked through looking in every room and closet for his "accomplice." The feeling of wanting to explode in indignation—a natural impulse for any man—seized Tony. But given his situation, he swallowed the urge, feeling his heart race. The tightness in his muscles seemed to spread to his chest. Only after Tony showed them his identification and enough pictures throughout the house of himself and his family did the policemen finally acknowledge that Tony was a homeowner, not a burglar.

The policemen apologized and left, but the anger that Tony had suppressed like a smoldering volcano had built to a white-hot rage.

Alone in his new house, the stress of the incident affected him physically that night as well. He could not sleep. Exhausted and still upset the next day, he took off from work. Try as he has to forget it, the incident is still fresh in Tony's memory, paining at him like a sore that won't heal. He constantly frets about its occurring again, in a setting that could add to his discomfort. "I am especially worried about the impact of being questioned like this in front of my wife and family since I have never told them about the event," he says.

Tony's story is typical of the many situations that cause psychological damage and worry in black men. Like him, many black men prefer to suppress their anger and rage, suffering the consequences, rather than open up and talk out their feelings. These "cool brothers" express their angry feelings in a number of nonproductive ways—overuse of tobacco, drowning the bile through drinking, or releasing the welled-up feelings in a burst of violence—often against loved ones. Talking through the feelings is not seen as an option because they want to appear strong and "manly." But understanding the forces that can cause sudden, even murderous rage—and more important, learning how to manage and control the impulse, may be the most important factors in the survival of African-American men, and, by extension, black people.

Anger, much like emotions such as anxiety and sadness, is a normal, natural, and basic emotional response to stress and provocations. It is experienced in situations that represent a threat or possible loss of some valuable possession (a physical object, right, relationship, or opinion)—through acts by others (a person, group, or society) that are perceived as being unjustifiable or as a violation of one's expectations and standards. Under these circumstances, especially if the loss is sudden, anger will be intensely experienced. The degree of anger is related to one's temperament, level of personal stress, how one has learned from parents and others to handle provocations, and the value placed on the possessions that are about to be taken away.

Injustices, betrayal, exploitation, manipulation and mistreatment, sexual harassment, and racism will cause anger. Threats to the ego such as a direct put-down or derogatory comments can also produce anger.

When Texas billionaire and former presidential candidate Ross Perot used the phrase "You people" in a speech to a convention of NAACP delegates in 1992, for example, he was startled by a chorus of angry boos from his mostly black audience. Repeated blows to the ego can create an angry black man with low self-esteem, a person who does not care about himself or anyone else. Such a state of despair allows for what appears to be random violent outbursts or withdrawal into hopelessness.

As Tony's case illustrates, angry reactions involve two things: psychological events, consisting of negative feelings and hateful thoughts, and biological reactions, such as elevated adrenaline levels, rapid heart rate, perspiration, muscle tension, and tightness in the chest. Anger is a basic emotion that supports our behavior in times of stress, frustration, and emergency. It alerts us to the presence of danger as well as prepares us to meet the danger through a basic, evolutionary process called the "fight or flight" response.

The fight/flight response is a set of biological changes that prepare the person for either flight from the danger and threat or an attack against it. The purpose of these biological stress responses—which humans share with all other animals—is to prepare the individual for the action that is about to occur. Such actions are motivated by a survival instinct. The body is now armed for physical assault, and the person is ready to either face the enemy head-on (fight) or run like hell (flight) to avoid being beat up. But in our civilized world today, often the "enemy" is not even a man but a piece of paper (e.g., an eviction notice, a long-overdue bill, a letter indicating that your position at work will be terminated, divorce papers).

What is the consequence of constantly arming ourselves to deal with events that don't have a real physical threat?

Some psychologists have argued that one of the results is that we become less capable of distinguishing between real and imagined or perceived dangers. Either way, we react to these threats with a set of built-in biological responses that may diminish rather than enhance our survival in these modern times.

Our survival capability is reduced simply because anger was designed to serve as a reaction to physical threats to our survival and not to *psychological* assaults to our pride, diminished self-respect, unfair criticisms and evaluations, frustration, humiliation, exploitations and manipulations.

Unfortunately, we respond *biologically* to these *psychological* attacks as if they were physical. For an entire range of reasons, both historical and contemporary, black men more often than not will harbor more anger than they are willing to admit. Like the temperature gauge in your car, you can either choose to respond to a trouble sign immediately or ignore it as if it were unimportant and will in some magical way start functioning correctly again. Ignoring those little red lights and gauges in the car can become costly. In my case, the engine in my Volkswagen van exploded while I was stuck in rush-hour traffic.

Many black men who disregard the warning signs of repressed anger can suffer similar dire consequences emotionally. The intensity of these hurts grows and becomes the cause of a multitude of explosive interpersonal problems. Many of these men develop adverse psychological symptoms akin to post–traumatic stress—a condition that is often found among men who have survived the traumatic experiences of war. Even the act of showing anger is deeply embedded in America's pyscho-racial history. Expressing anger is considered an acceptable way for men in the majority

6

culture to cope with feeling out of control. In fact, after the explosion, calmness is restored and men hope that all is forgiven. They would have you believe that their angry outbursts are a way of letting off steam to prevent a full-blown explosion and that it's nothing personal. Unfortunately, these bombs tend to go off frequently, and spouses, girlfriends, and innocent children are often the targets (as reflected in the steady increase in spousal and child abuse among all ethnic groups in the United States) because they are convenient and vulnerable.

Anger becomes a shield to hide other emotional responses such as pain or empathy. Being angry is so linked to aggression, in fact, that men in the majority culture grow up believing that expressing anger is what a man has to do to compete against other men on the basketball court, in college, or in the workplace. What gets confusing to black men is that the messages about anger and aggression that they receive are just the opposite. Black men learn that to survive and become successful in white America they must curb and suppress their feelings, especially anger.

What appears to be at the center of much of the suppressed anger and rage among black men is self-doubt, which makes a man distrust his worth and abilities. This is the kind of self-doubt that poisons the collective spirit and memory. It gathers in its wake all of the assorted disappointments, frustrations, deprivations, and racial hurts real or imagined in a man's life before it erupts as uncontrollable anger and rage. Two pivotal causes of anger, racism and learning to handle provocations by imitating the reactions of male role models, provide some of the fuel for the doubt that black men experience.

Information obtained from interviews with the black men described throughout this book provides strong confirmation of this point. For example, most of the men interviewed believed that the major cause of the anger and rage they experience is the violation of rights, unfair treatment, racism, and the way they have learned how to cope with frustration. However, just as many men believed that submerging their natural anger is the wisest choice, particularly when the

7

provocation involves a white person or a person of higher rank or authority. This effort to conceal any cracks in the facade of being the aggressive, "together," in-control brother is a constant with black men. Instead of dealing with anger at its source, they may

- take out their frustration on other blacks as reflected by some of the black-on-black murders
- use alcohol and drugs to cope with the bad feelings
- use wit and humor to minimize the seriousness of the situation
- identify with the source of the oppression and lash out at other blacks as a way of being accepted by the oppressor
- blame white people and racism for their problems
- stay cool, denying the situation and trying to remain unaffected by their feelings
- bury angry and hurt feelings so deeply that they result in chronic depression and hopelessness

None of these responses represent a full acknowledgment of the depth of the anger and rage experienced. Neither do they permit black men to use their anger—a natural response to provocation—to directly address the stressful events and restore balance in their lives and in their physiology. Serious problems occur as a consequence. Some of the ways to cope with stress are presented in chapter 11, "The Psychology of Staying Cool."

Suppressed feelings of anger often find expression in the homes of black men, or on the job. For many brothers these angry feelings can lead to poor health habits or exacerbate existing health problems. One of the most disastrous habits that is often used to cope with anger is drinking.

"I felt upset, angry, and hurt, but then I realized that there was nothing that I could do about this thing except to believe that a system that has more black men behind prison bars than it has in college couldn't possibly provide justice for me. I sure as hell did not believe that the system was going to treat me any different than any other black man," says Gregory.

When Gregory was twenty-five, he was stopped one night and arrested as he was driving home from work. Gregory fit the description of a black man who had murdered a white convenience-store manager during a robbery the day before. Gregory was jailed for several days, even though his alibi, a black male friend, could prove that the two of them were at the friend's house shooting pool at the time of the robbery and murder. After several days and statements from witnesses who described the villain as a man who looked nothing like Gregory, it finally dawned on the police that they had the wrong man.

Even though they apologized and spoke to Gregory's supervisors at work to avert any problems there, the damage had already been done.

After his release, Gregory responded to the event as if it had had no effect on him at all. He was a classic "cool brother" as he talked openly to his family and friends about his ordeal. However, that same day, he resumed a habit that he had worked for several years to eliminate—whiskey. He took his first drink in five years and got drunk. Gregory was driving down to the police station to give them a piece of his mind when he was pulled over and arrested for drunk driving. On reflection, Gregory now admits feeling "violated, helpless, and humiliated" when he was arrested as a murder suspect.

In both Tony's and Gregory's cases, there were many alternative responses to the rage and humiliation. Some of the techniques for coping with angry people (Chapter 9) would have been effective. For example, to emotionally distance themselves from feeling so hurt and humiliated, both Tony and Gregory could have used a *self-statement*, such as "I won't be manipulated into losing my cool," as a mental mantra to prevent their feelings from ruling the situation. They could also have drastically changed their thinking about the situation by looking at what was happening from the other person's point of view and using a self-empowering statement such as "I'm not going to let this person push my buttons."

9

Like Tony, and many other black men, Gregory expressed his anger in a way that got him in further trouble that could possibly have been prevented.

Racism

The pain and humiliation black men have had to deal with is a central part of the black experience in America. The history of black people in the United States is several hundred years of slavery, discrimination, and government-sanctioned racism only recently remediated through civil rights legislation and antihate laws.

Racism is a central part of the chronic, background stress and strain in the lives of all African-American men. Sometimes the racism is directly and overtly displayed. On other occasions, stress and strain is induced by the perception that racism is a factor in the outcome of a situation. Both experiences contribute to the greater exposure to chronic life stress for black men and the exaggerated angry reactions it can trigger.

But this pain and pathos does not only affect poor, impoverished black men who break the law. Attending college does not permit African-American males to escape second-class status in America, or the frustrations of racism. It does not matter how much education a black man has, where he went to college, or how much fame and fortune he has attained, he can expect to suffer some injustices in his life based entirely on the color of his skin. This situation, regardless of how it manifests, cannot help but cause him to be angry. For many different reasons, however, black men choose not to share the pain, anguish, and hurt they experience. Instead, they choose to be "cool," although the chances are quite good that many of them have felt very angry and helpless about being treated unfairly.

The scholarly multimillionaire and Wimbledon tennis champion Arthur Ashe, who died from an AIDS-related illness, revealed that the killer virus was not his heaviest burden. He wrote in his memoir, *Days of Grace*, that AIDS "is a burden, alright . . . but being black is the greatest burden I've had to bear. No question about it. Race has always been my biggest burden. Having to live as a minority in America. Even now it continues to feel like an extra weight tied around me. Race is for me a more onerous burden than AIDS."

One of the consequences of American history is that blacks, men in particular, still continue to experience a greater array of chronic stressors relative to other ethnic groups. Some of these chronic sources of stress include higher unemployment, higher poverty rates and low-income levels, lower-status occupations, lower social status, residential crowding, substandard housing, and residence in areas with higher levels of environmental toxins. The emotional turmoil and anguish associated with any one of these stressors is hard to cope with, but many black men deal with the cumulative effects of a number of these events daily, and quite often the emotional response to their loss of pride and dignity is anger. Why? Because for most black men the definition of manhood includes their ability to hold a job, provide for themselves and a family, and successfully interact with the system. Most men will perceive a man who is not doing these things as failing his first test of manhood. These unsuccessful men may even hate themselves and others because of their circumstances and failures.

This pattern of coping with angry feelings is possibly a remnant of an emotional and behavioral reaction style that was quite adaptive during slavery, where it was forbidden for black men to speak up or "talk back" to white people about their circumstances.

Black men in the not-too-distant past of slavery were trapped in a social and psychological situation where they felt threatened, angry, and harbored much hostility—yet these feelings had to be suppressed because their life or their family would be jeopardized. In the Jim Crow era black men had no doubt that they were living in a racist society: schools, housing, restaurants, rest rooms, and water fountains were segregated. Today, slavery and legal segregation is over, and yet the evidence of institutional racism radiates throughout the land.

In many communities across America, black men witness their neighbors, friends, and relatives fall victim to intentional as well as random acts of violence. There is no doubt that these men are highly disturbed as a consequence of witnessing shootings and killings. However, even the closest loved ones are not privy to these private fears and anxieties. So great is the burden of maintaining control and the image of strength.

But if these angry feelings are not verbally expressed, they do often find expression in the homes or workplaces of black men, and in some cases black men vent much of their hurt against themselves. While racism is indeed a factor that contributes to black men feeling stressed-out, it is not racism and prejudice that is directly killing black men. Black men are being killed predominantly by other black men. What's even more troubling is that many of the victims were socially acquainted with the perpetrators. Quite often the killer and victim were close friends or family members.

"The cost of keeping so many bad feelings to myself has been great, and it is hard to feel proud about being a man. Most of the problems I had growing up were because of racism—because of the way I got treated by white people and because of the way they seem to keep black people down," says Thomas.

Thomas, a thirty-five-year-old truck driver, moved to a small town in Florida from Detroit's inner city when he was twenty-five. Life, he said, was bad and hard growing up in Detroit, where his father was always unemployed or being harassed by white people. "After seeing so many people get shot, I had to get out of there before I got shot or had to shoot somebody in order to protect myself." In Thomas's case, he hid from the misery and emotional pain of losing his best friend to homicide when Thomas was seventeen by using crack cocaine and other drugs for nearly a decade. His habit had become so bad that he stole and did anything to get high, and yet he always bragged about being able to kick the habit anytime he chose to. Unfortunately the event that changed his life was the murder of a younger sister who was pregnant. She was shot to death and robbed by one of his fellow crack-addict friends as she was washing her clothes at a Laundromat.

For several weeks after his sister's death Thomas was deeply depressed and experienced much guilt about not having been a better big brother to his sister. Thomas also realized that he had never allowed himself to grieve after the earlier loss of his best friend, who was also murdered by a drug addict he thought was a close friend. It was like "everything came crashing down on me at once and I had nowhere to hide and nothing to do except face my problems," said Thomas. "I even refused to get high because of the shame and guilt that I was experiencing because of how my sister was murdered by a crack-head friend of mine. I was angry at myself and angry at my sister. I found myself being angrier than I had ever been in my life."

So why do black men suppress so much of their feelings when they know that they will eventually cause serious damage to themselves or to their relationships with family members or coworkers?

There is strong evidence that cultural and social factors such as those discussed are part of the explanation. But other factors, such as early childhood experiences of black men and the exposure to male role models with suppressive emotional-reaction styles are also likely to contribute to this phenomenon.

I Do As My Father Did

It has been argued that one of the major reasons for the excessive anger and violent behavior of black men is that they are simply mimicking the behaviors of their fathers or other important male role models. Just as we learn and acquire new behavioral skills such as tying shoes, hitting a ball, or driving a car by imitating what we see, our emotional reactions to frustrations and stress are developed in the same way. We learn most things from imitating the people who love and care about us the most—our family. For example, estimates from national studies have revealed that sons who witness their father's violence against their mother have a 1,000 percent higher rate of wife abuse than sons who do not. Also, there is very strong evidence that sons who are exposed to violence between their parents are more likely to exhibit both short-term and long-term adjustment problems such as academic difficulties, defiance, drug abuse, and delinquency. Being part of a home with a high degree of angry and hostile behavior may establish the foundations for some of the angry and violent behaviors that occur later in life.

"For all of my life I knew that I might have a problem with anger. All doubts were removed when I started raising my boys. Punishment, rather than praise, was the method that I first used to discipline my first son. Not only was the use of punishment ineffective and not working, I was frightened and started to lose my temper about everything. One of my fears was that I would hurt my sons, and the other fear was that I was adopting my father's ways of parenting. I was afraid that I was seeing myself as my father, who was very abusive to me and my two brothers."

Gerald, twenty-six, had approached child-rearing much as he had seen it done in his own youth. He describes his father as a "smoldering volcano that erupts with no warning and destroys everything and everyone that is nearby and some of the people that are watching from a distance."

Like many black men, including his father, Gerald could not always leave his anger and frustrations about work at his job. Instead, the conflicted feelings found their way into his family and into the bedroom with his wife, whom he slapped, cursed, yelled at, and beat up on several occasions. "I was fortunate to see my problems with controlling anger and to get help before the anguish that I was causing created some irreversible damage," says Gerald. "I know that my anger has caused a lot of problems in the past, but I thought that things would somehow change once I got married and settled down. But then my wife got pregnant and that caused some additional stress and worries." Even though he has a master's in business administration from a top university, it has been hard for Gerald to find a job that is in line with his educational accomplishments. He works as the manager of a clothing store, which he describes as a "job beneath my dignity, but one that pays the bills and feeds my two sons."

Gerald says that he was quite happy at first about having a son. Then later, even arguments over petty matters caused him to explode. "I was so upset and angry all of the time. Regardless of the situation or who was involved, I was angry, and they were going to get some of my feelings no matter what," said Gerald. "When my wife actually took the two boys and moved in with her mother, I finally took a good and honest look at myself and my problem."

During this time Gerald had numerous talks with his mother and was surprised to learn that his mother had had similar problems with Gerald's father. In the end, Gerald got some long-overdue psychotherapy for his problems and started counseling sessions so that he and his wife could work out their difficulties. Had he not done so, it is unlikely that Gerald would have broken the "intergenerational" pattern of coping with anger and frustration that has been passed along from fathers to sons.

Gerald was fortunate that through psychotherapy he realized that his brutalizing way of disciplining his boys was problematic and would eventually result in their developing similar ways of using threats and punishment to get their needs met. He was also lucky because one of the bitter aftereffects of this unbalanced way of coping with anger is that black males develop resentment and hostility toward the person who delivers the punishment. These negative feelings are then acted out indirectly in passive-aggressive and destructive ways.

It is quite possible that Gerald could have learned ways to better channel his anger without psychotherapy. For example, he could have used some of the techniques that are described in chapter 7, "Strategies for Stopping Anger Before It Escalates" and chapter 8, "Obstacles to Healing and Managing Anger." The techniques are often used to help men learn how to interrupt chains of aversive behaviors by teaching them how to identify the situations that "trigger" them to feel and act angry. Other techniques described in these chapters would have provided Gerald with ways to defuse anger and some proactive ways to solve problems that trigger angry reactions. Also, a man like Gerald could use the information provided in the "Self-Awareness Strategies and Exercises" section at the end of this chapter to educate himself and his sons about how they should express feelings of anger and rage. By doing so he would help his sons learn how to use proactive and problem-solving methods to cope with frustration and provocations.

We live in a time where millions of black males are being raised with absent fathers. Given that boys learn to do things by watching and imitating their parents and caregivers, then the absence of a father figure means that many black boys are not possibly learning the appropriate lessons for dealing with life. This in no way implies that black women should be blamed for their sons' unsuccessful transitions from boyhood to manhood. By all means, the major cause of the problem is the absence of fathers. Raising a child alone is difficult, but many black women overcome the problems and provide their sons the appropriate guidance so that they become successful men. The following chapter describes some of the challenges associated with raising a son alone and offers some prescriptions for developing the type of nurturing and loving relationship that will enable your son to learn how to be a man.

Prescriptions for Change

Much of the doubt that black men have about themselves and their abilities, as we have shown, has been acquired from their childhood experiences. Consequently, the solution, then, for dealing with the types of cultural, social, and familial issues that were discussed must come from within the individual and his family. Regardless of the number of "social programs" that are created to help black men, the real and enduring work must come from the healing of the hurts that have hindered the development of trust, love, and respect for one's family—regardless of the circumstances of the childhood experiences.

For a man to deal with his emotional development he must come to terms with who he really is, how other people perceive him, and what kind of man he wants to become. For many of us, there is a huge difference in these aspects of ourselves, and unfortunately much of the glue that holds these three things together is composed of hatred, frustration, disappointment, destructive family backgrounds, shame, and guilt, as opposed to love.

Basically, what is being said is that a real man must come to understand that the love that he gives to others he gives to himself. However, for a real man to give love he must also learn to love and accept himself.

For most of us there is no real way to change things that have happened in our past, and yet many brothers are constantly wishing that their past was somehow different. It is as if some black men have strongly adopted the idea that life and the concept of who they are is a fixed and static thing rather than a forever-changing process where no one moment or experience is ever exactly like any other moment or experience, and where there is always the potential for growth.

However, it is the memory of painful moments, comprised mostly of deep emotional hurts, that men use to drag their past into the present and their futures. Until a man accepts his hurts and talks out his feelings, he will be forever trying to hide from a part of himself that he must confront and learn to love in order for him to become a whole man.

Much has been written about what people can do to cope with anger in the short run, but it is whether a man, over time, can use his anger as an incentive and as fuel to achieve greater clarity and discover new and more self-empowering ways to deal with old problems and new ones when they arise that may be most significant. While the problems in managing and expressing anger that are contained in each man's experiences are not universal, you will undoubtedly recognize things that connect these with your own life and that of your son, husband, lover, brother, or someone else you know. For example, much of the emotional suffering that is depicted in these cases could have been averted if the men talked with family members about the events.

Tony, the black business executive, for example, was handcuffed and forced to follow the police officers through every room of his own home as they allegedly searched for his partner in crime. An event of this nature would undoubtedly cause any man some discomfort. The situation would also lead him to want to talk about the event to relieve some of his frustration.

However, for Tony to talk he would have to experience a "paradigm shift" that causes him to realize that he is focusing only on one outcome that could result from his talking with his wife.

A paradigm is a set of beliefs about the order of things in your world. In Tony's case, as it is with some of the other men, he is focusing only on being perceived as a weak man and the hurt to his "pride and dignity" that could result from letting his wife know about his encounter with the police. In essence, he has blinded himself to the possibility that talking about this event will lessen his anxiety and fear, strengthen the level of trust he has with his wife, and offer his wife an explanation for some of his unbalanced and bizarre ways of behaving each time he sees a police car or when they return home at night from social engagements.

Tony has failed to consider the possibility that other people, particularly those who love and care about him, may see the event from a different perspective or offer solutions that would enable him to use his anger and feelings to address this problem rather than seeing him as weak.

This also applies to the situation that Gregory encountered. Instead of responding to his arrest by getting drunk to hide his rage and humiliation, Gregory would have benefited greatly by talking about his true feelings with his family and friends. By getting drunk and then deciding to do something about his feelings, Gregory created a way to express himself without taking responsibility for his actions. "If it wasn't for my drinking, most people, including my family, would have never known how angry, embarrassed, and humiliated I was about being arrested like that," explains Gregory. His use of alcohol to lower his psychological defenses enough to permit him to act on his feelings introduces another factor that often complicates dealing with anger. This was also true for Thomas, who used crack cocaine and other drugs to hide his feelings about the murder of his sister and his best friend.

If talking about these events will relieve much of the pain and suffering that is experienced by black men, then what can you or others do to encourage black men to talk openly about their problems and challenges?

First of all, black men need to do as brother Malcolm X says: "Think for yourself, do for yourself, and stop blaming other people for your problems." Many of you are already reading this book, and that's a great start, but to evolve into a great man you have to focus on those qualities, values, and ways of coping that you want for yourself. One way to help develop your inner dialogue to your higher self is through the daily practice of meditation or some relaxation technique. A few basic techniques are described in chapter 11, "The Psychology of Staying Cool."

Through meditation you learn how to have quiet time away from all of the worries you have about the world—time to focus within. The techniques in chapter 11 will help you relax and provide you with some of the mental and physical energy that is necessary to effectively handle the problems that occur in your life. As a consequence of the greater mental clarity derived from meditation, you will be more adept at handling stressful situations that cause anger.

If you are a man reading this book, you need to encourage other men to better understand themselves by starting discussions about the information that is contained in this book. You can use the information in the section "Self-Awareness

Strategies and Exercises" to structure discussions with your male friends and coworkers about different ways of coping with anger and frustration. When you enter into these discussions, it is important to let the brother know that there are no right or wrong ways to express anger because each style has its good and bad points and that most men use some part of each style to cope with different situations. Another thing that you should consider is starting or joining a discussion group for men. You can use this book as a guide to probe into the different values and beliefs that black men have about "manhood." This type of exposure to black men who are clear about their roles as men and comfortable talking out their feelings can trigger the type of introspection that causes a shift in beliefs and values. Some of the men would also benefit, as Gerald did, from psychotherapy or counseling with a minister. Why? Because many of the "mixed-up" feelings that black men have about identity and manhood are associated with love and respect for parents and family on the one hand, and hatred, disrespect, and a lack of trust on the other hand. In most cases, the most self-empowering insights about how this situation came about can be gained in the safety of a fully trusting relationship with a psychotherapist. The big problem is that black men often refuse to seek out help because they are either afraid of the things they may find out about themselves or they don't trust counselors and doctors. As a consequence, they shy away from doctors and refuse to make healthy changes in their lifestyle and relationships.

In many cases, wives, girlfriends, female friends, and relatives provide the encouragement for black men to seek out help. A woman can be an invaluable source of encouragement for black men by simply being empathetic and willing to listen to and help her mate, male friend, or relative seek help for himself. In addition, black women can encourage the men in their lives to share their feelings through the use of what is called active listening or reflective listening. This is a nonjudgmental way of responding to comments made by another person. It simply involves the restatement of the comments with the purpose being to unquestionably let the other person know that you really have received their message. The real power of this method is in avoiding analyzing or summarizing the situation for them.

Secondly, one of the most powerful things a woman can do is ask about things that don't appear just right to her. Most men, for example, waste a great deal of time going around in circles trying to determine "why" an event occurred or "why" something did not work out as planned.

Imagine that you are driving home one night and you come to a road that is closed to all traffic. Let's say that you stop your car and begin to ponder, "Why is this road closed?" You can be assured that no matter what answers you come up with, you will not get any closer to your home. What I am getting at is that the real power is in asking your man (son, male relative) to focus on questions that can cause him to be proactive rather than reactive. Questions such as "What can I do to solve this problem and maintain my dignity?" "What can I do to make this situation perfect?" "What can I do at this very moment to bring greater happiness to all of the people involved?" "What can I do to prevent this situation from repeating?"

If you are a woman reading this book, you could encourage your man to better understand himself by having a few discussions with him about the content of these questions. If you are a mother with a son, my advice is for you to use the questionnaires and the information in the "Self-Awareness Strategies and Exercises" sections, located at the end of the chapters, to structure discussions with your son about his characteristic ways of coping with anger and frustration. When you enter into these discussions, it is important to let the brother know that there are many ways to express anger, with each style having its good and bad points and that most men use some part of each style to cope with different situations.

In learning effective ways to cope with anger it is important to remember that "being angry" or "getting angry" is a process, and as such it is natural for the ways to cope with anger to change as the process changes and as the reasons for the feelings come into focus. Unfortunately, most black men are not aware of this process, and they cling to their characteristic ways of coping without closely reflecting on whether what they are doing is making the situation better or worse. Essentially, many men lack flexibility in their ways of dealing with stress and frustration. While there are probably countless reasons for this rigidity, brothers must learn to be flexible in their approach if they are to effectively deal with anger and conflict.

In general, black men need to learn how to be proactive rather than reactive for their overall emotional development. Unlike the reactive brother who blames others, including his family, for his problems, the proactive man takes responsibility for his actions and effectiveness. He may have been raised in poverty with parents who could not read, but he understands that much of what he has become started as a thought that he put in motion. He accepts his upbringing and realizes that no rules say that because you are a black male raised in poverty, you can't grow up to be whatever you make up your mind to become.

In essence, the proactive man has little self-doubt because he has overcome many of the barriers that prevent other black men from getting to know a powerful and important part of themselves (see "Proactive Problem Solving" in chapter 7). Contrary to popular belief, the most powerful part of a man is his feelings—the fuel that turns thoughts about who you are, what you want to do, and what you want to become into actions.

As indicated earlier, hatred, frustration, betrayal, disappointment, destructive family backgrounds, shame, and guilt have overshadowed emotions like love and trust in too many black men. From a practical or grassroots perspective there is much that a black man, parent, grandparent, or any other relative can do to help a young man develop his true potential and real power.

The real secret is in knowing that the seeds for manhood develop inside of the soul and spirit of a man. When the spirit of a man or growing boy is finely tuned and well developed, nothing can stand in his path for righteousness, greatness, and success.

22

If you are a man reading this, then one way to help yourself develop more pride and respect for black men is to read stories about black men, particularly biographies. Reading one biography every week or two is not a costly adventure, and it is likely to decrease some mindless time that you spend watching television. An exceptional and rich source of information about historical black men before, during and after Christ can be found in a two-volume set called *World's Great Men of Color* by J. A. Rogers. This same advice can be used to help a son, father, brother, or any male relative.

Self-Awareness Strategies and Exercises

Take Notice of Yourself

Take some time to notice how you respond to events that are frustrating. Take note of what you do, what you say, and what you are thinking. When you get angry, do you boil inside and don't show it? Perhaps your style of coping with anger is easy to identify because you say things that you don't mean to say? Are you easily angered by what other people would consider a trivial event? Do you think that you have a temper? Perhaps when you get angry you are able to easily calm yourself to deal with the circumstances?

Take Your Temper Test

Each man handles anger and conflict in ways that have meaning to him. Nevertheless, expressing anger can be done constructively. Presented below are a few questions to help you get a better understanding of what causes anger in you. You need to complete the following questionnaire, referred to as the Temper Test. Remember the purpose of this step is to teach yourself how to recognize and get in touch with your feelings of anger and not to criticize yourself for not behaving the way you would have expected.

The Temper Test

The test is widely used in research to determine the role of stress and emotions in health and psychological problems. You can use this test to make a rough estimate of your characteristic way of coping with stress and frustration.

Directions: Read each question and then answer yes or no (or simply note in your mind) to indicate how you generally feel or act. There are no right or wrong answers.

How Do You Generally Act or Feel?

1. Are you quick tempered?
2. Do you feel annoyed when you are not given recognition for doing good work?
3. Do you have a fiery temper?
4. Do you feel infuriated when you do a good job and get a poor evaluation?
5. Are you a hotheaded person?
6. Does it makes you furious when you are criticized in front of others?
7. Do you get angry when you are slowed down by others' mistakes?
8. Do you fly off the handle?
9. When you get mad, do you say nasty things?
10. When you get frustrated, do you feel like hitting someone?

Score Yourself: Add up the points (0 for a NO response and 1 for a YES) for each item to get your total score, somewhere between 1 and 10. A person who scores 6 is just about average. If you score below 4, you're well down in the safe zones, perhaps unresponsive to situations that provoke others. But a score of 10 means you may be a hothead. If this is so, then you need to pay particularly close attention to the information in the Self-Awareness Strategies and Exercises. If you follow the advice, your chances of learning how to cope with your anger are great. However, your might consider seeking a professional counselor or therapist if your anger is interfering with your work, family life, or your health.

Total Points _____

Now that you have completed the questionnaire it would be wise to spend a few minutes reviewing your answer to each statement. The approach I recommend is to imagine yourself behaving as depicted by the statement and then to answer the following questions as they relate to your behavior.

1. Why do I act this way?
2. What does it cost me emotionally, physically, and financially when I act this way?
3. What does acting this way do to my relationships with people who care about me?
4. What will it cost me in the future (i.e., emotionally, physically, financially, and in my relationships with my family) if I don't change and continue to act the way that I do?

Take notice of how you feel when you are angry. Does your body posture change? What about your voice? Do you feel any tension or tightness in your chest, forehead, arms, or legs? Are there any changes in your breathing? Does your body feel warmer or sweaty? What about your facial and hand gestures? Are you more animated when you are angry and upset? Do you feel excited or do you feel sad when you get angry? When you get angry, what is it that you think that you are losing? Is it an object, your turf, an opinion, your rights, respect, approval by others, or someone's love?

Take notice of what you do when you are angry. Stop whatever you are doing, sit back, and take five to ten minutes to think about the last time that you got so angry that you were at the point of losing it. It is important for you to take a really deep look at the situation by honestly answering questions, like those below, that can offer you a more complete perspective about what you do when you are angry.

- What was the cause of your anger?
- Was it another person, yourself, or some object that caused your anger?
- What expectations were violated?
- How intense was your anger?
- How did you act?
- What did you say?
- Did you say things that you did not mean?
- Were you angrier than you were willing to admit?
- Did you keep your anger to yourself?
- Did you remain calm and act to solve the problem while staying calm?
- Did your actions make you feel better or worse?
- Did you see any similarities in your actions in this situation compared to your usual way of acting and behaving when you are angry?
- How do you generally act and behave when you get angry?
- What is the first thing that you do?
- Do you immediately yell at others and criticize them when you are angry?

Perhaps the first thing you do is to shift the blame for your feelings to someone or something? Maybe the first thing that you do is feel tension in your body or your voice? Or maybe you have lots of crazy self-criticizing thoughts.

Answering questions like these will help you get a fairly good idea of your habitual ways of acting when you are angry. So stop whatever you are doing and really take the opportunity to visualize in your mind the things that you did and said the last time that you became angry. If you stopped to do this exercise, you have started to learn about yourself and you have started to develop a conscious awareness of what you do to get angry and upset. What did you learn?

Given that everything we do starts as a thought that gets put into motion, it is important for black men to become aware of the different outcomes that can result from potentially aggravating situations. Better yet, it is essential for black men to know what they desire from a situation—be it an oppressive or racist encounter at work or a department store, a stressful relationship at home, or unfair treatment by a police officer. This is one of the essential elements for coping with any situation, and the more clear the desired outcome is the more likely it is that you will get what you want.

Make Decisions About What You Want

How clear are you about what you want to achieve by getting angry? If anger is an emotion that regulates behaviors between people, then what is it that you want to obtain by being angry? Much of what we do is motivated by unconscious needs and desires, but to get a better idea of what some of these desires are, you can ask yourself a few powerful questions, such as, What am I gaining by being angry? What pain and discomfort am I avoiding by being angry?

Make up your mind about what you want from those situations where you find that you are angry. Get a crystal clear image in your mind and see yourself behaving the way that you want. We are all driven by the need to avoid pain and to seek pleasure. Therefore, think about all that you gain from handling the situation well.

Even though there are an almost infinite number of ways for dealing with most situations, most people tend to look for one solution to solve the problem. Basically, many of us have been conditioned to believe that for every problem there is only one solution rather than many. Like everyone else, black men are imprisoned by what they perceive with their five senses. We have been taught to believe that if we

27

can see it, touch it, taste it, hear it, and smell it—then it must be real. The basic problem with this notion is that most of us take in small amounts of the information that is readily available to us. Because we are taking in only small bits and pieces, it is usually not possible for us to comprehend the whole situation. Furthermore, the bits and pieces we allow ourselves to take in are a product of how our minds have been conditioned to see, hear, taste, feel, and smell the world around us.

One of the things that a black man must do to overcome and go beyond problems with anger is to challenge his own limited and narrow-minded perception of the world. For example, a man who takes his dog out for a walk can be overwhelmed by the dog's reactions to sounds that he can't hear or smells that he can't detect, and yet the sounds and smells are there in the environment beyond the brother's conscious awareness. A more practical example might be the wife who is constantly trying new perfumes and new outfits to gain the attention of her mate, and yet he is oblivious to all of these things until the day that she says that she wants a divorce because he does not love or appreciate her. What is so fascinating about black men, and possibly all men, is that we tend to focus our attention on such a small amount of information about any issue, problem, or challenge.

All of us have been taught and conditioned to readily accept as truth anything that we are told. Unfortunately, many of the messengers of "truth" have not had anything good to say about black men. The message here is one of anguish and despair rather than love and hope. As a consequence, many black men continue to see themselves coping with stress and frustration with the same old destructive patterns that have been passed along from one generation to the next. Answering questions that clarify your feelings and what you do when you are angry will help you make some distinctions about what you want. However, the most important thing that you can do is to decide on what you really want and go for it.

There is a story about a man who fell into a deep hole and yelled constantly for almost a week for someone to throw him a rope. Well, no one came by and the man finally understood that no rope was forthcoming. So, what did he do? The brother was dirty, soaking wet, hungry, and tired of waiting for someone to help him out of the hole, so he got out by himself. What I am getting at is that every black man has the potential to be and do whatever he desires. The same power that traps a black man can also free him. Black men have always had this power, no matter what the obstacles, and the choice about how to use it has and will always be a conscious decision. The same thing applies to how a man deals with feelings of anger, frustration, and rage.

Stop Blaming Yourself and Others

Blaming someone for some unjust event assumes that there was only one way to handle a situation. It also assumes that there was some competition or jockeying around for who was right and wrong. Sure it matters who is responsible, but the goal is to learn from your mistakes and empower yourself to be a better person. Stop blaming other people for your emotional reactions. There is nothing wrong with feeling angry and upset.

The real problems with the expression of emotions start because most of the time we are not sure how to handle these feelings. As a consequence, one of the most counter-productive things that some of us do is to blame others for our feelings, which generally results in more anger, guilt, and a breakdown in communication. Take responsibility for your feelings. Use them as a guide or a signal that is alerting you that something is not quite right with a situation. Use your feelings as a friend that is there to help you rather than as an enemy that is there to destroy you.

Create Your Own Destiny

Picture in your mind the way that you really want to cope with feelings of anger and hostility. Imagine yourself acting the way that you choose to act rather than in the same old stereotypical way that has contributed to your problems. Take notice of the differences in the way that you usually act when angry and upset and the new way that you have chosen. Think of all of the emotional and personal losses that you will experience if you don't change how you have been coping with anger. Think of all the relationships that you will continue to destroy if you don't adopt the new way of coping. Think of how you will feel about yourself—how disappointed—if you don't change. You are not a robot that has only one way to respond to a situation; you are free to choose what you desire. However, you must first create a clear image in your mind of what you want because everything that you and I do starts as a thought.

2

Can a Single Mother Raise a Son to Be a Good Man?

Nearly thirty years ago, Daniel Patrick Moynihan, then an assistant secretary of labor, ignited a heated debate by declaring that fatherless homes were the "fundamental source of weakness of the Negro Community." At the time, one-quarter of African-American families were headed by women. Today, the situation is worse. A majority of black families with children—62 percent—are now headed by one parent, usually the mother. The situation is predicted to continue to decline. For example, the most recent census indicated that less than 75 percent of black women are likely to ever marry compared with 90 percent of whites.

The childbearing picture also continues to be bleak. For example, between 1960 and 1990, the proportion of young white women giving birth out of wedlock rose from 9 to 25 percent. While this was a remarkably faster rise than that for blacks, the rate for whites was still lower than the black rate of 42 percent in 1960 and 70 percent in 1989. As things stand, marriage and childbearing do not appear to go together for many African-Americans. A black child born today has only a one-in-five chance of growing up with two parents until the age of sixteen. What is also startling about this phenomenon is that out-of-wedlock births are not solely the problem of the entrenched underclass. For example, 22 percent of never-married black women with incomes above $75,000 a year have children out of wedlock, a rate that is almost ten times higher than for whites.

The reasons for the shortage of men in our communities are numerous. We lose too many men to homicide, suicide, death from drug abuse, industrial-related deaths from jobs in "hazardous areas," AIDS, and other health problems. When women and children exist in a larger world ruled by men and there are no men to look up to as role models, we have the right atmosphere for high levels of anger, anxiety, depression, and confusion about sex role identity. So, re-gardless of the reasons for the shortage of black men, the fact is that millions of black men are being raised without a father present. Therefore, the purpose of this chapter is to provide some insights about this problem. It's written for black men who were raised without a father and black women raising a son without a father. The material is also useful for single fathers.

Growing Up Without a Father

In the 1980s, comic actor Bill Cosby dominated the television Nielsen ratings with his portrayal of a warm and caring African-American father. In far too many instances in real life, the black father is a vague background figure who is minimally involved with his children. To a certain extent, this is also true in the case of the so-called "intact" family where the mother is the primary parental figure for the child even if the father is present. As a consequence, many black males are being raised with a strong feminine identity, and their deepest emotional relationships are with women— mother, grandmother, sister, or even teachers. The one fact that is clear about this is that black women are having a difficult time teaching black boys how to be men.

The lack of a significant relationship between a father and his son can stunt proper development of the expression of emotions, particularly anger and aggression.

Many men who were raised by a single mother believe that this relationship caused some of the feelings of anger, guilt, and shame in their mothers. Most single mothers are afraid that their sons will make the same mistake as their fathers or express their aggressive tendencies in a way that will get them killed. Many mothers are afraid that their sons may resent the chief disciplinarian, the person who sets the limits.

Things become more confusing when a mother communicates a double message. She may speak longingly of wanting her son to have a "man" in his life, while communicating a strong lack of trust and faith in the man's abilities to provide proper guidance for her son. The mother's anger that has become suppressed constitutes one piece of fuel for this confusion while fears about her capability of raising a son alone constitute the other.

Many men believe their mothers vented some of the frustration and bitterness they had about their son's father by giving the son a hard time. For example, Jason, thirty-seven and married for twelve years, explains that he had to work hard to overcome the shame and guilt experienced while growing up. "For most of my life, as a young boy, I would hear my mother talking to her friends about her poor judgment in men," explains Jason, who works as an airplane mechanic. Jason and his younger brother were raised by their mother after their father abandoned them. "It seems that my mother was always mad, and she took much of this out on me and my brother. She didn't physically abuse us, but she treated us badly. I guess what I'm trying to say is that she never showed me that she loved me. Instead she treated me and my brother as if it was *our* fault that her life wasn't like she expected."

While many single mothers work hard to not discourage their sons from developing a relationship with their fathers, it is difficult. Most memories of the ex-mate are associated with disappointment, pain, suffering, and hatred. To survive, the black male child sometimes learns how to disown and deny a major part of his deepest identification—his mother. He does this through a defense psychology called reaction formation—going to the opposite extreme. Rigidity and overcontrolled emotions are often the result of this coping process.

To deal with the confusion and conflict in the love/hate relationship black boys often have with their mother in the absence of the father, they suppress painful and disturbing emotional experiences. They learn how to live as an incomplete person, alienated from an important part of themselves. The black boy who develops an introspective attitude may soon discover that his frequent outbursts of anger have little effect on the real problem. Given this, he soon perceives himself as incapable and unworthy. Furthermore, if there is no strong black male role *model* to learn from during this crisis in development, the boy may grow into manhood burdened with the same vengeance and rage that destroyed his father, becoming part of a vicious cycle. To survive, black males are forced to function in an emotionally detached and extremely repressive manner. Rather than take responsibility for their anger, many men blame their mother for all of their problems.

The Lack of Basic Trust

One serious result of the absence of a father in the life of a boy is difficulty with developing what psychologists call basic trust. This loss of trust between father and son can potentially destroy trust and respect in all important relationships with other people, including mothers.

A black man with a great deal of trust believes in the goodness of people, expects that most people will be fair and kind in interacting with others. Black men who have internalized these beliefs are slow to feel anxious, resentful, irritable, or angry.

Some of the ill feelings that single mothers have about their sons' father are used as bricks to build an emotional wall between fathers and sons. Many men reported that they feared losing their mother's love and approval if they expressed a desire to have a relationship with their father. Consequently, these men learn how to effectively suppress and repress their strong feelings of outrage over this situation.

George speculates that he was basically angry growing up because what was rightly his (having a father) had been taken away from him or forced away from home by his mother. Even though his father lived in the same city, there was not much of a father-son relationship primarily because his father and mother grew to hate each other. "I grew up hating my father for leaving me alone with my mother, and I did not trust him to do the things that he promised," explains George. He also believed that the level of trust between his mother and him was hindered because he feared being unworthy of manhood since his only source of identity was a woman, his mother.

"I have listened to my mother say over and over again that she can't provide me with this wisdom to be a man, and yet, from my perspective, she has not made a concerted attempt to bring my father back home to provide me with the right role model so that I could learn the real rules of manhood," explained George. "As I reflect back on the trouble I got into as a boy, I now realize that most of it was to show my friends and my mother that my masculinity had not been blunted by being raised without a father."

Some black men share the perspective that their mother is responsible for all of their problems because the presence of a father would have prevented many of the bad things from happening or provided them with the opportunity to learn better ways of coping with life's problems. More importantly, many men hold their mothers responsible for not being capable of offering them the wisdom to be a successful and productive man.

Raised in a fatherless household, many black boys become extremely rigid in repressing the feminine side of their personality. This repressive response is also triggered because of a fear of hostile name-calling such as "sissy," "fag," or "momma's boy" by their peers.

George believed that his survival and acceptance by his male peers depended on his affecting a "tough guy" persona. Acting up in school, shoplifting, drug use, fighting, and hanging out with the wrong crowd became the "norm," explains George.

With few adult males around, some black boys rely on each other for information about sex and girls and so on—a classic example of "the blind leading the blind." Most of their knowledge is gained in secondhand fashion from older males such as a brother, cousin, an uncle, a neighbor, or from television and movies. Many of them also receive instruction from their mother's discussion about the "absent dad" who abandoned her to raise a child single-handedly.

Some black boys challenge the inconsistencies and myths about issues of "manhood," as presented by the "gang," and have a growing realization that their peers don't know as much about being a man as they thought. Still, for boys, the pressure to conform by joining gangs is great. Any reluctance to join a gang usually results in ridicule and name-calling. Equally difficult to cope with is the possibility that some peers take reluctance to join the gang as evidence that a woman (the mother) controls one's journey into manhood. Therefore, it should come as no surprise that one of the most common reactions to this situation is resentment and chronic anger.

A perceptive boy with a strong sense of self will seek out other peers or interested adults who, to a certain extent, are "outcasts" like himself, willing to buck the system. Protective factors such as quality schools, recreational services, and church involvement can reduce high-risk behaviors—truancy, fighting, or drug use. But one of the sad facts about being black in America is that many of the resources are not readily available to blacks. The level of anger, rage, and embitterment that is often associated with the loss of a father's love can turn some black men into walking "time bombs." For some men the fuse is so short, any event that is perceived as an attack on their abilities and self-esteem can trigger an explosion. Other men somehow learn to manage their hurt and avoid the pitfalls in being raised by a single mother.

Self-Reliance and the Supportive Home Environment

A single mother (or father) can be a successful parent for a man-child if her own level of self-reliance is strong. No matter what else goes on in her world, a self-reliant mother knows that she is the source of the happiness and success of her son. Self-reliance depends on knowing deep within yourself that other people, racism, poverty, etc., are not the causes of problems with your son. A self-reliant mother knows that her son is dependent upon her and that she is dependent on herself to get what she needs.

Single mothers of successful sons, according to many black men, have somehow learned to cope without having a man in their lives. This attitude may be related to religious beliefs or the development of a greater sense of self-awareness and self-love. Regardless of how this belief and attitude was acquired, for a single mother to use her own power and be self-reliant, she has to give up three things:

1. all self-hate, self-dislike, and self-disapproval
2. all need for approval from others
3. being inconsistent

When these three things are eliminated, a single mother or father would come to understand that loving themselves is the only approval necessary to move forward in life. Regardless of the immediate circumstances, each person can make a turnaround. This is possible because we are designed so that we can correct our mistakes and raise our consciousness and our self-awareness. This also applies to married women and men, too.

For a single mother to be self-reliant means that she has given up looking for love in the wrong places and depending on others for her happiness. It takes real courage for people to break away from dependency and to liberate themselves from their own fears. When a single mother does accomplish this, she becomes more sensitive and responsive to the other people in her life, and she can use her personal power to liberate others, particularly her children.

To be a self-reliant mother means being consistent. It means that a child can depend on her to keep promises. Of the three characteristics associated with self-reliance, being consistent is probably the hardest thing for a single mother to do. This is because so many single mothers have not had the chance to learn consistency from their own parents. But unless they are consistent with their sons, their sons will learn nothing about the consequences of their actions. This also applies to single fathers raising sons.

Many men expressed the opinion that their mothers were not afraid to allow them to make and experience mistakes. "One of the greatest things about my mother is that she taught me that making mistakes is how we learn," explains Ken. Although Ken was raised in an impoverished area of Houston, his mother created a home environment where Ken felt accepted, loved, and encouraged to learn how to take care of himself. It seems that early on in life Ken's mother instilled in him the same attitudes she has about self-reliance. "Rather than seeing my happiness or my anger as being caused by other people, places, and things, I quickly learned that I was the source of the events in my life," explains Ken. This lesson is one that was learned by many of the successful black men raised by single mothers. Another important lesson was the understanding that everyone at home had responsibilities. When a growing boy learns these lessons, he knows that there is no substitute for self-love, and he will avoid looking for the source of his strength in drugs, gangs, possessions, the need to be accepted by peers, or anything that leads him from recognizing his God within.

I Am Somebody and I Am Proud of My Mother

Many black males survive and thrive during the passage to manhood without guidance from a father without suffering any serious emotional or health problems. For example, Les Brown, the highly acclaimed speaker who talks to Fortune 500 companies and conducts personal and professional seminars around the country, grew up the hard way. Born into poverty, Brown was adopted and raised by a single woman. He was labeled "educable mentally retarded" as a youth. Yet he was able to control who he became, and he speaks with great affection about his mother, his role model and the source of his wisdom and strength.

Les Brown is a success story of a black boy who grew up without a father but whose strong connectedness and identity with his mother provided the catalyst and fuel for his climb to success. This is quite remarkable since most boys don't have a father and the situation doesn't seem to be getting better.

Rather than ignoring, cutting off, or denying his family background and roots, Les celebrated and fully accepted the challenges that life provided him. In doing so, Les apparently learned to be comfortable stretching the boundaries of his family roots rather than cutting them off. What he did was analogous to what people did in the good old days when a pair of new shoes fit too tightly—they were stretched by a machine to acquire a comfortable fit. In Les Brown's case, the machine used to stretch himself to new limits was his mind and imagination. This is the same machine that all black men must use to deal successfully with the sources of frustration and anger in their lives.

Prescriptions for Change

Despite the bleak picture painted by this chapter, not all sons raised by single mothers have deep emotional, social, and adjustment problems that lead them to a life of crime and drugs. The cohesiveness, closeness, and supportiveness of the family unit are some of the key factors associated with secure and stable children. While the presence of a "father figure" contributes strongly to how a family functions, a stable family is possible, even in the absence of a father.

If you are a single mother, don't get caught up in the myth that sons raised by single mothers don't stand a chance of developing into good men. Many good men, including the author, were raised by single mothers and are doing fine. One common element was being raised to be proud of the accomplishments of black men. Another thing that single mothers must do is create opportunities for their sons to spend time with black men who could serve as mentors— policemen, firemen, schoolteachers, coaches, ministers, even neighbors, are possible role models.

Talk to your sons and create an atmosphere of trust. A strong communication bond between mothers and sons is a must. Also, it is important that you learn to listen to your son and not always be the person talking and giving advice. My mother often initiated talks about values and created an atmosphere that took the focus off me. In developing the Values Clarification exercise that I use with parents, I drew on her approach. During these talks you simply ask your son to describe how men such as Jesus, Martin Luther King Jr., Booker T. Washington, Thurgood Marshall, Bill Cosby, Nelson Mandela, Malcolm X, your minister, or even the man next door would have responded to a certain situation. This exploration of values, beliefs, and proper behavior can open up a wonderful dialogue with your son. Going on a walk with your son is a wonderful way of getting him to talk about his problems. A single father raising a son can use these same techniques for strengthening the bond with his son.

Given the long list of accomplishments and contributions that black men have made in America, there are many examples for a young black boy to learn from. However, African-American history is not widely taught in most schools, so you will need to provide your son with the appropriate sources of information and not rely on what he is exposed to in school. As a parent you must demand that your son and other children be exposed to certain information. It's up to you as a parent to create a loving and supportive environment in which your son can succeed. But there will be no success unless you have communicated that he is responsible for his actions, that he does not exist in a vacuum, and that he must respect others to receive respect.

The only way that a mother can get to the heart of her son is by eliminating fear and treating him as a friend. All boys need love and environments where they feel secure and safe. They need guidance and discipline, and they need constant reinforcement of the idea that they can be the best that they can be. Some suggestions for the development of nurturing relationships with sons are

1. Give love unconditionally. When love is given there needs to be no string attached. Too often mothers are quick to put down or criticize their sons for what they are not doing, rather than trying to understand why they are behaving as they do. When love is given without criticism, the stage is set for the proper development of trust, respect, and friendship.
2. Encourage your son to get involved with organized sports. This activity will teach your son how to work as a team member and provide him a healthy outlet for releasing tension and aggression. Being a member of a team is also good for the spirit; boys who are involved

41

in positive social relationships are better adjusted than boys who don't have positive social outlets.

3. Establish high but realistic expectations. While the best example is what you do in your own life, you can select other people whom you respect as the model for what you expect of your son. Regardless of your circumstances, it is necessary for you to practice what you preach and do everything you can to be consistent.

4. Teach your son how to relate to women. Early in your son's life, you must begin to talk about the definitions of women as mothers, wives, workers, and lovers. He must also be introduced to the roles of men so that he understands that fathering children does not make him a man. This is likely to be difficult because of the conflict between the definitions of manhood he receives from his own father (or the absence thereof) and the society at large. The Values Clarification exercise that was previously described is a good technique for dealing with these issues.

5. Be honest. The truth is liberating and it is important for you to admit mistakes and failures. When you do this, you teach your son how to learn from failure. A good example to use to start a discussion about the positive side of failure is baseball. In baseball, the typical batting average is .300. What this means is that, on average, the batter only gets a hit three times out of ten and makes an out seven times. In this example, there are obviously more failures (outs) than there are successes (hits). You can use this and other examples to help your son understand that neither you nor he is perfect and incapable of mistakes and failures.

6. Establish a reward system for good behavior. This could be in the form of a weekly allowance or praise. If money is tight, don't worry, because praise works equally well. You can also combine praise for exceptional work with special privileges. If money is no problem, then open a savings account for your child as soon as he has enough money to start an account.

Encourage him to save one-third of his allowance so that he can begin to understand the value of money. Also, encourage him to give to those in need or to a church or social organization. The lesson of giving to receive is universal. Teaching your son how to benefit by giving is a powerful step toward the development of compassion and self-sufficiency.

7. Teach your son the lesson of forgiveness. This might be best accomplished by talking to your son about the problems you had with his father (or mother). Explain how you have forgiven his father for leaving you alone to raise him. Talk to your son about the difficulties and sacrifices you have experienced because of your dedication to making sure that he can be the best that he can be. If you are experiencing a lot of bitterness and anger because of how your son's father left you, then it is a good idea for you to review the forgiveness techniques that are described in chapter 12, "The Role of Spirituality in Managing Anger." It is also a good idea for your son to offer a forgiveness for the behavior of his father. This could result in the bond between you and your son being strengthened.

8. Teach your son how to solve conflicts without the use of violence. This book provides you with a number of techniques to achieve this goal. Regardless of what is happening in school, in films, or on television, it is important that you teach your son how to be aggressive without being violent. A black man can't compete and succeed in this world without healthy aggression. However, to learn to compete successfully, a growing boys needs to be surrounded with love. He also needs to learn how to appreciate himself and his people. As a parent, you can help him learn these lessons by not being afraid to show affection. Make the effort to tell your son how proud you are of him and how much you love him. While it is important to love unconditionally, it is equally important for you to set firm rules about the consequences of unacceptable behavior, particularly that associated with violence.

43

9. Help your son learn to be proud of black men. Provide him with truthful information about the accomplishments of African-American men. Some suggestions for accomplishing this goal are presented in the "Prescriptions for Change" section of chapter 1.

Self-Awareness Strategies and Exercises

Take Notice of Yourself

Take a moment and think about times in your life when you've felt invincible. Imagine yourself reenacting one of those situations, and try to figure out how to reexperience the same level of self-reliance and confidence that you originally experienced. What are you doing to feel self-reliant? Are you alone or with people? Does your level of confidence and self-reliance change when you are with different people? What causes your confidence to change?

How do you feel when you need to make a decision? Are you anxious or worried? Do you get angry at yourself or other people? Do you feel confident in your ability to make decisions, or do you run to someone else for help?

How do you feel about people who are confident in their ability to get things done? Are you comfortable being around such people, or are you more comfortable being around people who seem meek and helpless? Do you encourage others to become self-reliant?

Take a few moments and think back to when you were a child. Were you truly supported and loved? Did your parents encourage you to be independent and self-reliant? Did your parents encourage you to be consistent in your actions?

Now take a moment and review how you respond to children in your life. Are you supportive and loving? Do you welcome their growth and provide opportunities for them to become self-reliant, or do you shelter and protect them from making mistakes? Are you fearful that your children don't know enough to take care of themselves?

Take a few moments the next time you are with children

and observe your reactions. Are you comfortable with them? How does it make you feel when a child says, "I'd rather do this myself"?

Answering questions like those above is a powerful way to gain insights about your values. Regardless of whether you are a single mother or father, you need to understand who you are (e.g., your beliefs, values, hang-ups, prejudices, etc.) so that you can better help your son to understand and appreciate himself.

Make Decisions About What You Want

To get at the core of the situation, you need to understand that you make decisions about what you want in life. It is important to understand that each time you put off making a decision, you are avoiding taking responsibility for your actions. Ask yourself, "What will it cost me emotionally if I don't make decisions? What will my relationships with family, friends, and coworkers be if I continue to avoid making important decisions? How will I feel about myself if I avoid making decisions and taking responsibility for my actions? How will I feel about my children if they see that I avoid making decisions and taking responsibility?" How do you feel when your child does not take responsibility for his actions? Take a moment, close your eyes, and imagine the emotional pain that you and important people in your life will experience if you avoid making decisions. If you have trouble forming a mental picture of this situation, then let your mind ponder the things that your family, friends, and coworkers will think and say about you because you avoid making decisions. Use the feelings and thoughts this exercise causes to develop compelling reasons for you to make decisions and take actions to achieve what you want in your life.

Taking responsibility for your own thoughts, actions, and reactions to a situation is difficult for some people, particularly for people who tend to seek approval from others. Remember that to be self-reliant means giving up all of your needs for approval from other people. The chances are pretty slim that a child will learn this if he doesn't see his mother or father modeling this behavior.

Stop Blaming Yourself and Others

It is important for you to understand that it is your beliefs about making decisions and taking responsibility that determine whether you adopt actions and behaviors that will increase your sense of self-reliance. There is only yourself to blame if you don't make decisions or take responsibility and don't deal with the consequences of your lack of action.

Do you find yourself criticizing and blaming your children for things they do? Have you seriously thought about the fact that most of what you see in your children has been learned from you? Even if they are old enough to know better, you have had a major part in setting up how they behave. Stop blaming your children and take responsibility. When you stop blaming, you create a context in which change can occur. If your children engage in some behavior that is unwanted, then you simply need to teach them the consequences of the behavior and encourage them to think for themselves. They will then follow their natural inclination to avoid painful experiences. Accomplishing this means that you must be consistent and practice what you preach.

Create Your Own Destiny

Spend a few minutes thinking about all of the characteristics of being self-reliant and write out everything that enters your mind. Create a mental picture of what self-reliance means to you. Now imagine how you would respond to some of the situations in your life. Imagine yourself making decisions without asking for another's advice. See yourself earning ample money, paying all your bills, and so on. Visualize taking care of yourself. Imagine how it would feel to think for yourself and make your own decisions. Now imagine yourself being indecisive, weak, not sure of yourself, and blaming other people for your problems and mistakes. Take a few minutes and write out what you would think about yourself if you acted this way. Imagine what your life would be like if you always acted this way. Take a few minutes and describe the impact this would have on the development of your son. Take a look at the two lists you have and now make a decision and commitment to be a self-reliant person.

To complete this exercise probably caused you to experience some anxiety. Don't worry about it because this is normal. This occurs anytime a person makes an honest self-evaluation. However, if you are questioning your ability to become the self-reliant person that you want to be, then it is important for you to examine the meaningfulness of your chosen career. In chapter 11 there is a section entitled "Maintaining a Meaningful and Purposeful Life," which you should review. The exercise in that section will help you discover your unique talents.

3

Stretching
the Family Roots

Harold, thirty-eight, is a successful attorney and professor at a major university. In style, speech, and manner, he is the epitome of a middle-class, even privileged upbringing. But Harold grew up in a large, impoverished family in the Deep South, the third child and youngest son of six children. While the family had few amenities, there was love and a closeness between Harold, his two brothers, and three sisters. The children were encouraged to be good students and to use education as a means of breaking away from poverty. Only Harold, however, followed his family's exhortations to an unusually successful life. Now he considers himself so "different" from the rest of his family left behind in his small hometown that he barely sees them anymore. This produces not only alienation, but feelings of guilt as well. "All of my brothers and sisters are smart, and most are smarter than me, but none of them grew up wanting to leave home," Harold lamented. "They just accepted things and always acted like it was wrong for me to think about moving away.

But, I made up my mind a long time ago to get a good education, and never be poor."

Most of Harold's siblings are living the kind of hardscrabble life that marked their childhood. "I feel guilty and annoyed that I don't have the resources to help," Harold said. "I've tried to encourage my brothers and sisters to do better, and I use myself as an example, but it still hurts me that we have grown to be so different."

Harold's regret is not unusual among many black men today who have achieved a higher level of status than their parents. From owning certain luxury items (e.g., microwave ovens, cellular phones, laptop computers, and fax machines) to attending church, living near family members, or spending leisure time, for some black men the stark differences between their lives and those of their parents is almost like culture shock. The differences include whether to uproot family for career purposes, the types of foods to eat, marriage, and whether their mate will be of a different race.

The difference between black men and their parents is called status incongruity, and it can become a major source of stress, frustration, and anger for black men. In fact, it is possible that the more different African-American men are from their parents, the more likely they are to develop ineffective ways of communicating negative feelings, coping with life's problems, and maintaining a strong sense of self-identity.

It is a cruel paradox. On the one hand, accomplishing a better life than your father's is the essence of the American dream. But on the other hand, the greater success underscores the differences between you and your parents and family. At the same time family support is not available when it is most needed: to help cope with frustration and stress. As a consequence, black men are less prone to mobilize the support that is needed to cope with and reduce the deleterious effects of stressful events.

For some black men, the alienation they feel from families is rooted in the belief that relatives lacking comparable experiences can't comprehend the nature of the problem and therefore can't help fix it. Other brothers are "too proud" to admit frailties because they are expected to be sources of strength and counsel for less successful family members. Meanwhile, the bottled-up problems can escalate to such a level that no amount of intervention can fix the damage. A large part of the advice offered in chapter 11, "The Psychology of Staying Cool," can be used by men who have circumstances similar to Harold's.

In Harold's case, the alienation from his family that he attributes to being successful has been great. "There aren't too many days that I don't spend a lot of time thinking about how things are back home, and then when I phone home, I get depressed and agitated because I realize there is not much that I can do to change the situation." It was clear that Harold was not lonely or homesick. He is married, with a wonderful family and a great career. But Harold is angry and under a great deal of stress because his family (mother, father, and siblings) look to him to solve all their problems back home.

Harold's feelings of guilt were compounded by the way he chose to deal with the difference between himself and his family. "For a long time I thought that I could really help my brothers and sisters," he recalls. "I tried everything—every type of encouragement, incentive, and threat—until one day it became clear to me that the decision for my brothers and sisters to change or to remain the same was up to them and not me. This thought helps me to deal with the situation, but I still feel angry and upset because of the additional expectations they have about how I am supposed to help with problems back home."

Few human emotions are as distressful and painful as the feelings of guilt and personal disapproval from family members, some of whom may act as if they have been abandoned. For some black men, the voice of self-condemnation is in their conscious mind by day and invades their dreams by night. There tends to be little escape for these men from the unrelenting self-blame and hatred they impose on themselves for their mistakes, failures, and sins. Much of this self-imposed abuse can be effectively dealt with by evaluating the rules and values that family relationships are built upon.

The section "Overcoming Guilt" in chapter 8 includes an exercise directed at the identification of the rules that generate guilt. Two sections in chapter 9, "Coping With Shoulds" and "Enhancing Your Empathy," should also be reviewed.

The Fantasy Background

The shame and anguish that some black men feel about the differences in status between themselves and their family is so intense, some brothers never talk about their families. Rather than deal with the truth about their family background, they create false family histories more congruent with their new level of success. This was the case with Brian. Single, thirty-three, with a MBA from a top university, Brian grew up in a poor family. Although both his parents worked, there were many hard times for Brian and his two older brothers. Brian claims that he loves his family very much, but he is ashamed of them and the way that they live. He rarely visits and generally avoids having anything to do with them. Recently, Brian decided to cut himself off from his family altogether. He developed a "fantasy family" that possesses the "appropriate" social-economic characteristics for raising a successful son.

Brian blames his family for much of his anger and resentment. "It seems that my parents and my brother don't want to do anything other than struggle to just barely make a living," he said. "I've tried talking with them and I've tried to motivate them—to get them to take an interest in bettering themselves, but nothing has worked. What bothers me the most is that my brothers are smart enough to be anything that they want to be, but they won't even try. All of this has made it hard for me to feel attached to them." Ashamed and angry at his siblings, Brian prefers to lie about them when the subject comes up.

Brian's anger is reflected in how he treats people he is not related to. He claims that his family is probably unaware of his true feelings because he has internalized his hurt. But in believing that he can force negative feelings about his family from his conscious mind without ripping himself apart from within, Brian has made a crucial error.

The cramming of strong feelings into the unconscious mind is called repression, and it is often more hazardous than openly dealing with painful thoughts and emotions. Repressing feelings creates enormous pressure. They pop up somewhere in the form of depression, anxiety, tension, or in an entire range of physical disorders.

In Brian's case, repressed thoughts about his family are manifested in the form of his angry interactions with other people, a chronic depression that has been with him since college, and a number of health problems that baffle his doctors. "What hurts me the most is the ease with which I make up stories about my family and how I was raised," Brian said. "I get angry each time I make up something new, and I know that all of this is making me depressed. One of my biggest fears is that one day some person at work or a friend will discover that I have been living a lie and this will be held against me."

One of the things that was so distorted about Brian was the absence of guilt over how he deals with the differences between himself and his family. While admitting that he is angry and ashamed of his family, not once during our interview did he acknowledge feeling any guilt about how he deals with it. Brian's lack of remorse is masked by his adoption of a curious position: since "every successful brother acts like me, what I am doing can't be very harmful."

Unfortunately, Brian has failed to understand that the depression and anger he shows people are a direct result of the way he has mistreated his family. Brian has essentially locked himself into a vicious cycle where he feels damned if he does acknowledge how he feels about his family, and damned if he doesn't. To cope, he has tried to "intellectualize" his dilemma and resolve his guilt. He has chosen to use a rational criterion to make himself feel better. My behavior is okay, he tells himself, because other black men act the same way. A man such as Brian could greatly benefit by knowing more about the use of anger as a defense against inner feelings (see chapter 8, "Obstacles to Healing and Managing Anger," and chapter 9, "Coping With Angry People") and about the insights that are offered in chapter 11. If Brian's struggles remind you of yourself, it would be a good idea to pay particularly close attention to the section entitled "Living With Righteous Principles" in chapter 12.

By suppressing what may be part of the natural emotional responses and experiences associated with becoming more economically and socially successful than one's family, men like Brian have robbed themselves and their families of the opportunity for mutual growth. The prescriptions and techniques offered in chapter 10 as well as those at the end of this chapter are particularly useful for dealing with family problems.

Breaking Away from Family Pressures

Even black men raised in intact families, with successful parents, describe feeling pressured and somewhat disconnected from their parents as a result of incongruities between the status of their parents and their own desires and expectations. The emotional difficulties and alienation that result from the desire of parents for their sons to emulate their success can be great. In some cases, how a man deals with these parental expectations can either motivate him to achieve or cripple his chances for upward mobility.

"When I was growing up and got into a fight, I could always convince my parents, the teachers, and other people that it was the other person who started things and had a problem with their temper. It was easy to talk my parents into taking my side because I was a reflection of them and they did not want to be perceived as bad people or having a son who was a troublemaker," says Lester.

If a black man raised in an intact middle-upper-class family had a problem with anger, chances are he would probably smile and say, "Who, me? No, I never lose my cool. I don't have reason to be angry." But it is precisely this kind of man who often has the most serious problem with anger. He pouts and sulks; he may make sarcastic remarks or harbor secret grudges; he may even have grown up disliking or even hating his parents; but he refuses to admit any of this. Why would he have a problem with anger and rage when he grew up in a home where all of his needs were met—with parents who used their money and influence to shield him from the problems of the world?

Lester, twenty-nine, a high school janitor, is an example of such a man. Even though Lester grew up in a well-educated family with both parents, he barely got his high school diploma. His father is an engineer, his mother a college professor, his older sister a lawyer. Given his family background, Lester might have been expected to accomplish more in his life. Instead he has a serious drug problem and an extensive arrest record. Most of his problems with the law resulted from his temper. Yet, Lester admits that for most of his life he did not think that he had a problem with his anger: "I simply thought of myself as being better off and having more privileges than most other people because of my parents' status. No matter what I did, I knew that my parents would see to it that things would be okay. Because of this I would do things just to test my parents—to see just how much I could get away with."

During our interview it was obvious that his "temper" problem was possibly related to the sense of double jeopardy that he experienced while growing up. "It was like, my father would always say that he wanted me to work hard and be successful like him, but neither he nor my mother encouraged me. They always helped my sister with homework and encouraged her to make good grades, but they did not care whether I brought a book home." As a result of this incongruity, Lester was quite angry at his mother and father during most of his childhood. From his perspective, he believed that his parents "should" have known that he was angry about his treatment. "They let me get away with too much and never once told me that I was the cause of a fight or anything that I did wrong. They simply acted like I was not important enough to be corrected. Sure they talked to me about being successful, but they never quite reached out to help me with my problems. They treated me as if I was going to become a nobody, as if it was simply a matter of time before I did something that was too serious for them to fix."

Thus, many of his problems as an adult, in Lester's view, are a direct result of his anger at his parents. While he has tried to suppress it, anger surfaces often enough to destroy relationships with other people and to further distance him from his family. "I got so upset with my parents that I started doing things that would upset them, too. I just wanted to be accepted. Since they didn't act like they really loved me, I decided to be as different from them as I could."

Lester, sadly, was all too successful at becoming different from his parents. Unmarried, with few close friends, he is bitter that his "well-to-do" family didn't do a good job in preparing him to deal with life. "They spent much of their time protecting me from things and not enough time teaching me how to stand on my own two feet. They pretended that I did not have a problem, and today I don't know how to handle myself—I don't know how to express my true feelings." Lester believes problems with anger are the real reasons for his lack of success and the reason that he has not been capable of sustaining a happy marriage.

To a great extent, black men who cope with the status incongruities between themselves and family members in this manner are also being reactive rather than proactive about the circumstances in their lives. On the other hand, some black men who were raised to be successful struggle with the belief that they can't live up to their parents' expectations, no matter how successful they become. Take the case of Eugene. Although he owns three successful restaurants, Eugene's family still considers him an underachiever.

"They treat me as if they are embarrassed by the work that I do and that I should not act on things that do not meet with their approval," Eugene complains. "All of this has been going on for a while, and I am basically tired of them trying to control me."

Growing up in small beach town in Florida, Eugene, thirty-six, son of a successful physician father and a mother who was the principal at a local junior high school, spent his summers in Europe while most of his childhood friends were busy trying to find a job. He drove a fancy Ford Mustang convertible to high school before most of his classmates earned enough money to purchase their first bicycle. Even though he was a fairly good student, Eugene did not prepare himself for college. He stayed in trouble at school and hung out with people who had no clear ideas about the future. He was caught shoplifting at a toy store when he was fifteen and boasted about having one of the worst school attendance records in the history of his high school. Not surprisingly, Eugene was a big disappointment to his parents.

After high school, Eugene managed to open a small restaurant on the beach, ignoring advice from his parents, who preferred that he attend college. "At one point my parents were so upset over the idea that they did not speak to me," Eugene recalls. "I would call home to let them know how I was doing, and they would hang up on me."

Parental disapproval can be one of the toughest and most difficult things for people to manage. This is particularly true for those individuals, such as Eugene, whose parents have high expectations and an overriding need to be in control of their children's lives. The controlling parents may feel that it is necessary to control their children's destiny because the children have been the source of embarrassment, shame, and in some cases, hurt feelings that may bring back painful memories of their own childhood. Therefore, to keep from being hurt and prevent their children from being hurt, the parents attempt to control the behavior of the children. Despite their efforts, the controlling parents eventually drive their children away. Rather than love and compassion, the only emotion that is easily shown by the parents is anger or irritability. Even though these parents may constantly explain their motives and give all sorts of reasons for their actions and attitudes, this still does not get them what they want, which is the love and affection of their children.

To break away from parental bondage, Eugene adopted the belief that his success was not contingent upon his parents' approval. According to Eugene, it has not been easy to get his parents to accept him because they perceive him as resigning himself to a position in life that is below their standards and expectations. Eugene has apparently done a good job in handling his situation with his parents because he says that his relationship with them has improved and that he remains hopeful that one day they will come to fully accept him.

Prescriptions for Change: Dealing With Family Pains

Most of us have to make decisions about how we deal with the past because of its painful nature. If a man carries strong feelings about something that happened long ago, it may hinder his ability to live in the present. He has to get rid of these feelings because they have no real value to him, only the value that he gives to them. Most motivational experts claim that "the past does not dictate the future," and yet many black men believe that to be perceived as successful they have to disown their past, cutting off all family links. This is especially true for those black men who have gone on difficult and incredibly cruel journeys to achieve their dreams.

The goal of this section is to help you expand your consciousness so that you may grow to become more accepting of your past, regardless of the differences you perceive between what you have become and where you came from. The exercises are designed to help you drop the burden that you have carried about differences between you and your family. They are designed to help you deal with the notion that it is the person you have become, not the things you have achieved, that is most important. The family relationships of all of the men depicted in the cases (Brian, Lester, Eugene) would have been different had they used the techniques described in the following sections.

Keeping the Channels of Communication Open

First of all, the single most important thing in dealing with status incongruities is to prevent the adjustment problems from occurring. This can be accomplished by the maintenance of good communication about the importance of self-discipline, religious and spiritual development, family pride, and heritage in the foundation of one's successes. Some guides for maintaining good communication are provided in the "Prescriptions for Change" section of chapter 4.

It is important to remind black men that our roots go far deeper than the immediacy of a few generations that have survived hardships after being forcibly taken from our homeland in Africa. It is also important to remind black men that the accomplishments of black men and their contributions to humanity have been great, as have been the sacrifices that every generation of black people have made to facilitate the successes of the next generation. These truths have not always been passed on from one generation of black men to the next. For this reason, some of our problems with black men would be prevented if every black person, a parent or not, took on the responsibility of sharing in the upbringing of our young men and women. It is through this type of extended parentage that our young men can grow up to be proud, strong, and deeply connected to their family. They would also have greater access to the wisdom that has been passed from several generations of black people because there would be more family members willing to help give our young men a future. Without instilling these attitudes and practices, how can we expect black men to feel connected to us or their heritage? Why would we expect them to stretch their family roots to new depths when they feel confused about their family roots?

Establish Some Family Traditions

Secondly, there is a strong need for black families to establish some traditional practices that create the right atmosphere for keeping family members informed about each other and strongly connected. Many of our young people have only vague ideas about their family heritage or the rich history of African-Americans. It is important that all of us do whatever we can to help prevent the breakdown of black family values, beliefs, and traditions. Even though some black men may not know exactly what they can do to keep their families connected, their role in this process is major because it is through them that the next generation of black men will learn how to stay connected to their families as they move up the economic and social ladder. Some suggestions for reestablishing and maintaining family unity include

> family reunions
> regular visits home during holidays
> frequent phone calls
> sending special greeting cards for birthdays
> sending cards and gifts to acknowledge anniversaries
> acknowledgment of personal accomplishments of family members

Some families have developed a family newsletter that several times throughout the year describes accomplishments, marriages, births, graduations, advances at work, and other changes among family members. Other families use the major holidays to impose their family traditions, while others use Kwanzaa as a point of stabilizing family values, issues, and concerns. In brief, Kwanzaa is a unique

American holiday, observed from December 26 through January 1, that pays tribute to the rich cultural roots of Americans of African ancestry. Kwanzaa means "the first" or "the first fruit of the harvest," in the East African language of Kiswahili. Kwanzaa was founded in 1966 by Dr. Maulana Karenga, a black-studies professor who describes himself as a cultural nationalist. Kwanzaa originated as a cultural idea and an expression of the nationalist Us organization, which was headed by Dr. Karenga. Kwanzaa is unique in that it is neither religious, political, nor heroic but rather a cultural holiday that is based on seven fundamental principles that are referred to as the Nguzo Saba and may serve as guides for daily living.

The seven principles of Kwanzaa are listed below:

1. Umoja (unity). To strive for and maintain unity in the family, community, nation, and race.
2. Kujichagulia (self-determination). To define ourselves, name ourselves, create for ourselves, and speak for ourselves instead of being named, created for, and spoken for by others.
3. Ujima (collective work and responsibility). To build and maintain our community together and make our sisters' and brothers' problems our problems and to solve them together.
4. Ujamaa (cooperative economics). To build and maintain our own stores, shops, and other businesses and to profit from them together.
5. Nia (purpose). To make our collective vocation the building and developing of our community in order to restore our people to their traditional greatness.
6. Kuumba (creativity). To do as much as we can, in the way we can, to leave our community more beautiful and beneficial than we inherited it.
7. Imani (faith). To believe with all our hearts in our people, our parents, our teachers, our leaders, and the righteousness and victory of our struggle.

While some African-Americans may not agree with all of the principles of Kwanzaa or even know what it is, the celebration of this event is a wonderful way to develop family unity. Some families use these principles as guides for daily living throughout the year. An excellent resource book for those of you unfamiliar with Kwanzaa is *Kwanzaa: Origin, Concepts, Practice* by Maulana Karenga (Kawida Publications, 1977).

Learn How to Forgive

Another major lesson that black men must internalize is the power of forgiving. It is an immutable mental and spiritual law that when there is a perceived "gap" between a man and his family, there is a forgiveness problem. A man must forgive if he wants to become a real man. Regardless of the negativity surrounding the circumstances that a man was raised in, he needs to learn how to let go of animosity, bad feelings, and all uncomfortable thoughts about his past. Brian is a perfect example of a man and his family who would receive tremendous benefits if Brian simply practiced forgiveness.

Forgiveness dissolves the negative attitudes and memories that are lodged in the conscious and subconscious levels of our mind. Unless a mental and emotional cleansing takes place, negative emotions will lead to ill health.

Some brothers refuse to forgive their families for their impoverished upbringing because they say that the act of forgiveness is unpleasant and embarrassing. However, the forgiveness ceremony is neither unpleasant nor embarrassing, and it can be very simple. To forgive does not mean that you have to bow and scrape to those who you feel have offended you. To forgive means to "give for," to "replace" the ill feeling, to gain a sense of peace and harmony again. In most cases, you need no contact with those involved in your forgiveness act. If such an occasion does arise, it can facilitate your healing because it provides you with an opportunity to practice handling a difficult situation while controlling your anger. As you change your attitudes toward others, they will unconsciously change their attitudes toward you.

Material Things Don't Make
You a Good Man

Finally, we must teach our men that it is the process of becoming a successful man rather than the things that a successful man has achieved that matters most. I am not saying that material wealth is unimportant, because our father, the one and only father, God, is giving us whatever we desire. If we desire material wealth, fine. If we don't, then that's okay, too. However, many of our men have fallen victim to the false belief that it is the things that they have acquired rather than the righteousness of the process of becoming successful that separates them from their families. Whereas a successful man may see himself as better than other people, including his family, because of his fame and fortune, a righteous man perceives himself as being no different from others and as a member of one family where God is the father of all.

Our men also need more exposure to Christian values and principles, particularly those that focus on the idea that prosperity emanates from consciousness. In essence, our men and boys need to be firmly rooted in values, beliefs, attitudes, and practices that enable them to deal with any challenge they face.

Basically, if a man knows who he is, then he knows that his problems and the solutions to his problems require him to look within himself and detach himself from his concerns about the outside appearance of the challenge. Sure, it would be wonderful if we could change the world and solve our problems, which is a noble thing to do. But, if we want to change the world, we have to first change ourselves . . . change our thinking . . . and change our consciousness. What could a man gain by changing his consciousness? He would realize that the real problem is how he has been conditioned to see the world. He has a limited perception of who he is. He knows that his emotional states are dependent upon what and how he focuses his attention. Most of us are consciously aware of only a small amount of what is going on around us at any given time. Most of the time we ignore most of what's happening and focus on bits and pieces of the whole situation. As we do this, it becomes nearly impossible for us to fully perceive and understand the issues and challenges we face.

The Power of Our Questions

Each of us has the power to focus on the positives and the great things that are going on rather than the negatives. Basically, we can do this because whatever we pay attention to is what we are going to get out of life. What we focus on is determined by our beliefs and how we have learned to evaluate things. All of us make evaluations, and we do this by asking ourselves questions. Four of the fundamental questions most of us ask ourselves are

1. Who am I?
2. Where did I come from?
3. What do I want?
4. Where am I going?

Asking these questions, a man opens himself up to receive help and answers from the most powerful computer of all: his brain. Many brothers don't regularly perceive the answers to their questions because they are caught up in the belief that they can't achieve their goals because they are black. Some of us don't hear the answers to our questions because we get so caught up in worrying, thinking, and trying to figure out why we have not solved the problem. In many cases, black men don't perceive the answers to their questions because they ask themselves questions that presuppose that they will be limited in how they deal with the challenge. For example, imagine that you have tried to get a family member to get a bit more education or to adopt a healthier way of eating. Imagine asking yourself, "Why can't I get this family member to get into school?" Or, "Why can't I convince this family member to eat healthier foods?"

I hope that you can see that both of these questions presuppose that you "can't" get the family member to change and that every answer that you come up with will be negative. It's simple to get what you want out of life, and it's simple to keep a strong connection with your family in spite of whatever differences you perceive separate you from them. So, how can you overcome these differences? Part of the answer is in learning to ask yourself questions that are powerful, questions that open your mind to search for all possible solutions to the challenge. Rather than these "why" questions, we need to ask ourself questions such as "What can I do to motivate my family to eat healthier meals?" "How can I educate my family to be more concerned about their eating habits?" Basically, the "why" questions will do nothing but cause more frustration and anger. For example, imagine that you are driving home from work and one of the roads is closed. A big sign says Road Closed. Well, my friends, if you ask yourself why is that road closed, you will get nowhere. You can get out of your car and ask yourself that same question (Why is my road closed?) for the next forty days and nights, and I guarantee that whatever answers your brain comes up with, they will not get you any closer to home. You will get home when you ask yourself questions that offer you power—a power that you already have, to deal with any challenge that comes up in life. Our questions are important because they do three things for us:

1. Asking questions instantly changes what a person is focusing on. No matter what is going on, when you ask yourself questions, you focus on more than the few bits and pieces of the situation. For example, rather than asking yourself why you can't get your family to improve themselves and get more education,

ask the question "What can I do to motivate my family to become more educated?"

2. The second thing that questions do is change what we are deleting. To get caught up in negativity and unhappiness, you only need to delete all of the great and wonderful things about being a *spiritual being* and focus on the negatives. Sure, some negative things are going on out there. But, if we continue to focus on the "why" questions, then we will continue to go around in a circle and not get our needs met, much like what would happen at that Road Closed sign.

3. The third thing that questions do is to help us get access to the resources that we need to make happen whatever we want. Again, the solutions to everything we desire are already here, but you won't get access to your power with weak, nonempowering questions. Many philosophers have commented that nature does not reveal its secrets, it only responds to a method of questioning. Our questions have the power to release us from bondage . . . from being imprisoned by our own minds.

Many years ago a popular television ad for the United Negro College Fund reminded us, "A mind is a terrible thing to waste." Well, my friends, the UNCF had it right. Now its time for us to realize that the Mind Is a Powerful Thing Not to Use to Its Fullest Potential. Our thoughts are what we are, so let's think properly and ask the right questions.

The Greek philosopher Heraclitus once wryly observed, "You cannot ever step into the same river twice, because the river is constantly being changed by new water rushing in." The same is true for you and your decisions about what you want to do about the perceived differences that you have allowed to separate you from your family or any other problem that you are being challenged by. The truth is that the past influences but does not dictate your future. Whatever was there last year, last month, yesterday, or even a few moments ago is gone. All of us are much more like a river than anything frozen in time and space.

Self-Awareness Strategies and Exercises

Take Notice of Yourself

Take some time to notice how you respond to events that involve you and your family. Observe the way your life is now and see if you can find the patterns that brought you to this place. Notice those things that you like about your relationship with your family members and those things that you want to change. Make a list of the problems you have, and beside each problem, list the way you would like it to be. Take note of what you do, what you say, and what you are thinking when you do this. Take notice of how you feel when you think about your family. Do you get angry or upset about the circumstances in your family? Do you boil inside and not show it? Perhaps you feel fear. Do you feel that it is impossible for you to be close to your family?

Make Decisions About What You Want

Accept that you have created the relationship between your family and yourself to this point. You know how the relationships with your family members are going to turn out. You know that it's up to you to change how you have been dealing with the situation. How clear are you about what you want from your family? If you don't know what you want, that is okay, because much of what we do is motivated by unconscious needs and desires. To get a better idea of what some of these desires are, you can ask yourself a few powerful questions such as "What am I gaining by creating distance between me and my family?" "What pain and discomfort am I avoiding by distancing myself from my family?"

Stop Blaming Yourself and Others

Take responsibility for your actions and feelings. Stop blaming your family for how you have been dealing with your successes. Stop blaming them for how you have distanced yourself from them. Stop blaming them for whatever you see in them that is different in you. Rather than focusing on their faults and shortcomings, focus on their strengths and their uniqueness. Use them as a guide or a signal that is alerting you that there is something that is not quite right with a situation. Use your feelings as a friend who is there to help you rather than as an enemy who is there to destroy you.

Create Your Own Destiny

Go back to your list of problems and the solutions you want. Beside each problem write the steps you think you will need to take to successfully deal with the challenge. Picture in your mind the way that you really want the relationship with your family to be. Get a crystal clear image in your mind and see yourself behaving the way that you want. Imagine yourself acting the way that you choose to act rather than in the same old stereotypical way that has contributed to your problems.

Take notice of the differences between the way that you usually act and the new way that you have chosen. Take time every day to visualize the way that you want the relationships with your family to be. Think of all of the emotional and personal losses you'll experience if you don't change how you have been responding to your family. Think of all of the people (your mother, father, brothers, and sisters) whom you will continue to destroy and let down if you don't adopt some new ways of coping. Decide on what you really want and go for it. Don't let the past dictate your future relationship with your family. Think of how you will feel about yourself—how disappointed, how frustrated, how guilty—if you continue to distance yourself from your family. Remember that you are free to choose what you desire and how you want the relationship with your family to be.

4

Black Women

Black women and black men seem to be at war, using each other to work out some of the frustration, faulty expectations, and rage they encounter adjusting to life in white America. Black women bear the brunt of the ill feelings black men build up from society's treatment, directly when many black men simply refuse to become self-sufficient, and indirectly when their men withhold the full commitment black women yearn for. Instead of seeing society as the enemy, many brothers have worked hard to "verbally murder" black women in an attempt to control and dominate them. Rather than offer support, value, and love to the women in their lives, black men have contributed to an environment that nurtures fear, hate, manipulation, and dishonesty. It is no wonder both parties are miserable. Consequently, the relationships between black men and black women tend to be a reflection of the crisis that resides behind the cool facade of black men—a crisis fueled mainly by the lack of understanding of self and the perpetuation of relationships based on guilt, domination, and control.

The economic dislocations that began in the 1970s were devastating to black men. The decline in the number of manufacturing jobs that had lured vast numbers of black men to the North resulted in a sharp drop in meaningful employment. This national shift from an industrial to a service base also seriously affected the black family and the relationship between black men and women. Many black men were robbed of the opportunity to establish themselves as a breadwinner for their families, and as a result there was a dramatic increase in the problems that occur between black men and women. Ironically, just as the job market and the doors of opportunity closed for black men, they opened for black women, who went to college while black men lost their lives at war, got hooked on drugs, or were lured into the fast-money drug trade as a way to support themselves and their families.

Corporate America was apparently more willing to accept college-educated black women than black men. The entry into the business world of black women was pushed along on the tide of the "women's movement," while racism and discrimination in corporate America helped to keep black men locked out of the mainstream. In other words, jobs that were given to black women came at the expense of black men. Basically, corporate America took the position that it would look better if they could have two minorities, "two for the cost of one," a woman who was black, rather than a black man. Today black families are paying the cost. This job gap has also created other problems, such as a "lack of self-reliance," in the relationship between black men and black women.

Despite the economic battle between black men and women, the desire to marry remains a potent dream for single African-Americans adults. For example, a recent *Newsweek* poll of African-American adults indicated that approximately 88 percent wanted to get married. In this same poll a large percentage of the people surveyed (51%) believe that the major reasons young black people are not getting married today is because women can't find enough eligible men. Not surprisingly, some 49% of the people polled believed that not having enough money to set up a household was also a major reason why blacks are not marrying.

According to the most recent U.S. Census Bureau figures, among nonmarried African-Americans ages eighteen to thirty-nine there were 3,654,000 women compared to 3,352,000 men. This computes to ninety-two available African-American men for every one hundred women—eight fewer men. Obviously, this ratio does not indicate a huge shortage of African-American men. However, when we consider the proportion of black men who are incarcerated, addicted to drugs, homosexual, involved with nonblack women, uneducated and unemployable, there is a shortage of African-American men for the available black women. The situation worsens for women as they age because the marriage rate appears to be related to the sex ratio. For example, even though the ratio of males to females is relatively even at ages fourteen to seventeen, by ages thirty to thirty-four there are only seventy-seven African-American men for every one hundred African-American women; a large proportion of these women have exceeded the educational and economic development of the men.

"I didn't think that it was going to cost me too much emotionally to be a nice black man who never gets angry at anybody. I thought that I could make the marriage work, but I didn't fit into my wife's life. She is always on the go, working and socializing. All I wanted was to be a happy husband and father, but she was always pushing me to try new things and to be something that I am not. I guess that all of this was too overwhelming for me to deal with, and I found myself being angry most of the time."

James, thirty-eight, is an automobile mechanic whose wife is about to divorce him. James surprisingly started psychotherapy at the request of his wife, to learn how to separate his problems at work from his problems at home. Although James is fully aware that his wife, a busy corporate executive, has filed for divorce and is planning to move to another state with his son, initially he denied having any feelings about the situation. However, after prodding, James admitted that he is "upset and worried about the situation" and that "there is nothing" that he can do to solve his marital problems. "It's almost over and I know that it's mostly my fault. I just could not keep up with her, and that's what got me into trouble," James lamented. "At least, I think that this is the reason that I am so damn angry all of the time. I tried to fit into her life, but I always felt out of place."

James is like a lot of black men who were taught that anger is wrong, especially hostility toward a woman. He was also raised with the belief that anger was a problem only when it became visible to others. Thus, James had progressively hidden from his own feelings about the failed marriage. He had repressed so much hurt, in fact, that James described himself as being "numb." His basic problem was that he failed to use opportunities with his wife to learn how his anger might be used to get his needs met. His suppressive nature created a situation where conflicts were rarely resolved in a satisfying way. "I never seemed to feel comfortable when my wife and I had arguments," James related. "I basically didn't know what to do in order to deal with the situation. So I would generally just listen to her and then leave home and go have a drink or two. I gave up trying to talk about our problems because I would always end up losing my temper and blowing up."

According to James, his behavior is "nearly identical" to how his father dealt with problems. "I never thought much about my father primarily because he was an alcoholic, but I realize that I have adopted many of his ways," James said. Much like his father, James skillfully uses his anger to mobilize support for his side during disputes. Rather than directly addressing the real reasons for his being upset, James claims that he would create situations where other people could fight his battles. "Instead of dealing with the situation head-on, I remember my father talking about how victimized he was to anyone who would listen. I am sure that he did this to gain their sympathy," explains James. James described a similar situation from his own life. He once spent an entire Thanksgiving vacation nagging his wife and openly complaining to her mother and other family members about her lack of support for his contributions to their family. "I was upset and I just wanted to get a few things off my chest. All that I wanted was for someone to listen to me and to know some of the difficulties I was having." James admitted having had a few too many drinks, which helped fuel his outburst. The real motive for his behavior at the Thanksgiving gathering was to "generate enough sympathy from my wife's family so that someone would take my side and retaliate against my wife."

James's behavior "spoiled" the entire vacation and resulted in a "heated" argument with his wife. His indirect approach in dealing with his anger also created an awkward situation for everyone, including his nine-year-old son, who was so disturbed by the situation that he became ill. James's attempt at coping with anger always seemed to create situations that constantly minimized his chances for developing a trusting relationship with his wife. He constantly felt boxed in: damned if he expressed strong feelings, and damned if he repressed them. In the end, James felt that he was "the loser" because his wife refused to communicate with him or mocked his efforts to change. According to James, this escalated the situation. He hurled epithets that he later regretted.

James typifies a number of "cool brothers." Their outward appearance of being in control masks an inward turmoil marked by rage, jealousy, envy, and a diminished sense of self-worth. The basic problems of the cool brother are related to a belief that relationships with other people will suffer if they express anger and hurt feelings. Sadly, they never consider the possibility that a relationship could actually be *strengthened* by directly dealing with these emotions. In James's case, the price of his pacification was huge—he lost his family, he started to drink heavily, and difficulties on the job and health problems soon followed.

Many of the emotional and health problems that black men like James suffer from are the result of poorly managed anger. What is more troubling, many of these brothers fail to recognize the difficulty they have in controlling anger or expressing feelings.

In James's case, some of his feelings of helplessness and anger derived from the fact that his professional wife earned more money. "I thought that I could adjust to her making more money than me, but I always felt uptight when we talked about money." According to James, just discussing money with his wife angered him. "I would get upset when she talked about who controlled the household, particularly when we were with family members. It seems that she would use these times to criticize my capacity to support the family. What I did in return was to give her a hard time or try to stay away from her." Although James said he never resorted to physical abuse, he threatened his wife with assault.

Regardless of the trigger for their arguments, the underlying problem between James and his wife appeared to be an issue of "control." What was unusual about James is that he attempted to assert control through other people. However, as you have seen, his wife refused to accept his threats of abuse and moved on with her life. In the end, neither of them learned from their mistakes.

"I am forever being accused of things, like seeing other women and being dishonest, but I am as faithful as can be. But, I can't take her stuff anymore. There is never a break from the complaints about what I should be doing or what other couples are doing, where they are traveling and vacationing, and their wedding plans. I would like to be able to give her things, but I am a working man and I don't make that much money."

David, thirty-three, a salesman in a clothing store, has been engaged to and living with "his woman" for three years. David suffers from some of the same problems that James manifested—he is a quiet man who is content with where he is in his development—and yet it angers him that "his woman" has surpassed him in her economic and career development. During the past five years, while David was at home watching television and contemplating what his life should be, his woman managed to find a college scholarship, earn a degree in mass communications, and land a great job with a large salary and fantastic benefits. "I love her, but I can't marry her because she is doing far better than me financially, and her job in telecommunications is far more stable than mine. This angers me a bit because I have tried real hard to find a better job." Even though he has a college degree, David has had a difficult time finding a job that is congruent with his education. He admits that staying in the relationship will be difficult because he feels he is competing with his woman. He also simmers at the thought that his fiancée believes she holds the power in the relationship because of her salary.

Rather than talk about his feelings, David expresses his anger through passive-aggressive means. His main strategy is harassment and sabotage, and he skillfully avoids large-scale confrontations with his woman. Gradually, his woman is worn down and made to feel she is the source of their troubles. "I think that I was always trying to get back at her for making me feel so small and insignificant. Some of the things I did to irritate her were so silly, like leaving her gas tank on empty after I used her car or not telling her about important telephone messages from her family or people at work. There was also a time or two when I was supposed to meet her at a particular place and I didn't show up." David says that he did these things to get back at his girlfriend because she was constantly "telling" him what to do and how to do things to better his life. "I would try to deal with her, but it seems that she never listens to me. She was more concerned about me doing the things that would make us measure up to other people rather than the things that would bring us closer."

Black men such as David who use a "guerrilla fighter" approach to coping with anger leave little possibility for a healthy resolution of conflicts because they habitually strike at the other person's vulnerabilities. They use anger as a shield to hide real feelings of inferiority. For example, David described a recent situation in which he was accused of aiding a shoplifter because he does not "pay attention" to black customers at the store he works in. In this instance a black woman walked out with over $2,000 of merchandise, marking the third time in two months that the store was robbed. Everyone blamed David because each of the previous thefts took place during his shift. "I was mad as hell about this thing. I felt hurt and humiliated for being blamed for this thing, and I knew that I was being blamed because I am the only black person working in the store."

Despite David's concern, he never told his girlfriend about this event, but he did remember her questioning him about his mood as well as standing her up for an event that he had promised to attend. "I knew at the time that this would hurt her. I never thought that I would be the kind of man that would hurt someone else in order to vent my own frustrations, but that's what I do," explains David. David didn't explain why he was upset, even when he was confronted by his girlfriend. Instead, he blew up at her and accused her of not trusting him and tried to make her feel guilty for something she did not do.

David evidently did not tell his girlfriend about the event at work because he did not want to be "put down and made to feel like a fool." Like many other black men, David has difficulty dealing with women who are outspoken and independent. Rather than seeing the advantages and strengths of having an independent woman in their lives, these brothers perceive these sisters as trying to dictate their behavior or denying their autonomous identity. "I didn't talk to her about this because she uses things like this to remind me of the other mistakes that I have made. Rather than supporting me, she would have related to me by putting me down or reminding me that I need to be working somewhere else because I have a college degree."

In both David's and James's cases, their relationships with black women were hampered because deep down inside these brothers felt as if their dignity were destroyed. Both reported feeling as if they were imprisoned by their feelings and a bit helpless about their chances of becoming the men their women wanted them to be. Their big problem is a lack of self-reliance. From another perspective, what both David and James were projecting is a "sagging self-image" and a sense that they could not compete successfully against their women. This latter attitude has become very prevalent among some black men because of the economic problems black men face. Most black men often cope with the situation by boiling inside, maintaining their "cool" facade. Some of us, regardless of the amount of frustration and humiliation, refuse to show the hurt and anguish that we are experiencing, while others take out their anger on their women.

What needs to be done to prevent the pain, confusion, and emotional suffering from recurring? In thinking about David and James, one has to wonder if their problems with women stem more from their beliefs and attitudes about money, self-worth, and manhood or from "communication problems" that are usually the cause of conflict in a relationship.

Both men have problems expressing their true feelings about loss of control and self-respect. Both have a difficult time dealing with women who are better educated and more "economically" successful than themselves. As a consequence, they have difficulty asking or allowing their partners to nurture and support them. Unfortunately, they live in a time where it generally takes two paychecks to run a home and where women desire economic freedom as strongly as men.

James is fortunate in that he is seeking help for his anger problems through psychotherapy. There are, however, a number of techniques that James and David could have used to help change how they dealt with the situations that triggered their angry reactions. First of all, both men would have found great benefit from using the proactive problem-solving strategies that are described in chapter 7. In James's case, much of his anger could possibly have been prevented if he had developed a greater sense of awareness of the problems that triggered his anger. Once this had been accomplished, he could have used some of the *quick methods* to defuse anger that are presented in chapter 7. Simply listening without talking or talking more slowly in a softer voice could have worked to change the nature of the angry interactions James had with his wife. If these didn't work to cool him off, he could have tried to modify his thoughts or to change his physical response to the situation by changing his posture, stretching, or walking around the room. He could also have called a *time-out* and indicated that it would be best to deal with the situation at a later time. Another technique that he could have used is *thought stopping.* This distracts you from the train of angry thought and images before you lose your cool.

If James or David reminds you of yourself, then using the techniques presented at the end of this chapter can help improve your communication style, but it is still necessary for you to examine some of the techniques described in chapter 7. It is also recommended that you read certain sections in chapter 9, "Coping With Angry People."

My Woman, Her Children, and Me

A large percentage of black women who are interested in marriage already have children. This is a major complication since a large number of black men are not capable of supporting a family because of underemployment or unemployment. Compounding the problem is that some women believe that it is easier to support a child with welfare by remaining single. Black men's attitudes about starting a family with a woman who already has children is still another significant barrier that hinders the development of strong relationships between black men and black women.

It appears that regardless of their income and educational attainments, black men prefer to seek marriage-minded relationships with women who don't have children. However, some brave brothers have ventured into this area and have developed some successful relationships and marriages with black women and their children.

"Everything was going okay and things felt right, and then she told me she had a four-year-old daughter. I never would have guessed that she had a child, but then again I never pictured myself falling in love with a woman who has a child."

77

Reginald, thirty, works as a biomedical research assistant and plans to earn a doctoral degree and greater economic freedom. Life was simple, carefree, and nonstressful after Reginald earned his bachelor's degree almost a year ago. A handsome man, he works out nearly every day and takes pride in his accomplishments and fitness. In addition to his regular work, he earns a few dollars every weekend as a musician. He has a great sense of humor.

Up until a year ago Reginald was engaged to a woman he had met while in college, but after graduation she landed a job in another city and another man. "I was devastated after she broke off the engagement, but life goes on and I knew that I would find the right woman." After a few weeks of enjoying the single life, Reginald was introduced to a woman he had often seen at the church he attends. "When I was introduced to her, I didn't know what to say, but we talked for nearly two hours after the church service. I don't know what we talked about, but I felt connected and I knew that she was a nice lady. Since she never talked about children, I was shocked when she told me about the difficulties she had finding a baby-sitter as we prepared for our first date." After dating for nearly a year, Reginald, convinced that he had found his soul mate and best friend, asked for her hand in marriage.

Given the real shortage of desirable black men, a large percentage of black women may not have the option to pick and choose a partner as the male does. The choices for some black women are even more limited if she already has children from a previous marriage or out of wedlock. Regardless of the woman's economic situation, the extent to which a black man will seek a marriage-minded relationship with such a woman is determined by his earning capability and his self-esteem. In Reginald's case, he earned enough money to support himself, but he was afraid of the added expenses of having both a wife and child. "I worried about this the entire time we were dating, and there were times when I thought that I would be better off finding someone without a child. At times I found myself actually feeling angry, depressed, and a bit used because I would have to support another man's child."

Reginald is a bright man, and one great thing that he has going for him is his desire for his partner to meet him as an equal. By this I mean that Reginald's relationship does not appear to be motivated by the belief that he can restore dignity and joy to a woman who is downtrodden simply by getting involved with her. He has come to understand that the basis for a smooth relationship is honest communication and the ability to listen to a partner. "I realized that this relationship was going to have some special challenges, but I love her and I am committed to her child. I also know that this relationship can work as long as we both are honest with each other."

According to Reginald, it's been tough for his wife to stay focused on their relationship because most of her friends are without men and telling her that she would be better off raising the child alone. He realizes that there is a lot of pressure for her to fall into the same pattern as other women in her family. "I know these things because we talk all of the time and because she has been open about her fears and concerns." It appears that through all of the talks with his wife he has learned to trust himself and to open up. By trusting himself he has learned to let her know about his fear and his feeling about raising another man's child. "At first I thought that by just talking about our problems things would be solved, but I had to keep telling myself that it takes time to change. I knew she was motivated to change and I realized that criticizing her for spending time with her friends was not going to solve anything, so I give her all of my support and love. By respecting her and treating her like the queen that she really is, she is becoming more like that queen she wants to be."

Reginald has avoided falling into the trap of believing that he can rescue and "save" a woman from pain and suffering. He realizes that his masculinity is not tarnished by admitting that he is afraid of dealing with a challenging situation. By honestly communicating his feelings he has discovered a way to overcome the hurt and anger he has about "raising another man's child." He has also come to understand that change occurs gradually and that criticizing his wife's effort would be counterproductive. "Rather than criticizing each other when we argue about things, we talk about how we want things to be, and we have learned how to not take things so seriously." This is very different for Reginald because he was raised believing that a man should be serious and just tell his woman how to act and behave. However, to cope with the challenges of being married, he and his wife turn their conflicts into a game by seeing who can come up with the best and funniest way to deal with a problem. "We always come up with ways to make things better, and somehow we seem to have some fun and laugh a lot about how serious we sometimes can be about our problems. Sometimes I find that we are laughing so hard that I can't even remember what started the argument."

Sam, forty, married for four years and the manager of a health club, is another brother whose ideal mate came with a package—two children. His case was unusual because to have this relationship he had to overcome his fears of an abusive ex-husband and cope with a woman whose relationship with God is first in her life. "From the first time we met, I knew that she had children, but I had no idea that her ex-husband was still causing her a bad time. This scared me because of all the murders you hear about these days, but once a man finds the woman he is looking for, it seems that nothing can stop him from being with her." Despite a stressful situation in which it was almost impossible to nurture a loving relationship, Sam endured, and he appears to be enjoying a happy relationship that is supportive and challenging. "What I have learned most from my wife is how to forgive people for causing pain. She is my greatest friend and teacher, and I admire how she was so calm and together through all of the mess she put up with from her ex-husband. Through all his threats she kept asking God to forgive him."

Before meeting his wife, Sam had not given much thought to God and religion. "It actually angered me to have to deal with her and to have her praying for him when he was the cause of so much hurt." However, since coming together with his wife, he has incorporated some of her qualities and he has learned that through the love of God all things are possible. "My wife has taught me that loving means giving and sacrifice. Once I learned to give of myself, I overcame a lot of personal problems and worries. I have truly learned that anything is possible when you believe in the power of God."

The Circle of None: The Fear of Commitment

A growing number of black men are realizing that, based on the statistics, they are a commodity. As a consequence, some brothers are turning a depressing situation into one where they can exploit and use black women. Some black men realize that the only way for some black women to have a relationship with a man is for them to share a man with another woman or several other women. With this being the case, then why should the African-American male not have two, three, four, or even more women? If black women are willing to settle for less than a one-to-one fully committed relationship, then why should the few available "good men" not have multiple partners? This is the type of confused argument that has contributed to the idea of sharing men as an alternative way for African-American men and women to mingle.

Whereas the sharing of men may be a possible solution to the shortage of "good men," the health implications of the "man-sharing" arrangement may be detrimental to the survival of the race because of the emergence of HIV/AIDS in the African-American community. We as a people have faced many problems and obstacles to our survival, but HIV/AIDS is a problem that must immediately be dealt with by refuting myths about the sexuality of African-Americans and by accepting certain realities about sex and politics.

Because politics and sex are often deeply intertwined with racism and racial superiority, the health and economic consequences of HIV/AIDS on the black family are likely to be one of our most difficult challenges. Basically, the HIV/AIDS epidemic has taken its toll on the black family because it provided another means of reducing the number of available black men and created another reason for black men and women not to trust one another. It has also created a large number of children who have lost one or both of their parents to the epidemic. Again, the consequences are the same—the black family unit suffers. Another frightening aspect of the AIDS epidemic is that some brothers, despite being highly knowledgeable about how AIDS is spread, continue to maintain relationships with several women. They do this because so few "good" men are available and they use this to manipulate women into having dead-end relationships.

"All of a sudden it seemed like black women lost respect for black men. So, why should I or any brother continue to act like a gentleman and respect the ladies when they treat us like dogs. Since they don't appear to have any respect for me, or black men in general, then I don't see any reason why I should be serious about a relationship."

Jerome, thirty-five, describes himself as a handsome, well-educated ladies' man who is fun to be with and not interested in being married and tied down to one woman. He served four years in the navy and has been a successful car salesman for over ten years. "I realize that I can be with as many black women as I want because there are so few men like myself. I have a good education, a steady job, and I buy a new car every few years. As I see things, any sister would be proud to be with me." Jerome's attitude is typical of many black men who constantly find themselves surrounded by beautiful and single black women. Jerome's behavior, to some extent, is similar to that of a rooster who wakes up one day to find himself in a house full of hens.

Jerome claims that until a year ago he was very marriage minded and very much involved with a woman. "Things were really going well, and then, all of a sudden, she started acting funny and treating me poorly. It was hard enough to be treated this way by her, but it seems like all of her female friends treated me with disrespect." As it turns out, this was not the first time that Jerome had been "treated poorly" by women. His last girlfriend evidently saw through his friendly facade and realized that Jerome was not serious about having a monogamous relationship. "She told all of her friends about me and about how much she loved me, and the next moment she was putting me down in public."

It's possible to have some understanding for Jerome's attitude toward women and possible even to develop a bit of empathy for his situation. However, his behavior may be strongly related to his fear of making a commitment, and his rhetoric about the shortage of "good men" may simply be a smoke screen that he uses to hide the truth from himself and other people. But, what is the truth? What happened during his development to cause him to fear having a committed relationship?

Jerome was raised without a father who could help him define what it means to be a man. As a consequence, Jerome, like many other black males today, learned about the values of a relationship from his peers on the street. Without a positive father role model there was little chance for him to learn the values of a commitment between a man and a woman in a relationship. Growing up in the streets, particularly in the inner city of Baltimore where Jerome was raised, African-American males learn the lesson that women are whores and handmaidens who want to have children as a means of proving that they are adults. Some brothers have also used something of a backward logic to conclude that some black women want to have children so that they, the mother and the child, can be taken care of by welfare.

As with a large number of black men who were raised without a father present, Jerome has nurtured the attitude that courting and having a relationship with a woman is a game in which the object is to perfect a rap that seduces women and contributes to one's sexual conquests. While it may be a bitter pill for some of us to swallow, having a succession of senseless sexual conquests is what having a relationship boils down to for some brothers. As Jerome passionately explains, "The whole thing between black men and women is a game. They only want men who can measure up and provide them with material things, and I only want single, well-educated, beautiful women with no dependents. If a black man takes a honest look at the situation, as I have, he would see that it makes no sense to get tied down to one woman when there are so many beautiful sisters that he can be with."

Unfortunately, there are no winners and only losers in the game described by Jerome. Black women lose because they are basically abandoned by black men, and this stirs up more anger, more hurt, and more animosity about dealing with black men. The brothers lose because the attitudes and behavior of men like Jerome continue to reinforce a vicious cycle that will always keep grown men acting like boys who don't take responsibility for their actions, behaviors and development.

Rather than expressing excuses, despair, and self-pity about the present predicament, black men must learn how to step beyond the prison of their own intellect and seize the moment—take responsibility for their actions or lack thereof as they mingle with black women. It becomes so easy for the brothers to blame their problems on things outside of themselves because many were born economically underprivileged and raised without fathers to teach them about self-reliance. They have also used this as a permanent grievance, which permits them to spend a lifetime sulking, harboring hostile feelings, and cursing their fate.

Rather than doing something to empower themselves to overcome these challenges, some brothers use their past problems as a permanent excuse for all of their weaknesses and failures. In most cases these men take out their anger on other people. Sad to say, some brothers attempt to turn the situation around and claim that black women are the cause of their problems. "If they want to be treated nicely and like ladies, then they should treat us with respect. The disrespect they—black women—get is their own fault," explains Jerome.

As things stand, there are no permanent fixtures in the path between black men and black women. Old problems and wounds are constantly being replaced with new and more demanding challenges. For example, in addition to the problems of discrimination and racism, some black men are now attempting to manage relationships where the woman rather than the man is the chief breadwinner for the family. This trend will continue for a while because of the low number of black males who graduate from college or trade schools and because of the high mortality primarily from AIDS and homicide. One of the consequences of all of this is that the old essential question "What's happened to all of the good black men?" may be changing to "Where are the black men who can deal with well-educated, career-focused, and strong-minded black women?"

In contrast to men like Jerome are brothers who have overcome their fear of commitment, failure, and their desire to project their manhood through the clothes they wear or the car they drive. Some of these brothers have also overcome their fears of having a relationship with a black woman who has more education and is more financially secure than they are. It is important to know more about how these brothers cope with this arrangement because it is likely to be the rule rather than the exception.

Superwoman and Her Man

"I've been told by the brothers that I am a lucky man to be married to a successful woman who makes lots of money, owns a big house, and will give me anything that I desire. Hearing this sort of thing used to make me angry and cause me to feel a bit strange because I knew that behind this comment the fellows were really putting me down because my wife, who is a physician, is the reason for my affluent lifestyle."

George, thirty-eight, a dental assistant, has three children and has been married since he was twenty-two. "I met my wife-to-be as she was about to enter medical school and I had no idea that she and I would stay together and eventually get married. There were many times when I thought that she would find someone in medical school, who was more compatible. But, deep down in my heart I knew that we had something that no man could ever take." This thing that George is talking about is something that is deeper than love and involves what some people may call "old-fashioned" values about what a "commitment" between a man and a woman is all about.

As it turns out, once George and his future wife realized that they were serious about each other, they made a commitment to develop a relationship with marriage being one of the products of their union and raising children being another. "I realized that we didn't have to rush into anything or prove anything, so we took our time to get to know each other's values and beliefs about life as well as our likes and dislikes. I felt a little uneasy about the situation at first because she was attending medical school to become a doctor, but I gave her all of my support."

According to George, while his wife was in medical school, her classmates made jokes several times about her dumping him when she got her MD. "What was so awful about this is that some of the white fellows would make these statements in my presence. I have gotten over my doubts about my wife's commitment, and I don't feel ashamed, intimidated, or embarrassed about my marriage and relationships with my family. But, there were times when I felt pretty low and I did question myself about being able to stay with my wife."

Unlike the cases of David and James, George has learned that his manhood is in no way shaped or affected by having a mate who has received more formal education or who makes more money than him. "I deeply love my wife and children, and I feel special that my wife and I have the opportunity to provide our children with all of the things we didn't have." George also feels lucky that he has a wife with a career because he knows that otherwise he would not have the time to spend with his two boys. "In these days and times black boys need all of the guidance they can get, and my wife and I are fortunate to have the income and security that affords me the opportunity to spend quality time with my sons," explains George.

George is fortunate in that he has developed to the point where he understands that the typical image of what a man is supposed to be is incomprehensible and insane. Such a man is supposed to be aggressive, controlling everything and everyone, unemotional, unaffected by things, and always competing to win at all cost.

Some black men and women have allowed themselves to adopt this image of a man as a measuring stick. The truth is that a "real man" has liberated himself from the point of view that it is the external image of things that defines him. Basically, what a man believes in private and practices daily is what determines the external reflection of his inner character. "I don't think that I or any man can deal with a self-sufficient woman if he is not secure in his identify as a man. By this I mean that a real man does not have to create a glossy and fake image of himself because his moral character and his inner character are consistent with his outward expression of himself. It's like buying a nice piece of wood furniture that doesn't need all of that glossy covering because the wood used to make the piece was of good quality. And everybody knows that it's the cheap and inferior piece of wood that needs to be dressed up and polished to have the appearance of a quality product," explains George.

The development of these positive attitudes did not necessarily come easily for George. His wife would, on occasion, mock him for his failure to contribute as much money as she did to the household. According to George, she would make comments such as "I am not worth as much as she is" and "I don't work as hard as she does." These comments, more than anything else, caused this brother grief and stirred up his anger and insecurities. For example, at times George was so angered by the comments that he would not speak to his wife or sleep with her. "I knew that each time she made comments like this she was under a lot of pressure or feeling stressed-out. It was difficult for me not to let my anger fly, but I knew that being angry at her wouldn't do anything except make the situation worse."

Rather than falling into the trap of being caught up with his own anger, George learned to simply be quiet and to question his wife about her feelings and what was happening at work. "Each time I did this, I learned how to reduce my own distress and my wife learned how she sometimes used her income as a weapon to hurt me. This was very hard for me to do since my initial response was to become angry when I felt criticized or accused of something I didn't do."

From the description above it should be clear that George coped with his anger by changing what he and his wife focused on when they felt frustrated. He was able to accomplish this by using questions that empowered the situations rather than questions like "Why are you angry at me?" or "What did I do wrong?" that presupposed that he was responsible for his wife's anger. "Standing behind our relationship is trust and a strong belief in the desire to help each other through whatever problems and obstacles life creates. Early on I learned a lot by helping my wife get through college and medical school. I worked two jobs to support my family and help pay her tuition. While I was doing this, all of my so-called friends gladly told me that I was crazy because she would leave me once she got her degree."

The relationship George has with himself and his wife is similar to how Darnell has evolved. Darnell, forty-one, drives a school bus for a living and has been married for twenty-three years to his high school sweetheart. He is a proud father of four children and is comfortable being in a relationship with a woman who is the chief breadwinner for the family. His wife is a successful and busy corporate attorney with a six-figure income. According to Darnell, what is unique about his wife is that she has a strong sense of who she is, how Darnell helped her stay in college, and his contributions to their relationship and family.

Over the years Darnell has endured many hardships,

threats to his manhood, and heightened insecurities about his job stemming from his limited education. "Each year I panic because of the teacher strikes and because of the threats and talk about the cutbacks the schools need to make." While he has had several opportunities to better himself by attending college, he would have had to put his needs ahead of the needs of his family. "I've got mad about this at times, but I made a commitment to my wife and family, and I knew that my wife was also committed to our relationship and family. I knew from the first day we met that my wife rather than me would be the person making the money, and I have never had any regrets about helping her reach her dream."

Darnell clearly has accomplished something that many brothers would perceive as being a threat to their manhood. He has also discovered that as long as he is clear about himself, then it does not matter what job he does or how much education he has. "In the long run I know that my wife loves me for who I am and not the size of my paycheck. I know that she loves me because of how I have cared for our family, and she knows that I love her and that I respect her talents and that I would do anything to help her meet her goals."

To some people it might appear that Darnell is getting the short end of things because of his tendency to give and his capacity for helping. However, in the long run Darnell has been blessed with a beautiful and healthy family, and he has a life that most men would envy. "We have paid our dues. We don't have any financial worries and we are very comfortable. Even though I don't bring home as much as she does, we both make decisions about what we are doing with our money. This is the one thing that I thought we would have some difficulties with, but we respect each other too much and there has never been a problem. She has never once told me what to do, and it makes me feel very proud when she asks my advice about decisions concerning her work."

The ease with which Darnell discussed his relationship is a credit to himself and his wife. In these days and times, black men have strong fears of appearing weak or dominated, especially by black women. For many black men and black women the source of the conflicts in their relationship is their different views about work and money.

When a man's and a woman's priorities are incongruent, the bonds are not likely to last. But if they share the same attitudes and vision, they are usually capable of overcoming their differences. In Darnell's case, the tie that bound him and his wife was their attitude about raising a family. Both he and his wife were raised in poor families, and they promised that they would support each other and develop their independence. "Basically, my wife and I see our family as being the only thing that matters. Up until now that has meant that I spend more time taking care of the children and making sure that our house is okay. I know that a lot of brothers would have a difficult time doing this because they are not as committed to black women and black families as they need to be."

Prescriptions for Change: Nurturing Healthy Relationships With Black Women

The challenges facing black men and black women are enormous and require a renewed commitment for mutual respect, loyalty, devotion, and love for one another. Furthermore, a transformation of faulty beliefs and our sagging self-image is necessary. When a man seeks unconditional love and support from a woman, he attracts to himself the treatment, circumstances, and women who duplicate the beliefs, images, and judgments he has about himself. Therefore, to transform a relationship a man must first have a complete relationship with himself. Before he can be loved, trusted, respected, accepted, supported, and adored by another, he must feel these things about himself.

Some black men are so sensitive to the perceived threats against their masculinity by white society that they rebel against any authority figure. The difficulties stemming from this problem have been enormous for black men. One consequence is that black men often feel uneasy dealing with strong and independent black women who are sometimes the chief wage earners for their family. Some brothers have overcome this challenge because they understand the power of a commitment. They have come to understand that having a commitment means sacrifice, being loyal and faithful, dealing with the good and bad times, communicating from the level of the heart, and thinking about their partner and their family rather than themselves. Making a commitment is a choice that involves compromise, giving up feeling helpless, and the realization that everything and everyone changes according to his or her speed and level of development.

It seems that black men who make a real commitment to black women do so because they have a great trust in themselves and their woman. For some brothers the respect for women is a reflection of the respect and love they have for themselves. These men have come to understand that a woman is not a mirror image of them, but a refection of the quality of their inner happiness and their self-respect.

If a black man wants to have and maintain a loving relationship with a black woman, he must understand that his relationship will have absolutely nothing to do with luck or the popular wisdom about people being "made for each other." A lasting love and relationship are built on friendliness, happiness, trust, and compassion. Here are some of the simple things that men like you and those described in the earlier part of the chapter can do to nurture these qualities.

Learn to Listen Without Talking

One of the major reasons that love wanes is neglect, and one of the principal kinds of neglect is the inability to listen well. Some psychotherapists have proclaimed that the number one way a man may succeed in fulfilling a woman's primary love need is through communication. By actively listening to his partner, a man can effectively show a woman that he cares about her, that he respects her, that he is devoted to her, and that he is there to support her and provide her with reassurance.

One simple and effective way to enhance your listening abilities and create a great atmosphere for dialogue is for you and your partner to eat something before having important conversations. Low blood sugar causes epinephrine (adrenaline) release in your bloodstream and, according to some authorities, may cause some people to have a short temper, become more frustrated, and make it more difficult to think clearly. After eating a healthy meal or snack, you'll often be better able to head off arguments and listen more attentively and lovingly.

Listening well is one of the rules of communication that makes it difficult for conflicts to occur and often results in people feeling satisfied about the resolutions that are reached. Other rules that minimize conflict include not interrupting your partner when he or she is speaking, staying focused on what is being said rather than what you think, respecting differences of opinion, helping a partner validate his or her feelings, and fighting fair and not using conflicts as an opportunity to hurt your partner or bring up problems from the past.

Relate Eye to Eye

One of the most important ways a man can affirm his connection to a woman or any loved one is eye to eye. The eyes express how much and in what way we value our relationships with other people. Our eye contact tells other people how much we trust them and whether or not we are being completely open and honest about important issues. Regardless of how old you become, you will never cease to need unconditional, simple valuing in another's eyes—and in your own eyes. Some philosophers have even claimed that the eyes are the windows to the soul.

Know Your Communication Style

One of the major difficulties black men have with black women, regardless of how the problem rises to the surface, is poor and nonassertive communication. Seldom can couples achieve the type of intimacy they desire without communicating assertively, because the goal of assertive communication is to express feelings and needs clearly and directly without lashing out or overlooking the partner's viewpoint. Unfortunately, most brothers (and sisters) don't communicate assertively, and their styles of communication and dealing with conflict tend to be either be passive, aggressive, or passive-aggressive.

Black men who use the passive approach to dealing with conflict have difficulties expressing their feelings, and they often neglect their own needs. They do anything to appear nice and to avoid confrontations simply because they don't know how to openly express themselves. This was the approach used mostly by James, who would hold in his anger to appear nice.

Aggressive men are often angry and hostile in defense of their own interests. They are basically self-centered individuals who go to extremes to make certain they get their way. These brothers often attempt to dominate their partners through sarcastic remarks, put-downs, threats, and verbal attacks.

While it may appear that only overly aggressive men are likely to be abusive, male spouse abusers are often characterized as being passive as well as passive-aggressive in how they deal with their anger and hostility.

Passive-aggressive men, as is the case with David and Jerome, are manipulative and irresponsible, usually as a response to an inability to honestly express feelings. Nevertheless, they are determined to get their needs met, often at the expense of other people, including the women in their lives.

To gain a different perspective about how you communicate, consider the following incident:

1. Your wife or partner is four hours late coming home and did not phone you. When she finally arrives, she does not give you much of a reason for being late. *How would you respond?*

    a. You quietly ignore her and pretend that nothing unusual has happened.

This is a passive response and it clearly tells the wife that you are not to be taken seriously and that your needs are unimportant. Some of the clues that accompany the passive response include a weak voice, failure to make eye contact, and excessive fidgeting.

    b. You get angry and say, "I have been waiting and worrying about you for the last four hours. Where in the hell have you been?"

This is an aggressive response, often spoken in a louder than usual voice, with such nonverbal behaviors as finger-pointing, hands on the hips, and moving the neck from side to side.

    c. You are so angry you say little to your wife, but you think of ways of getting her back for causing you to wait and worry about her.

This is the approach taken by passive-aggressive men. A typical passive-aggressive response for a man is to arrive late to an event he didn't want to attend or completely forget about the commitment he made. Some of the associated nonverbal behavior includes rolling the eyes, folding the arms across the chest, and sighing. A common reaction of men who use the passive-aggressive style is for them to displace their anger by lashing out at someone who was not involved in the provocation.

d. You tell her directly and clearly how you feel about her not calling home, saying, "Because I want us to understand each other, I want you to know that I am angry that you didn't bother to call me because I was worried that something might have happened to you."

This is an assertive response and is an effective way to express feelings and thoughts without attacking or withdrawing from the other person. This response is also quite effective in minimizing conflict because it invites further discussion and creates the groundwork for negotiation. In this situation, it is important to be honest and to create a nonthreatening climate so that meaningful dialogue with nonconflicting nonverbal cues can occur. Direct eye contact is made, both partners are relaxed, and they listen attentively because they are respectful of each other. Another characteristic is that each partner tends to use "I" messages (e.g., "I felt upset," rather than "You upset me") that show ownership of their feelings rather than blaming ("you") messages that tend to offend the listener.

If you have trouble identifying your communication style, following are some other situations that are common sources of conflict. In parentheses you will find the response style that is characteristics of your choice.

---

2. Your spouse tells you that she is going to a business meeting, and you later find out that she had dinner with an old boyfriend. *How would you respond?*
   a. Tell her why this caused you to be angry. (assertive)
   b. Keep this to yourself because of your fears about what it may mean. (passive)
   c. Talk to one of her girlfriends about the situation. (passive-aggressive)
   d. Don't ask for an explanation, but tell her to pack her bags and leave or have her things packed and placed outside when she comes home. (aggressive)

3. You want to have sex, but your partner does not. *How do you respond?*
   a. I know that you don't want to have sex, but I want to right now. (aggressive)
   b. It's okay that you don't want sex, but don't ask me for anything. (passive-aggressive)
   c. I know that you like to have sex—is anything bothering you? (assertive)
   d. Say nothing and go to sleep. (passive)

4. You are angry and upset because of problems at work and you want support from your partner. *How would you respond?*
   a. Say nothing when you arrive home. (passive)
   b. Complain about your partner's lack of sensitivity. (aggressive)
   c. Explain that you had a bad day and that you need a hug. (assertive)
   d. Go play basketball. (passive-aggressive)

5. You are upset because you overheard your spouse on the phone talking to a family member about how much more money she makes than you. *How would you respond?*
   a. Say nothing. (passive)
   b. Tell her to get off of the phone. (aggressive)
   c. Let her know that you want to have sex. (passive-aggressive)
   d. Wait until she is off of the phone and ask about the conversation you overheard. (assertive)

While it may appear that it takes a "conscious" effort to communicate assertively, the real art to assertive communication lies with the types of questions men (or women) ask themselves about the conflicts they encounter. For example, here are some powerful questions a man can ask himself when he is experiencing difficulties with a woman or if he wants to avoid finding himself in a difficult situation:

- Do I know what is really happening?
- What has been miscommunicated?
- What do I want from this situation?
- What are my feelings?
- What am I angry about?
- What am I afraid of losing?
- What can I learn from this interaction?

In addition to questions such as these, a man can also practice distancing himself from the conflict and challenges by using the following technique.

Look slowly around the room and say to yourself, "What I am saying does not mean anything. What she is saying does not mean anything. What I am thinking does not mean anything. The way that she says things does not mean anything. Why? Because I am never angry for the reasons I think. I am never afraid for the reasons I think. I am not worried for the reasons I think. I am not sad about this for the reasons I think. I am not upset for the reasons I think." This is an excellent exercise that can be practiced daily until the "fantasized" wall that separates you from a loved one vanishes. To practice this exercise simply requires you to sit quietly for a few minutes each day and examine your mind for whatever is distressing you, regardless of how much or how little you think it is doing so. As you search your mind, you focus on situations and then practice the distancing technique.

Creating a Healthy Transition Between Work and Home

Today, more and more couples rush home from work, hurry to prepare dinner, flip through the newspaper, eat quickly while watching television, and then plunge into their nightly round of scheduled errands and activities—exercise class, catching up on paperwork, paying the bills. The one ingredient that is missing in these relationships is a transition period where a husband and wife can sit together, without the television in the background, and regain their sense of togetherness and harmony while recovering from the day's work.

For most of us the amount of time we need to make this transition can be as little as fifteen or twenty minutes. While there are many things a couple can do to create a healthy transition between the tensions and pressures of the work world and home, one method that is highly recommended is to incorporate a meditation/relaxation period into the daily routine. In our home, we schedule ninety minutes at the end of the day, 5:30 P.M. to 7:00 P.M., where there is no television, music, or any intrusions from the world outside that we deal with. Phone calls that come to us are saved on the answering machine. Instead of attending to the troubles of the world, we use this time to turn our attention to meditation, yoga, working out, and our spiritual and self-development reading. Although we don't have children yet, several of our close friends have set rules like this for their families, and they are exceptionally happy with the results. When you think about it, what parent wouldn't be happy to have a scheduled time at the end of every day when they can hear a pin drop in their own house?

If you have trouble finding the time for meditation, here are some other things that you can do to increase the harmony between you and your spouse or partner:

- Kiss and greet each other whenever leaving and returning home.
- Have dinner in a settled atmosphere without the noise of a television.
- Spend time together preparing meals, doing dishes, or puttering around the lawn or garden.
- Go for early-morning or evening walks.
- Sit together quietly, listening to music you both enjoy, sipping a cup of tea or a glass of wine.
- Stretch out on the sofa and hold each other—fully clothed, with nothing unsnapped, unhooked, or unzipped—in a "spoon" position, with one person wrapping arms around the other from behind.

- Share a warm bath or gentle rhythmic massage for fifteen to twenty minutes prior to sexual intimacy.

Self-Awareness Strategies and Exercises

Take Notice of Yourself

Take a moment here and ponder how you respond in your various relationships with women. Answering the following questions will give you a good idea of how you respond to women.

- Do you want to be in control?
- Do you react with anger, guilt, and sadness to manipulate women?
- Do you sometimes feel as if you are competing with women?
- Do you sometimes feel powerless in your relationships with women?
- Do you feel misunderstood by women?
- Are you happy or unhappy with the relationships you have with women in your life?
- Which one of your relationships with women is the best?
- What makes it the best?
- Which relationships are the source of anger and conflict?
- What makes them this way?
- Do you behave differently in the relationships with women that are good versus those that are conflicted? If so, why?
- What do you gain by acting differently?
- Do you think that the way that you behave determines whether your relationships with women are good or conflicted?
- Do you act differently with the women you work with compared to other women?

- What is your behavior like when you have a woman supervising your work?
- Does this situation bother you?
- Does it cause you to feel uneasy or angry?
- Does it cause you to feel less than a man?

Take a few moments and look for differences in your behavior, attitudes, beliefs, and feelings as you interact with women in your life.

- Do you see any patterns in your attitudes and beliefs?
- Are you doing anything that hinders the development of a happy and trusting relationship? Why are you doing these things?
- What pain and hurt are you avoiding by doing these things?
- Does it make you feel angry to see a man and woman happy together? Be honest with yourself. What would you say to this man if you had a chance? Are you jealous of this situation?

Take a few moments each day for the next week to recall how you feel about your relationships with the different women in your life. Slowly think about the things that make each relationship different. Think about what you can do to make each relationship more peaceful, wonderful, and lovable.

Make Decisions About What You Want

Take full responsibility for what goes on in your relationships with women. If the relationships you have with women are painful and conflicted then it's because you have created them to be this way. If these relationships are superficial and phony, then you have to take responsibility for them and say to yourself, "I want to have superficial and phony relationships with the women in my life." Whatever your responses are to your relationships with women, this is the way that you are now because you have chosen to be this way. If you always feel confused when you are with women, say to yourself, "I choose to feel confused with this woman." If you are hung up about "control," say, "I choose to try to control this woman." If you are angry at women, say to yourself, "I choose to be angry at women." Whatever your feelings, behaviors, and attitudes are about women, accept them and take responsibility for what goes on in your relationships with women. Accept that this is the way that you are because you have made either a conscious or subconscious choice to be this way. Just as you have made these choices, you can choose to have any type of relationship you desire with women. But, then, what is it that you really want from a relationship with a woman? Do you want love? Are you looking for someone to make you feel whole? Do you want someone to accept you for what you really are, or do you prefer a woman who wants you because of the man that you want to become? Are you looking to control someone, or do you want a woman to control you and save you from the awful things in this world?

Stop Blaming Yourself and Others

It is so easy for a black man to blame black women for his difficulties, but the truth is that each black man is responsible for his own behaviors, attitudes, and beliefs. There is nothing wrong about the feelings you have about black women. These are feelings that you have created as a result of the beliefs that you hold about relationships with women. Stop blaming black women for what happens to you or other black men. When you do this, you only create problems for yourself and place more obstacles between you and the relationship that you desire.

Take a few moments and reflect on the fact that you are always responsible for your behavior. Every relationship you have with a woman is a relationship you have with a spiritual being who, as is the case with yourself, is responsible for her actions. You can try to blame a woman for what happens to you, but this only compounds the problems and alienates you from your real self. That real self is spirit, knows no imperfections, and has but one purpose, and that is to express eternal love for every person and everything.

Create Your Own Destiny

Think about how you would like your relationships with black women to be. Create a clean mental picture. Visualize yourself with the various women in your life. What would you like to say to them? How do you want to respond to them? What feelings do you have about these relationships? Now, make contrasts between the way you want your relationships with black women to be with the way they are now. Do you see any differences in your behaviors, attitudes, feelings, and beliefs? Take a moment and really see the man you are, the man that other people see, and the man that you want to become. Are there any differences in these three versions of yourself? Which version of yourself do you allow to run your relationships with black women? To know this more fully you must be willing to know all about yourself and accept your strengths and inadequacies. You must be willing to be alone with yourself so that you can learn to love yourself. Once this is accomplished, you can then bring more love into your relationships with black women.

5

Rage
in the Workplace

Job stress and how it relates to suppressed anger in black men is one of the most difficult subjects to investigate. There is as much variability in the type of work that people perform as there is in the people performing the tasks. Nevertheless, some central issues factor into work-related anger in black men regardless of their job, their level of education and training, or their rank at work. For many black men the anger they experience at work is produced because of a perception of an ever-present low level of institutional racism, invisible but palpable nonetheless. While many brothers often experience uncomfortable feelings that appear to have no apparent cause, they are suspicious of the motives of their white counterparts. The causes of their disquiet are seldom uncovered. In some circumstances, however, the reasons surface and the real villain is identified as racism.

William is a thirty-seven-year-old corporate attorney, one of ten blacks in a firm of thirty lawyers. Even though a third of the firm's lawyers are black, there are no black or women partners. One morning, William overheard a conversation between two of the partners in the firm. Essentially one was complaining to the other about the slow progress of a project that William was directing. In defense of William the second partner said, "You know how things are with our niggers. It takes them longer to do the work." William was stunned. But what to do about this blatant example of racism? Should he angrily confront the partners or complain to their peers?

William quietly completed his work while he boiled inside. He left work at the end of the day and turned in his resignation a few days later. Ten years later, William says that he still feels angry and humiliated about this event, but he is also convinced that his response was the proper one. "Rather than lose it and act out my anger and disgust, I decided to terminate my employment and offer my talents to a firm that was often a competitor for the same contracts. Upon reflection on this event, I realize that I was angry enough to have actually hurt someone," explains William. But instead of getting into an ugly confrontation, William contained his anger and calmly thought during the remainder of the day about how to deal with this situation. "I always felt a bit guarded at work, like there was something going on underneath the surface—something private that was not to be shared with blacks—of my interactions with many of the white lawyers," he said. "There were times that I wondered about whether they felt comfortable having black attorneys at the firm, but I never expected to hear the things I heard that particular day."

Even well-educated, successful black men worry that someday the anger that simmers within will come pouring out with an intensity that it threatens the foundation upon which their success is built. Many brothers would have reacted quite differently to the situation William was confronted with. Some may have challenged the partners about the racial slur, which could have resulted in injuries, and perhaps loss of job and income. A lengthy discrimination suit could have been started with no guarantee that the injustice would be addressed. William made a conscious choice to not let his anger fly, but to change jobs so that he was in a better position to attack the institutionalized racial practices that had led the law firm to not promote minority lawyers. William was unlucky, in a sense, because the hasty resignation from his job did not give him much time to prepare for his departure. Also, by staying longer his leaving might well have been more to his advantage.

Even though each of us at times has some doubts about the power of our thoughts in shaping our lives, there is much power in self-fulfilling prophecies and not considering things beyond the boundaries of one's own self-imposed limitations. This is true for expectations about gaining employment, winning a basketball game, passing a difficult exam, moving beyond addictive and destructive relationships, as well as using emotionally charged moments constructively, to address the causes of the anger and hurt we feel.

"I was obviously very upset and angry about the conversation between these two men, but I decided that there was a better way to deal with the situation and to confront them about their racist attitudes. I took a position with one of the firm's major competitors and eventually gathered enough information from the other minority lawyers to file a discrimination case. As a consequence, I was able to alert other ethnic minorities about these attitudes, which dissuaded several top-of-the-line attorneys from seeking positions with this firm," explains William.

Many African-American men could benefit from William's example of developing an action plan that moved him beyond his anger and prevented his feelings from ruling his life. In contrast to William, Lloyd wears his anger like a badge of honor.

At thirty-eight, Lloyd is a department store manager who has a long history of poor relationships, fighting, and job instability. "I have a temper and it does not take much for me to become angry," says Lloyd.

So far Lloyd is fortunate his uncontrolled temper hasn't resulted in physical violence. This style of coping with anger is referred to as anger-out. It is characterized by frequent and impulsive anger and is expressed in aggressive behaviors toward people or objects.

For Lloyd, anger was usually expressed verbally in the form of insults, threats, criticism, sarcasm, and profanity, often aimed at a coworker's "weak point." Most of the people who suffered his angry outbursts had no idea why because Lloyd was adept at masking the issues. It's as if Lloyd would rather figure out a way to stab you in the back in a public place than talk to you face-to-face.

Lloyd was remarkably insightful about the causes of his anger: "My parents are very smart and successful, and I simply did not think that I could live up to their standards. So what I did was constantly start trouble at school." Even though he had good insights, Lloyd was slow to understand the impact of his anger on others. "I knew that I had a temper, but when I got angry at someone at work, I always thought that I was justified. I knew that my reasons were right, and more often than not my reasons for behaving the way I did had to do with the way that white people treated me at work—as if they were better than me."

Black men often pay a severe price for expressing angry feelings at work. It can damage the chances for advancement, promotions, and the perception of being someone who can fit in and be accepted. Many of the men interviewed expressed the opinion that no matter how hard they worked or how much education they acquired, they did not feel accepted by their nonblack coworkers because of their race. The anger that is generated by this awareness is quite intense, and yet it simmers within these men with little chance of being expressed.

For those black men who have not learned how to be assertive without being overly aggressive, expressing anger in the workplace often results in their dismissal. But the consequences of repeatedly repressing anger can be the loss of self-respect, increased self-doubt, and the realization that one is not "in control." This sets in motion a vicious cycle that reinforces the desire to keep unpleasant feelings to one's self and to not rock the boat.

The Nature of Work

As a worker, a man is protecting his self-respect and fulfilling a duty. His sense of self-respect and dignity is not terribly tarnished—even in the case of menial, unrewarding, dehumanizing, and unchallenging work that leads nowhere—because he is a man with a job. It is still the case today that a man's worth to himself and his family is measured by his job, achievements, and his earnings. For this reason, it is quite common for black men to describe being laid off or fired as an "assault" because of the resulting diminution of self-respect, pride, and self-worth..

Being without a stable job is difficult and stressful for anyone, but for some brothers the job becomes the source of their stress, aggravations, and frustrations. In many cases the underlying cause of the stress is racism. For example, one of the situations that causes black men to experience much frustration and anger at work occurs when an important decision they have made about a project is undermined (i.e., changed without their awareness or input) by their boss, even though they were supposed to be in charge of the project. "I was particularly upset about one particular project that we had put together to educate kids in the inner-city schools. We had gone so far as to inform the principals, teachers, and students about the program when out of the blue the program was brought to an immediate stop. I was so humiliated and embarrassed by this event that I could hardly look in the faces of people at work for almost a month," says Cleveland.

Cleveland, thirty-six, is the director of a drug abuse program for a large city. When he took the position, he was told by the supervisor that he would have control of the program and be able to establish his own drug abuse initiatives. As it turns out, each of his initiatives has been undermined without any strong justification by the same supervisor who assured him that he would have autonomy. This has resulted in Cleveland's feeling angry, upset, embarrassed, humiliated,

107

and betrayed. "I considered the possibility that the behavior of my boss has some racist intent. I thought about other things, too, but there are no justifiable reasons for him to block my programs other than the fact that I am black. I am good, and the programs that I have put together are not only good, but my staff and I believe that they will be effective."

This sort of situation makes a man feel useless, as if he is wasting his time and going around in circles. For some brothers, the level of frustration is so acute that they eventually lose their temper and their "cool" facade or they leave their job. In either case, these men have failed to consider the possibility that they have been manipulated into acting and behaving as if they were not worthy of the position that they had worked so hard to attain. "I know that I have worked hard at my job, but I don't seem to get the respect that I deserve. The stress at my job gets unbearable at times because I feel that much of my work efforts are undermined by my colleagues, who sometimes deliberately block my progress," explains Cleveland.

Many black men expressed the opinion that they thought that some white people, particularly males, don't want to see black men be promoted to positions of authority either because that would prevent some white person from being promoted or they simply don't want to be told what to do by a black man. "They act as if the company will fall apart if there were black people making decisions at the top. They treat us as if we are not capable of doing the job. What is so pathetic about all of this is that most of them were trained to do their jobs by a black person," says Cleveland.

Being Left Out of the Good-Old-Boy Network

Black men are often put in situations at work where important decisions are made outside of the work environment, but they don't feel invited to be part of these "inner circles" or "good-old-boy" networks. In fact, many of the men who were interviewed said that they feel as if they are not invited or encouraged to develop social relationships that extend beyond work. "They treat me as if I am good enough to help them look good and get a high mark at work, but they don't want to have anything to do with me outside of work," explains Cleveland.

What becomes problematic for black men is that they ultimately miss the opportunity to gain advantages at work through the informal exchange of valuable information that takes place outside of work. Another negative effect of this sort of undermining is that black men start to believe that they can't trust people at work. Once the level of trust between people is diminished, it is very difficult for work relationships or any types of relationship to function effectively. Quite often the lack of trust that develops from these types of encounters results in a lot of paranoid thinking about the motives of other people and contributes to the further destruction of relationships at work and at home.

According to many of the men, these situations occur often enough that it is important to have a set of standard methods readily available to cope with the situation. They can vary from downplaying the importance of the situation ("perhaps he made a mistake and overlooked my role on the project" or "they forgot to invite me to the weekend gathering at the boss's home"), telling themselves things to belittle the boss ("this situation is not that bad because he is incompetent"), using humor to soften the insult, or silent prayers and affirmations.

What is important about all of these methods is that none of them involve a direct confrontation. By far, most of the methods used by black men to cope with anger at work usually involve the suppression of feelings. While this may appear to be the best method for keeping peace at work, the suppression of anger often results in a man's feeling depressed, anxious, somewhat hopeless, and fearful about how to handle the situation if it should arise again.

For many black men these mixed-up feelings can't always be suppressed and bypassed at work, and they end up being directed at innocent coworkers. Take Carl, thirty-three, for example. He eventually quit an accounting job rather than be fired because of the anger he could hardly contain in the office. "I was constantly blamed by a white boss for mistakes I did not make. I thought that being a college graduate would protect me from this sort of thing, but I was wrong. At times I was so angry and so low that I could hardly work, and then one day I could not take it anymore. I told my boss off and quit the job because they made me feel stupid. The thing that I dislike most about the way that I left is the fact that I took out my anger on some of the coworkers who had nothing to do with how I was being treated."

"Sometimes," says Danny, twenty-eight, an airplane mechanic, "I think they're trying to lure me into doing something stupid—something to get me fired. I've received obscene notes and drawings and overheard derogatory conversations about niggers that were meant for me to hear. When I do experience these things, I can feel them staring at me, waiting for me to react violently, like a puppet on a string without a brain. Sure, I'm angry and I want to punch somebody, but I've got a wife and two sons. To get through this mess I think of them."

It is easy to say in retrospect what a black man "should" have done about a situation at work in which his authority is challenged or where he feels left out of important decisions, but the threat to his job security is intense and reflects all of the worries that are tied up in the belief that blacks "are the last to be hired and the first to be fired." Many black men often feel as if they are in a double bind with feelings of anger because of strong expectations about how conflicts should be settled. The predominant view is that they will be penalized, victimized, or even fired from their job if they point out inequities at work.

For many brothers, actions are motivated by their fear, and in many instances the fear is so intense that it prevents the brother from taking any initiative to address the situation. This type of fear produces a situation where the brothers harbor much resentment because they can't openly express their feelings. Further anger and resentment are developed as a consequence of this realization, but these feelings can't be expressed either because of the possible loss of a job or promotions.

On the Road to a Promotion

A source of frustration and stress for many black men is being unjustifiably denied a raise or a promotion. This situation becomes more insulting in some cases because it is common knowledge that a white coworker with less experience was given a big pay raise with a promotion and is now supervising the very person who provided him with the training to do the job. The insult to injury is worse because it is public knowledge that they trained this individual to successfully perform the job, and yet they were not perceived as being good enough or qualified for the promotion.

Most black men who talked about these situations say they experienced a tremendous rage because they were made to feel less useful, less powerful, and less valuable than someone with little or no experience who happened to be white. The frustration, humiliation, and shame that results from such situations is intense and generally provides much fuel for the anger that burns deep within black men.

Stanley, thirty-eight, has been working as an administrator of a social-work agency of a large city for fourteen years and has been serving as the interim director for the past year. According to Stanley, his department has had three directors over the past eight years, and all of them had significantly less experience than him. "Now I am being told that a man that I trained a few years ago will be joining us as the new director of the program. This is hard for me to believe and accept since everyone knows that I am the most qualified person for the position. I have worked hard and I deserve to be the director. I really believe that if I wasn't black, I would be promoted to this new position. Hell, I could be anything other than a black man—Asian, Hispanic, Mexican—and I think they would have given me the job."

After much discussion it became clear that the most aggravating thing about this situation is that the newly appointed director knew nothing about the field before he was trained by Stanley. "In a very strange way I feel a bit guilty and shameful for being so stupid as to believe that this department would want a black man at the top. Sometimes I forget that I am black and that the world does not openly support me, my thoughts, my behaviors, or my desire for success. Sometimes I forget that there are people out there who would find amusement in seeing me hunted down by bloodhounds."

The situation with Stanley is similar to the situation with Bruce, forty-two, one of the most senior physicians employed at a community health center. Bruce has been at the center for eight years and was once the interim director for six months. However, once the directorship position became available, a white physician who had been at the center for only two years was given the position. "I was angry and humiliated, and I don't know how I kept from exploding. I guess I kept saying that they will always find a way to remind us who is in charge. I guess that I tried to distance myself from my hurt feelings by reminding myself that I have too much to lose by losing my temper about a situation that I can't control."

In the end, Bruce continued his work, even though it bothers him daily that a white man with far less experience than him was promoted to a position that he was qualified to fill. "All of this makes me feel that even though I am doing the same job, because I'm black, I can't be as smart as a white man." One of the effects of the internal doubt that is generated from these situations is that the anger and rage that's suppressed at work finds a way to be expressed at home. "The situation at work is the cause of many of the arguments over petty things. I would come home and get on my wife's case about anything, and the next thing I know I would be yelling, losing it, and on my way to an explosion . . . when all I wanted to do was to not feel so low because of how I am treated at work because I'm black."

To guard against the feelings of inadequacy that arise

when their goals are blocked, many black men shift the cause of their anger and rage from themselves to other people. By doing this it becomes quite easy to focus on what caused the problems rather than who could not fix things. In this regard, the self is saved from embarrassment and shame. While this process works well for some circumstances that are private, in other situations the shifting of the cause of the failures from the self to other people is problematic. For example, what is a black man to do if one of the consequences of anger that is expressed over an unfair job evaluation is that he is suspended without pay or fired? In this case, it is difficult for him not to question his honor and self-worth. Why? Because being laid off and unemployed crushes his image as a capable provider for his family. This was exactly what prevented Stanley and many other brothers from leaving their job to pursue other positions. "I was angry enough to leave many times, but each time I seriously considered leaving, I realized that there was no guarantee that I would find a job so that I could support my family. In the end I knew that the best thing for me to do was to not rock the boat and not let them know how angry and upset I was about being almost forced into a position to feel dependent on others for my survival," explains Stanley.

The Stress of Being Laid Off

In today's workplace, another threat to job stability is that many large companies have to cut back and reduce the size of their workforce. Some people's job skills are so limited that locating a new position with a salary that is both worthy of their years of experience and education level is exceedingly difficult.

"After all the years and everything that I have given to my company, you would think that they would find a way to keep me on, but they don't give a damn about me. If I was white, I am sure they would have helped me out in a

much better way so that I could have retired with full benefits, but this whole thing is a mess. A big mess to use black
men, promise them a good retirement for long years of hard
work, and then they figure out a way to remove us before
we can reap the benefits.''

Andrew, forty, is an electronics engineer who has recently
celebrated his ten-year wedding anniversary. He and his
wife have a comfortable lifestyle and no worries about how
they will pay the college tuition for their three children. He
is a levelheaded, clean-cut, Christian man—the type who
would hardly be considered a suicide risk. Nevertheless, two
years ago Andrew nearly killed himself. Only the unexpected return home from school of one of his children startled him into misfiring the gun.

Over a stormy seventeen-year work history, Andrew felt
fortunate not to be affected by the massive layoffs in the
automobile industry. However, the situation had radically
changed during the past few years. Two years ago, for example, Andrew was given the unpleasant choice of taking
early retirement with substantial losses or face being terminated with few or no benefits. Even though Andrew took
the option of the early retirement with plans to start a second career, he was depressed and angry over having to lose
his job—a job that gave him much more than a paycheck.
''After leaving my job I felt detached from things, as if there
was not much purpose in my days. I tried to find the energy
to get going and think about finding a new job, but I just
could not seem to make the move. I was just too damn
angry and upset to get myself together. The thing that kept
me angry was the idea that I was laid off because I'm black.''

During our interview it was obvious that Andrew lost far
more than a steady paycheck when he lost his job. He lost
his identity, his illusion of freedom, his self-respect, and the
respect and admiration of his family and friends. ''For nearly
two months after losing my job I became a hermit and seldom went outside of the house because I did not want people to know that I was not working. I was drinking heavy
and thinking lots of crazy thoughts and being hard on my
family. My wife tried to assure me that this phase in my

life would pass, but I felt like a fly caught in a spider's web with nowhere to hide or to protect my pride."

After drinking steadily for several days, he got out his gun and was about to shoot himself when he was startled by his oldest son, who had come home from school to get a homework assignment. "If my attention had not been pulled away from what I was doing, I am sure that I would have killed myself as opposed to shooting myself in the shoulder," explains Andrew in a quiet and subdued voice.

When the circumstances of a black man's life are made public, as in being laid off or forced to take an early retirement, he usually experiences humiliation of the most intense form. To become unemployed, go through a divorce, or flunk out of college contributes to his already diminished sense of self-worth, power, and control. To defend themselves, black men conveniently shift the blame from the self and their own inadequacies to the "system" and "racism" or the wife that we promised to love until death. We defend ourselves because we take pride not only in our accomplishments, but in the acknowledgment of our worth by our friends, family, and the community.

Andrew was fortunate to pick himself up and restore balance in his life by renewing his faith in God. Even though he went to church every Sunday and read the Bible every now and then, Andrew says that he was not a real Christian because he didn't really have faith in God and that he was never sure that he understood what God really was. "I realize that most of my life I have been all worked up about how things were going to turn out in the future. I had some belief in God, but I realize that I was praying to God as if he was my servant—like he was supposed to stop everything and attend solely to my wishes. I guess what I am trying to say is that I was not really practicing a Christian lifestyle," Andrew observed.

In talking with this man it was clear to me that he was given a second chance to live and develop his faith in God and his love for his family. It was also clear that it has been difficult for Andrew and other black men to sustain a belief in a God that was given to them by the people who enslaved, beat, and punished them and murdered their families. Dealing with the humiliation and rage related to slavery, racism, and segregation has been hard enough. Yet black men are encouraged to be patient, to be humble, and to wait for this God to answer their prayers.

Andrew's second career has nothing to do with electronics. He currently works as a crisis counselor for his church and a crisis hot line in the city where he lives. The money is not as much as he made in his former job, but Andrew is a wealthier man because he is helping people make better decisions about how they cope with stressful and personal problems. "Without the help and support of my family and my renewed belief in God, I realize that I would not be here today," Andrew said. "I guess that I stopped believing that I would be useful to them when I lost my job."

Focus on Finding Solutions to Problems Rather Than the Problems

"Sure, I get upset by many of the things that interfere with my progress on projects, but I address the problems rather than allow my feelings to get the upper hand and rule how I treat other people. I learned a long time ago that I could manage my temper by focusing on the problem and by asking myself questions such as 'What can I do to solve this problem and allow myself to remain happy?' and 'What can I do to solve this problem and prevent this thing from repeating itself?'"

Steve, thirty-nine, a married college professor, would be described by most people as being easygoing and laid-back. Yet he says that he is easily angered and has a temper. His life as a professor is very demanding given that he teaches full-time, conducts research, publishes his work in scientific journals, and finds quality time with his wife and two children. Even though he is constantly under pressure and working to meet deadlines, he rarely allows the pressure of his work to ruffle his feathers.

Steve's style of coping with anger is characterized by a concerted attempt to restrain and control angry feelings and to think quickly and calmly about solving whatever problems caused the anger to arise in the first place. For example, black men who use this style to cope with anger express their discomfort about unjust events and will do whatever it takes to deal with the issues that caused the event to surface, in a calm manner. They focus, as Steve does, on what they can do to fix things and prevent similar situations from occurring in the future. "Rather than dwell on my angry feelings, I discovered that I could use questions to help me think more clearly about the consequences of my actions and to transcend my anger and stay focused on removing the obstacles that are hindering my work."

Interestingly enough, Steve also uses this method of questioning to deal with problems in his relationship with his wife, and he believes that this is the single most important thing that he does to enable himself to stay clear of anger. "It is so terribly easy to get caught up blaming somebody else for my feelings, but when I don't let my anger interfere with resolving the conflicts that stirred my ill feelings, I realize that it was those times that I was taking responsibility for my actions. This is what black men must do—take responsibility for their behavior—in order for them to better control their tempers," said Steve.

Like many black men who graduated from prominent universities during the seventies and early eighties, Larry, thirty-six, believed that a handful of degrees as well as his success as an accountant would shield him from racism. "I knew that racism existed, but I thought being a graduate from a top university would put me at a different level so that the only thing I had to do to prove myself was a good job. Well, I was wrong, and I quickly discovered that most whites thought that I was incapable of handling major accounts and important clients." Larry endured a stunning indignity when a client with whom he had only done business over the telephone met him for the first time. "I will never forget the man," Larry says. "He gained his wealth from a string of fancy restaurants and a friend referred him to me. When I arrived at his office, one of the first things I noticed was that there were no people of color—it was lily-white."

After waiting in the reception room for nearly an hour, Larry started to think that something was not right. "I begin to wonder if he knew that I was black since I don't sound black over the telephone. When he finally came out to greet me, he shook my hand and didn't even bother to apologize for having me wait. What really got me upset was when he told me that he had decided to do business with another accountant. This all seemed a bit unusual because of the way we talked on the telephone, so I asked why. 'I changed my mind,' he said, and it immediately became clear to me that this man was not going to trust a black man to help him make decisions about his money."

It is never easy for a black man to dismiss the frustration and humiliation he experiences as a result of confronting situations such as these. The natural reaction is to strike back at the demoralization and threat to his dignity and manhood. "It seems that I have to take a stand every day," says Larry. "But too often, I can't get it out of my mind, and if it wasn't for the thoughts about my family, I know that I would eventually explode and destroy my chances of making a better living for myself and my family."

Like many of the other brothers who have experienced rage in the workplace, Larry sought strength from within his family to survive. "I know that reaching out for help goes against the grain of being macho, but talking to my wife about the things I encounter allows me to be introspective and less impulsive about how I decide to handle a situation. To cope with the awful things, I have promised myself that no matter how obsessed and defensive I get because of how someone has insulted me, I will remind myself that I am not in this alone—I have a family and what I do or don't do will have an effect on them."

Prescriptions for Change

Perhaps the greatest challenge facing black men in the workplace today is figuring out when the expression of anger is right. Most of the feelings we experience when we are angry change as the intensity of anger and the circumstances that cause the angry feelings change. As a consequence, many of the black men who cope with provocations by talking out their feelings may also keep things to themselves under certain circumstances. At other times they are capable of bypassing angry feelings altogether. Whereas the experience of anger is a process, the manner by which this process unfolds depends to a great extent on whether a man is comfortable accepting how he may be using anger as a way of avoiding the painful feelings of hurt, uncertainty, sorrow, sadness, shame, guilt, and fear he harbors about situations he has encountered at work or throughout his life. Because of this latter point it is important to question yourself about the feelings that you experience in response to events at work. This will enable you to gain a better perspective on the problem and cause you to take a deeper and more critical look at your contribution to the problem. By doing this you will be more likely to choose how you want to continue to respond to the situation.

To effectively deal with rage in the workplace can at times require a lot of effort. The following suggestions were put together to make it a bit easier and less stressful to manage anger. Basically, a man who engages in the following six steps (Step 1: Recognition of Feelings of Displeasure; Step 2: Suppress Taking Any Immediate Action; Step 3: Identifying the Cause of Anger; Step 4: Evaluate Whether the Angry Feelings Are Legitimate; Step 5: Positive Confrontations; Step 6: To Forgive and Forget) stands a better chance of learning how to use his anger to get his needs met than the man who allows his feelings to rule his thoughts and actions. Although the steps can be used to cope with any situation that causes anger, a specific example about how to use these steps to deal with rage in the workplace will be analyzed. The six steps are discussed below so you can gain a better idea of how they can be used effectively.

Six Steps for Managing Anger in the Workplace

I. Recognition of Feelings of Displeasure

The purpose of this step is to learn how to get in touch with your feelings rather than to judge whether they are right or wrong. Most men are well aware they feel hurt, uncomfortable, or uneasy. However, many brothers have repressed feelings of anger for so long that most of these feelings are described as "feeling funny or confused." Sometimes it may be necessary for a man to look at the situation and see how he handles it in order to discover the kinds of feelings that produced his behavior.

The test presented below can be used to determine the extent to which your experience with stress and frustration in your workplace causes you to feel angry.

Causes of Angry Feelings at Work

Directions: A number of social situations that occur in the workplace are given below. Read each situation and then circle (or simply note in your mind) the answer that best indicates the degree of anger you would feel in the situation. There are no right or wrong answers.

1. You are criticized by your boss in front of your coworkers.
    1. I would not feel angry.
    2. I would feel somewhat angry.
    3. I would feel moderately angry.
    4. I would feel very angry and furious.
2. You are criticized by a coworker in front of others.
    1. I would not feel angry.

    2. I would feel somewhat angry.

    3. I would feel moderately angry.

    4. I would feel very angry and furious.

3. You have done a great job on a project, but you receive a poor evaluation.

    1. I would not feel angry.

    2. I would feel somewhat angry.

    3. I would feel moderately angry.

    4. I would feel very angry and furious.

4. Someone other than your boss makes a rule about your work on a project.

    1. I would not feel angry.

    2. I would feel somewhat angry.

    3. I would feel moderately angry.

    4. I would feel very angry and furious.

5. A coworker disagrees with how you want to handle some work.

    1. I would not feel angry.

    2. I would feel somewhat angry.

    3. I would feel moderately angry.

    4. I would feel very angry and furious.

6. A person supervising your work gets angry at you for reasons you don't understand.

    1. I would not feel angry.

    2. I would feel somewhat angry.

    3. I would feel moderately angry.

    4. I would feel very angry and furious.

7. Someone insults you or your family.

    1. I would not feel angry.

    2. I would feel somewhat angry.

    3. I would feel moderately angry.

    4. I would feel very angry and furious.

8. Someone you trained is promoted faster than you and you believe it's because he or she is white.

    1. I would not feel angry.

    2. I would feel somewhat angry.

    3. I would feel moderately angry.

    4. I would feel very angry and furious.

9. Another coworker takes credit for work that you completed.

    1. I would not feel angry.

    2. I would feel somewhat angry.
    3. I would feel moderately angry.
    4. I would feel very angry and furious.
10. Your boss or coworker changed decisions you made on a project without letting you know.
    1. I would not feel angry.
    2. I would feel somewhat angry.
    3. I would feel moderately angry.
    4. I would feel very angry and furious.
11. You are under pressure or stress to complete some task.
    1. I would not feel angry.
    2. I would feel somewhat angry.
    3. I would feel moderately angry.
    4. I would feel very angry and furious.
12. You are placed in a situation where coworkers are telling racist jokes.
    1. I would not feel angry.
    2. I would feel somewhat angry.
    3. I would feel moderately angry.
    4. I would feel very angry and furious.
13. Your nonblack colleagues don't make time to spend with you.
    1. I would not feel angry.
    2. I would feel somewhat angry.
    3. I would feel moderately angry.
    4. I would feel very angry and furious.
14. You discover obscene drawings of black people, left where someone knew that you would find them.
    1. I would not feel angry.
    2. I would feel somewhat angry.
    3. I would feel moderately angry.
    4. I would feel very angry and furious.

Score yourself: Give yourself 1 point for choosing the first response, 2 points for choosing the second response, 3 points for choosing the third response, and 4 points for choosing the fourth response. Add up the points (1–4) for each item to get your total score, somewhere between 14 and 56. Total Points _____. A person who scores 38 is just about average.

If you score below 26, you are well down in the safe zone—
not prone to become angry in a number of these situations. A
score above 40 means that you may be a hothead—prone to
respond to frustrating situations at work with intense feelings
of anger.

If you scored in the hothead zone, then your next step
is to take one of the work situations where the amount of
anger you would experience is either a 3 (I would feel
moderately angry) or 4 (I would feel very angry and furious). The situation I will use to help you understand how
to use the remaining steps to manage rage at work involves a combination of the circumstances presented in
situations 9 and 10. In this example, *a white coworker
changed some of the decisions you made on a project without
letting you know, and then he took credit for the work you did
and the completion of the project.*

Take a moment and imagine how this situation would
make you feel. Now imagine talking to this person about
the situation. What I want you to do is imagine yourself
asking for what you want. The *opening line* that I want you
to use is, "I'm feeling angry and upset because you went
behind my back and took credit for my work. What I think I
would like is for you to talk to our boss and let him know
that you made some decisions without informing me and that
you then took credit for my work. The second thing that I
want is for you to write me and our boss a formal letter
of apology."

It is important for you to ask for something specific and
to limit your request to one or two things. Use good voice
control and keep your voice low in volume without communicating blame, contempt, or sarcasm so that you can guard
against escalations. If you get resistance, then your fallback
position will become clear as you read on about the next
step for handling rage in the workplace.

To help you deal with the specific situations you identified
as causing anger in your workplace, it is a good idea for

you to practice visualizing each situation. Practice generating opening lines for coping with the situations.

2. Suppress Taking Any Immediate Action

It has been said that "a fool gives full vent to his anger, but a wise man quietly holds it back." Regardless of the intensity of the hurt feelings, it is important to suppress taking any action until you have thought through the situation, the possible consequences of your actions, and have control over what you will say and do about the situation. The whole idea is to defer taking action without losing touch with the problem. It is analogous to the proverbial counting to ten or a hundred. At times this step may take only a few seconds or minutes, but at other times it may take hours or possibly days.

Rather than act as if nothing is bothering you when you feel angry and upset, it would be best to practice an opening line like "What you did upset me, but I need to think about it more before I say anything about it" or "Something about this bothers me, but it's not clear to me yet. Maybe when I've had a chance to think it over, we can talk about it." If we take the example identified in step one, then either of these opening lines will let the coworker know that this is a problem for you and for them, and it alerts the coworker to think about what was said and done.

If we don't say anything, quite often the specific issues that caused us to feel upset are forgotten because we did not mark them as a problem for ourselves and the other person involved. When the situations are not marked, it is easy to feel vaguely upset later without knowing why and then be unable to resolve the problem.

Now let's take the situation we identified in step one and figure out how to suppress impulsive reactions. First of all, the most important thing to do is to keep in mind that you are negotiating for what you want. Your interaction with the coworker is not a confrontation, but an opportunity for you to state what is bothering you and to indicate the specific things that need to occur for you to feel better about the situation.

3. Identifying the Cause of Anger

Once you have learned how to recognize feelings of displeasure and to suppress taking any actions until you have thought through the situation, it is time to focus on the causes of anger. Basically, the major lesson is to focus on answering some powerful questions: "What is causing the angry feelings?" "What is it that is making me feel upset or disturbed?" "What did I lose to make me feel this way?" "What valuable thing—object, opinion, rights, etc.—am I thinking that I will lose?"

Because anger can so easily be displaced to someone or something that has nothing to do with the real cause of the distress, it is important for you to practice answering these questions about the things that make you feel angry or hurt. I'm sure that you all are familiar with the following chain reaction: the boss yelled at the employee, who got angry at home with his wife, who took it out on their son, who kicked the dog, who soiled the new rug and is now being forced to live outside in a tiny two-foot-by-two-foot doghouse.

To get yourself to effectively focus on the "what" of anger, I suggest that you write out the issues as well as talk over the problem with your spouse, a friend, or a coworker whom you trust. Be creative about how you deal with this step because it will be difficult for you to proceed any further until you have learned how to identify the causes of your anger, hurt, displeasure, irritations. What you learn in this step is how to take care of yourself. Once you have identified the cause of your anger, then you can use an opening line like "If (whatever the problem is) goes on, I'll have to (state your solution) in order to take care of myself." Using the example we identified earlier, the opening line could be, "If you continue to let the boss think that you are responsible for completing the project, I'll have to write a formal complaint about your lack of ethics in order to take care of myself."

As you practice step three, it is important for you to understand that you are taking care of yourself. Your reactions are not something you do to the other person, it's your way of doing something for yourself. You are behaving in a way to solve the problem, and your reaction to the other person is not a pushy ultimatum or a punishment.

4. Evaluate Whether the Angry Feelings Are Legitimate

The basic issue is determining whether the reasons for feeling angry are good enough to justify the feelings. To determine whether there is adequate basis for one's angry feelings is difficult and a real challenge for most men. The real secret is to encourage yourself to deal honestly with yourself and other people. In doing so you will be more comfortable sorting out the extent to which you are responsible for the problems that caused your angry feelings and the degree to which other people are responsible. Seldom when we get angry are we 100 percent right and the other person 100 percent wrong. Typically, there are multiple factors causing the problem and several different ways to view the situation.

One way to encourage a man to acquire the habit of evaluating whether angry feelings are legitimate is to have him ask himself a few questions such as "What was my role in this event?" "I know that I am not totally right or wrong, so why am I angry?" "Assume for a moment that the other person is right. Then would I still feel upset and angry?" Using these questions to address the situation we described earlier would enable you to you get information about what concerns and worries you about the situation. Perhaps you would consider the reasons why the person took credit for your work. Maybe he thought the decisions he made behind your back were necessary to complete the project. Could it be that the project was dragging on and he simply wanted to help you finish it? Is he a bigot and wants to hurt your reputation with the boss? Whatever reasons you come up with, it is important for you to assume for a moment that nothing was wrong about his behavior in order for you to determine whether the reasons for your anger are justified. If you feel justified, then it is important for you to take actions to resolve these feelings.

For most of us, the problems that stir us to feel angry and conflicted are usually resolved as we go through the above steps. For some of us, there is a strong need to take further action to handle angry feelings constructively. The typical man deals with conflict by one of the following methods: (1) he expresses his anger outwardly—"I hate you, and I will get you back you so-and-so"; (2) he runs or withdraws from the situation—"I am going home and I am taking my computer games with me"; (3) he verbally gives in to the other person—"Okay, you win," but in reality he is extremely angry and upset with the situation. In most cases, a lot of resentment is hidden, which magnifies the problem and makes it extremely difficult to handle the conflict.

It is important to remember that it is your responsibility to let other people know how you feel about issues. When you feel something strongly, it is up to you to express it. You are asking for all kinds of trouble if you assume that the other person knows how strongly you feel, unless you actually put it into words and express your feelings directly. Sometimes when a man does this, having a confrontation is a necessary part of the process. Confrontation is usually difficult for most men, particularly when it involves people we care about. Confrontation is not necessarily a hostile or painful experience; it can be done in a tender, loving, and forgiving manner.

5. Positive Confrontations

As indicated earlier, two important things to understand before trying to deal with anger are that conflict is both normal and inevitable. Intellectually, most of us understand that being irritated, annoyed, or upset is a normal part of life.

Even though this is the case, most of us look upon being angry, having conflict, and experiencing a confrontation as an abnormal thing. Much like anger and conflict, confrontation is also necessary at times. Don't take what I am saying wrong. It is always best to be kind, tenderhearted, loving, and forgiving to each other. Unfortunately, some people we deal with don't share this collective understanding of one of the major purposes of life—to do whatever you do for love, happiness, and bliss. There are also times when each of us is entrapped by the wrongdoings of others, and the resultant threats to our pride, dignity, and self-respect are so intense that many feelings of anger and rage are rapidly vented.

Again I want to emphasize that there are no rules that say that confrontation has to be a hostile and painful experience. While some people may be afraid of and uncomfortable about confronting other people, confrontation can be done without attacking another person.

As you prepare yourself to learn about dealing with confrontations, it is necessary that you keep in mind that confrontation can vary widely from a gentle, private resolution of an issue to a strong, possibly unpleasant situation involving other people. Basically, there are three steps to confronting people. The first is to clearly and honestly inform the other person about the issue that affected you and that person. Most of the time a simple statement is all that it takes to resolve a situation effectively, even in cases where other people have deliberately taken advantage of you.

The second step is to convey your feelings. Feeling angry is quite often a secondary set of feelings or reactions to some situation that usually involved insult, put-down, deprivation, betrayal, or frustration of some wish. This is precisely the type of situation we created at the beginning of this section, and the opening lines at steps one and two were used to confront the person and convey your feelings.

Remember that anger is a warning signal that something is not quite right and some adjustments are necessary for you to feel more at ease about a situation. Quite often these adjustments involve other people and one of the most constructive ways to deal with anger is to get in touch with the primary feeling and then share this with the person who needs to be confronted. The real art to the process is to communicate your feelings without blaming the other person. For example, take a few minutes and ponder how different you would feel if you were confronted by someone with an "I feel" message such as "I get the feeling that I'm being blamed for something that I did not do," as compared to a "blaming" message such as "You always blame me for everything that goes wrong." The "I feel" messages are wonderful and direct ways of letting other people know how you feel, and they do a fairly good job at getting to the primary feeling that is underneath the anger. In contrast, the blaming messages usually come off as being judgmental, critical, attacking, and they don't give the other person room to do anything other than to become hostile and to defend themselves.

The "I feel" messages help everyone involved to get in touch with their primary feelings. Once this occurs, it is usually quite easy to deal with the real issues and solve the problem rather than to get stuck dealing with the superficial issues that quite often have very little to do with the cause of the problems. The "I feel" message was used in the first step for handling rage in the workplace. Quite often this message serves to identify feelings, sets the stage for the suppression of any impulsive actions, and establishes a positive confrontation. If there is no resistance at step one, then feelings of anger are not likely to escalate because you have taken care of yourself and addressed the problem rather than allowing yourself to be ruled by your emotions.

In the event that the confrontation has generated a defensive reaction from the other person or that you feel your anger boiling, the best advice is to use an opening line like "I feel we're starting to get upset. I want to stop and cool off for a while." Use this opportunity to physically leave the situation. It is important that you practice this opening line and commit it to memory. Also, it is important for you to set a time limit for how long you will be gone. While you are away, you can practice some of the relaxation and stress reduction techniques that are described in chapter 11 and the quick methods to defuse anger that are offered in chapter 7, "Strategies for Stopping Anger Before It Escalates."

My experience has been that people who really love and care about one another confront each other in ways that show each other how to give and receive love. This brings us to the third and strongest way to confront, which is to rebuke in love with the aim being reconciliation. Even though you may dislike or even hate what the person is doing, you care deeply about the person.

6. To Forgive and Forget

Well, you have had the confrontation. Sometimes a strong compromise is needed because we have become aware of the other person's feelings and we are faced with a different perspective on the issue. In some cases the other person is completely at fault, and yet there is a need to move forward and resolve the conflict rather than constantly bicker over small details. The best possible solution to the problem, both for yourself and for the other person, is to willingly hold no grudges and drop the issue. In essence, we let the other person know that we are willing to forgive and forget about the situation. Sometimes other people are informed about the situation and how you have chosen to resolve it. In the example used throughout this section it would be a good idea to inform your boss about your feelings and how you resolved the situation with the other person.

Many people have misconceptions about what forgiveness really involves. Often people, when trying to forgive another person, try to talk themselves into thinking that what the other person did wasn't really wrong, or that the other person didn't really mean to do whatever they did, or that the resultant anger is an overreaction to what the other person did. Regardless of who was at fault, forgiving means that we actively choose to give up our grudges despite the seriousness of the injustice done to us. Forgiving doesn't mean that the person at fault doesn't need to "suffer" the lawful or natural consequences of their actions. By all means, you can forgive and still allow justice to be administered. However, no matter how many steps you have taken for dealing with anger, if you don't learn to forgive the people who caused your anguish and forget the situation, there are going to be repercussions sooner or later.

Most of the time the person who is angry and holding the grudge suffers the most because the other person quite often doesn't even know about it, and even if they do, they seldom care. So the best advice is to practice being a person who can forgive and forget rather than hold grudges that most often cause more harm to you than the person you are angry at.

Because most of us spend the biggest part of our time at work, the relationships we have with those at work take on tremendous importance. Ideally, the work setting offers magnificent opportunities for a man to gain self-esteem and self-appreciation, and best of all, a sense of being a productive person. However, what too often happens is that the work setting becomes a place in which a black man's abilities are stifled and undermined, and where his self-confidence and self-worth are destroyed. As revealed in this chapter, some brothers have found ways to cope with the indignities, racial slurs, and unfair treatment they experience at work, while others have become walking-wounded victims of the assault upon their manhood.

If a black man is to function as a winner in the work environment, he has to start with how he defines the purpose of his work and the organization he works for. While the person at the top (the boss) is the one who creates, monitors, and maintains the environment, it is important that black men take responsibility for making certain that the boss knows that they know what the organizational purpose is, and what the goals of the company are, and understand the individual rewards for being an employee of the company. Beyond this point, things in our society become a bit foggy because most bosses don't deal with the idea that everything in life is set up as a opportunity for growth and development. The bosses may not see that the essential purpose of work is for a man to experience enlightenment, while the secondary purpose of work is for a man to create a service or a product for the community so that he can make a livelihood and help the members of the community.

While many bosses may not see their company from this perspective, it is important that black men transcend the petty situations that arise at work by seeing that everything in life—their job, their money, their relationships at work—comes out of their level of spiritual consciousness and their own intention. This is the type of awareness that challenges the barriers and obstacles and makes possible mastery of seemingly impossible tasks in some of the most racist workplaces. This is the spirit that has propelled many black men to continue working even though feelings of anger have nearly eaten away the fabric of their being. Essentially, the happiest brothers are those who are working, not just going to a job but really working. They are not necessarily working for higher pay and shorter hours. The bottom line is that they want to be recognized for the work they are doing—they are working for acceptance, love, understanding, support, and the freedom to be all that they can be. However, the black man also understands that there will frequently be people at work who will either consciously or subconsciously try to lure him into doing something so that he is either fired or reprimanded.

When a black man is enlightened as a person, he feels sufficiently complete within himself to allow the same space for his coworkers, regardless of their attitudes or their level of enlightenment. Unfortunately, most people have no idea of what enlightenment is all about, and most are not conscious of their own capabilities. As a consequence, the unenlightened black man sees his job setting only as a place to get the job done and be paid. He doesn't see the job setting as a place for him to grow, to make and correct errors, or as a place for people to be supported in their mistakes and their successes. To transcend these errors in judgment a man must understand his emotional development and come to terms with who he is, how other people perceive him, and what kind of man he wants to become. Many of the suggestions offered in the "Prescriptions for Change" section of chapter 1, "Why Are Black Men Angry?" are useful for developing insight about self-development.

Self-Awareness Strategies and Exercises

To go beyond the senseless and simple things that cause anger to arise in the workplace, it is important to look at the organization to which you belong as a place for self-enlightenment. Regardless of the circumstances and obstacles that you encounter, it is important to keep in mind that it is your attitude and your character that determine your life experiences at work. A man's unfortunate acceptance of mediocrity and self-defeating beliefs about his capacity to bring a higher purpose into his work environment will forever make him feel that the external world has power over him. When a man adopts a life of excellence, he truly believes that his flow of life at work is an expression of God and his love. Obstacles and challenges to the purpose of work that are caused by racist attitudes and unfair employment practices are readily seen as the manifestations of weak-minded individuals who have not found their spiritual enlightenment. This is perhaps one of the most powerful attitudes of an enlightened black man and one that will always protect and transport him beyond the temporary anguish, embitterment, humiliation, uncertainty, sorrow, sadness, shame, guilt, and fear that he so often encounters in the workplace.

Take Notice of Yourself

To understand how race affects you at work you need to take notice of how you perceive your work environment. Note who is in charge at your job.

- How do you feel about this person? Are you comfortable with his or her authority?

133

- Do you feel that he or she is supportive or suppressive? Do you like this person?
- Is this person of another race or ethnic group than yourself? Do you feel that the race or ethnicity of this person makes it more or less difficult for you to assert yourself at work?
- Does your boss encourage you to be all that you can be, or does he or she act fearful that you may rise to take his or her job?
- Have you ever socialized with your boss away from work?
- At your job are you often put into a situation where you are forced to talk about the culture of other racial groups while ignoring your own culture just to get along with your coworkers?
- Do you spend time with your white colleagues away from work?
- Does the way that nonblack people at work respond to you make you feel alienated?

Now look at your responses to the questionnaire where you identified the causes of anger at work. This time mentally note whether the way that you feel about each event has anything to do with your being black or the way that you have been treated on your job because you are black. How do you feel about this? Do you believe that your feelings are legitimate? Whatever is going on at your job you must accept responsibility for.

Choose now at this very moment to accept the responsibility for whatever the stress is you have experienced. Choose to feel angry, frustrated, fearful, humiliated, uncertain, or whatever you feel about the situation at work. It is okay to have feelings about the events that you experience at work. Choose this time to recognize your feelings of displeasure. If you fear that someone else may get your job, say, "I choose to be afraid that another person may get my job." It is important to take responsibility for your feelings and accept them.

Some additional questions pertaining to the effects of race and racism on your work are presented below. It is important for you to be honest about how you would respond to the situation. This is necessary for you to understand how race and racism affect you.

- Do you think that your race affects the praise you receive or don't receive for your work?
    - If so, how?
    - Do you believe that this has something to do with you or your supervisor?
    - Do you think that things will always be this way?
    - Do you believe that you have any control over whether this happens to you?
- Have you ever experienced racism at work or known of someone who has?
    - How did this affect you? How did this affect your relationships with coworkers?
    - How did this affect your relationship with the person in charge (the boss)?
- What did you do about the racism you experienced at work?
- Did you communicate honestly and openly or did you avoid confrontation or call it something else?
- Did you take out your feeling on your coworkers or a family member at home?

Regardless of whatever you did to cope with racism in the past, your response does not have to be impulsive. Remember that there is nothing wrong with being angry; the problem is in what we do to cope with it. If being angry about the experience of racism at work has caused you to lose out on opportunities, then it is important for you to examine what you did to cope with your anger. Use the steps for coping that were presented earlier to try and figure out how you could have responded differently to the situation. Pay particularly close attention to steps two through five. You should also consider some of the techniques for modifying your thoughts about anger that are presented in chapter 7, "Strategies for Stopping Anger Before It Escalates." These techniques are based on the idea that by mentally rehearsing the coping responses, you can avert your anger and stay focused on the problem. However, the first thing that you need to do is to make up your mind about what you want.

Make Decisions About What You Want

Whatever is going on in your work relationships, it is important for you to accept responsibility for it. If you are in a nonsupportive and suppressive work environment, that is your choosing. Say, "I choose to work here." If you encountered racism at your job and then took all of your feelings home where you dumped them on your family, that, too, was your choice. Admit it: "I choose to dump my anger on my family." If you were passed over for a promotion that you deserve and you did nothing about it but feel bitter and resentful, this, too, was your decision. Say to yourself, "I choose to do nothing about being passed over for a promotion that I deserve."

It is up to you to think about what you want before you do it and not after the fact. One way to do this is to schedule a few minutes every day so that you can focus on the things that are going on in your life. It is important to get a clear mental image of what you want from a situation and how you plan to acquire it. I am not talking about simply saying to yourself what you want. While this is important, you've got to get worked up and excited about what you want, and you basically have to act as if you have already been enhanced by your source and have received what you desired. Some of the exercises that are described in chapter 11, "The Psychology of Staying Cool," can be used to help you relax and clear your mind so that you can think more critically about how you plan to deal with important events in your life.

Stop Blaming Others

Don't make other people pay for your mistakes, because they are not responsible for your life; you are. Each time you stop to blame another person you are taking time and effort away from your quest to achieve your goals. If you keep moving and know where you are going, the chances are greater that you will reach your destination. Remember that you are in control of your life and that you create your own opportunities to live it the way you want.

Create Your Own Destiny

Make a list of the things that you want to change at your job. Use this list to visualize exactly the way you want things to be. Vividly picture yourself in the various situations at work, and imagine yourself responding in the way you want to respond. Imagine just how your response will make you feel. Imagine how happy and powerful you will feel when you take charge of your situation and respond to situations the way you want. Picture how it will be when the changes come about. How will you act? What will you say? What will others say to you? Have some fun and remember that the past, no matter how brutal and unfair, does not completely dictate your future. It is important for you to set aside a few minutes each day to mentally practice acting and behaving the way that you want to be. Use the exercises in chapter 8, "Obstacles to Healing and Managing Anger," to cleanse and prepare your mind to create your destiny.

6

Health and Emotional Well-Being

Anger, as we have noted, is a natural and basic emotion that supports us in times of stress, when our physical safety is challenged, enhancing our capacity for survival. Unfortunately, it takes a greater effort to cope with threats to our egos, pride, and self-esteem than it takes to cope with physical danger. These psychological threats, which are the root causes of anger and rage among black men, have a lasting effect because they are forever stored in our memories. This chronic anger contributes to the development of a variety of ills—digestive disorders, hypertension, heart disease, susceptibility to infections, rashes, headaches, and many more.

One way to visualize the wear and tear on the human body during intense episodes of anger is to think about the erosion of parts in an automobile that are neglected. Imagine for a moment that you are examining a car that was regularly serviced, well maintained, and carefully driven by a "little old lady"—and is now in the hands of a eighteen-year-old boy. This young man believes in rap music, hanging out with the boys, and that the cops are not smart enough to catch him speeding. Unlike the little old lady, he does not change the oil every three months or give the car a tune-up or schedule routine maintenance. What would be your guess about the condition of the car after a few months of steady use? You guessed it—the car will be in bad shape. There would probably be a buildup of sludge in the fuel line and the carburetor. The engine is strained, and it probably knocks and spits because of the uneven flow of fuel and air. Good gas mileage is a fond memory. The brakes are worn down, the electrical system is probably strained, and the battery will die.

The body can undergo similar devastation when it experiences massive disruptions in routine functions that are caused by stress, frustration, and episodes of anger. Individuals who are ineffective in managing and expressing anger are more likely to engage in behaviors that are reminiscent of the fight-or-flight defense reaction. In addition to the wear and tear on the body, anger and stress in daily life can also foster hostile attitudes that create troubling interactions with other people.

Sometimes black men are unable to recognize anger in their lives, but they sense that they have been under immense stress and have experienced much frustration. If you are one of those brothers who usually feels stressed-out rather than actually angry, then it might be helpful for you to substitute the word *stressed-out* for the word *anger* as you continue with this book.

The Psychobiology of Anger

The experience of chronic anger is thought to increase the heart rate, blood pressure, and respiration and to provide blood for the muscles needed to engage in an attack or to defend against the loss of one's highly valued possessions. During episodes of anger, the muscles become more tense, the pupils dilate, and there is a strong outpouring of hormones such as adrenaline into the body. Many of these hormones have a negative effect on the body when they are secreted in high concentrations. For example, when cortisol, one of the hormones associated with stress, occurs in high concentrations, it is believed to worsen and speed up the processes associated with atherosclerosis (hardening of the arteries) and coronary artery disease.

Other evidence shows that heart attack victims have high levels of cortisol and other hormones, which suggests that the heart attack may be partially related to excessive stress. Evidence from a number of research studies shows that many of the hormones associated with stress interfere with the ways the body prepares itself to fight off infections. Some evidence suggests that the progression of cancer and even AIDS is made worse because of how individuals deal with the stress and frustrations in their lives.

Chronically high levels of certain stress hormones (epinephrine and norepinephrine) stimulate the sympathetic nervous system to shunt blood from the skin, liver, and digestive tract to the heart, lungs, and skeletal muscles. Blood pressure is elevated, and glucose is dumped into the blood system to provide energy for confrontation or escape. During episodes of stress, blood is shunted away from the liver, making it less efficient in clearing the blood of cholesterol, thus contributing to the fatty deposits in the arteries.

Each of the major physiological systems of the body is disrupted during episodes of intense anger and stress. The billions of living cells in the body are organized in structures called organs, and each individual organ performs a unique set of biological functions. Organs that perform similar functions are referred to as a system. The operation of most systems is maintained by a process called homeostasis, which is the attainment of a relatively stable state of equilibrium or balance in the systems that control the body.

Any condition that disrupts the balance will automatically set in motion countermeasures to restore balance. It is believed that during these times excessive emotional reactions such as anger and hostility may have their most deadly impact on the body. For example, the cardiovascular system serves the body by circulating oxygen and nutrients and removing waste products. These functions are vital because the cells of the body must ingest oxygen and nutrients and excrete toxic waste products in order to maintain normal metabolic activity.

Another vital system that is disrupted during episodes of intense anger is respiration, the exchange of gases within the cells of the body. Even though the term *respiratory system* is commonly used to denote the lungs, it actually consists of every living cell in the body. So essentially all living cells are disrupted when a person is emotionally disturbed by frustrating events. Even the two basic functions of the gastrointestinal system, which are to chemically break down the complex products contained in food into simpler forms and to expel products that cannot be digested, are disrupted by anger. The efficiency with which the body regulates its core temperature is similarly disrupted.

An excellent example that is often used to explain how the homeostatic process works to maintain balance in the body is the control of body temperature. Most of the body's physiological systems function most efficiently at 98.6 degrees Fahrenheit, although some operate better at slightly lower or higher temperatures. Sperm requires a temperature of exactly 98.6 degrees; they are stored in testicles that hang in a scrotal sac outside the body. And the scrotum has an automatic reaction to temperature changes. For example, in hot weather or when body heat has increased due to exercise, physical exertion, or a hot shower, the scrotum expands and the testes are automatically lowered away from the body. By contrast, the scrotal sac contracts when a man enters a cold environment such as a cold shower. The testes are brought closer to the body for warmth and protection. The sperm would die if this automatic homeostatic process was greatly disrupted because of excessive anger and stress or other factors.

Not all of the links between emotions and health are understood, and there are skeptics, but thousands of articles published in some of the leading American medical journals support the idea of a connection. If our emotions are expressed through bodily processes that are under the influence of the nervous system, then the first danger to health and life may stem from our emotions, rather than an invading germ.

Although there are various theories about stress, each leans heavily on two components that appear to be closely related. The first is the involvement of the fight-or-flight response during the initial phase of the reaction to threat—be it physical or psychological. The second is that the final pathways by which stress has an effect on disease will involve hyperarousal of physiologic and biochemical functions.

Stress and intense emotional experiences, such as anger, alter hormonal patterns, immune function, cardiovascular function, and other physiological patterns that are key aspects of the causes of illness. The wear and tear on the body that is brought on by anger is associated with both acute and chronic diseases. However, it appears that it is the manner in which anger is handled and expressed that is more strongly related to illness.

Camouflaged Anger

Much of the stress in our lives is anger in a camouflaged form that may be expressed as bitterness, cynicism, envy, feeling overwhelmed, depression, or a sense of helplessness. Many of the brothers who bury their anger often fail to recognize the indicators of anger in their lives and instead choose to use the words *stressed-out, hyped,* or *geeked* to describe their suffering. They don't recognize as anger the little twinge they experience when a coworker inserts an ever-so-carefully-phrased insult in the middle of a conversation or the vague bitterness at their wife and kids for not appreciating all of the things that they do for them. They don't recognize as anger the sense of helplessness and doom that they experience when they think about the living situations for black people or the crap that black men have to put up with to survive in America. They don't recognize as anger the tightness in their chest and the clenched fist they have when they view television programs that constantly portray black men as drug dealers and thieves. They don't recognize as anger the uncomfortable feelings brought on by department store clerks who act as if they are about to rob the establishment.

If you are one of those men who don't recognize anger in your life, review the Self-Awareness Exercises in chapter 1. Pay particular attention to your responses to the Temper Test. You should also revisit the section in chapter 5 entitled "Managing Anger in the Workplace," and note how you respond to the questions concerning the causes of anger at work. If you then perceive that there is too much anger in your life, then it's time to learn how to cope with it. Reviewing the exercises presented in the "Prescriptions for Change" section of the previous chapters would be a good place to start. I also suggest that you move forward to the material in chapter 11, "The Psychology of Staying Cool." That chapter contains a number of techniques that you can easily learn to better manage stress in your life and to prevent anger from killing you.

Is Anger Related to Ill Health Among Black Men?

The idea that emotions are related to illness has received considerable attention over the past fifty years. However, only recently has medical research looked at whether the manner in which black men cope with feelings of anger and rage is associated with the excessive levels of ill health and personal problems we suffer. Most of the information linking emotions and health among black men focuses on high blood pressure and hypertension.

Doctors have always suspected an association between anger and high blood pressure. To understand how anger elevates blood pressure, it's important to first examine how blood pressure works in your body. Blood pressure is simply the pressure exerted by the blood on the walls of the blood vessels. Two different pressures are expressed as two numbers, such as 120/80 or 140/90. The higher number represents the systolic blood pressure of your blood as it surges through the arteries during each heartbeat. You feel that wave of pressure as you touch the pulse in your wrist. The lower number is a measurement of the diastolic pressure in the artery between heartbeats. A blood pressure of 120/80 means that the pressure in the arteries is 120 at the time of the heart's contraction and 80 between heartbeats.

Although the association between anger and hypertension has been demonstrated by many studies on various patient populations, it was the pioneering Motor City Study that led the inquiry into the association between anger-coping styles and health problems among black Americans. In the Motor City study, conducted in Detroit in the early 1970s, the relationship between the manner in which anger is expressed and hypertension was examined for over one thousand adults who resided in high and low stress areas of Detroit.

Motor City Madness and Hypertension

The level of stress in the Detroit study was determined by the degree of crime, juvenile delinquency, divorce, population density, and general dissatisfaction with the area in which the participants resided. Researchers predicted that the amount of hypertension would be greater among black people who did not openly express their anger. The results confirmed the predictions and showed that the relationship between suppressed anger and hypertension held constant regardless of the source of anger and frustration. In other words, hypertension occurred more often among individuals who suppressed their anger whether they were being treated unfairly by their landlords, their boss, a coworker, their spouse, or a policeman. However, higher levels were more likely for those individuals who lived in the high stress areas of the city.

Another important finding in this study was that blood pressure was highest in persons with high levels of job strain or family strain who had a tendency to suppress angry feelings when provoked. A linkage between anger and hypertension has been observed in several other studies as well. What is most disturbing is the data showing that the linkage between anger and high blood pressure even occurs among black youth. My own research with over thirteen hundred adolescents demonstrated that blood pressure is high among black youngsters who frequently experience angry feelings that are suppressed. In addition to higher blood pressure, these black adolescents are more likely to smoke cigarettes and be overweight.

National Survey of Black Americans

The National Survey of Black Americans (NSBA) was directed by researchers at the University of Michigan and constituted the first nationally representative mental health survey of the adult (eighteen years and older) black population. The sample of adults was assembled in such a way as to ensure that every black household had an equal chance of being selected to participate. Researchers and investigators at the University of Michigan have used information from the NSBA to determine whether anger was related to health problems (arthritis, ulcers, cancer, hypertension, diabetes, liver difficulties, kidney problems, stroke, circulatory problems in the arms or legs, and sickle-cell disease) that are relatively common among black Americans.

One particularly exciting aspect of the study is that the results revealed that the rates of hypertension, the most frequently occurring health problem, were higher among black Americans who kept angry feelings to themselves. In addition, anger expression was related to many other health problems included in the survey, as well as cigarette smoking and heavy consumption of alcohol.

The relationship between anger expression and health problems was found to be independent of (not changed by) the person's age and gender, or whether the individual lived in a large urban city or a small, rural town. The only factors that changed the relationship between health problems and anger was whether the person was unemployed or had experienced other stressful events. In this case, black Americans who were unemployed (43 percent of the respondents in the NSBA were unemployed at the time of the study in 1979–80) or who had recently experienced family problems were more likely to have a higher number of health problems if they had conflicts about the expression of anger.

Overall, the conclusion from the NSBA and other studies is that black Americans who are at increased risk for health problems may be identified by how often anger is experienced and expressed during periods of emotional distress, and that a high degree of "life strain" makes the situation worse.

Hypertension is especially critical because of the large number of African-Americans who have this deadly disease (approximately one out of every three adults). Hypertension is indeed a silent killer because many people with it are unaware they have it, and as a consequence the condition goes untreated and can contribute to heart disease, strokes, kidney disease, and even blindness. Nevertheless, hypertension can be treated, often without medications, because of the strong relationship between hypertension and lifestyle— dietary and exercise habits.

Only recently have we considered whether techniques that help people manage anger and stress can also be used to help black people with their hypertension. As is the case with many self-care or preventive health techniques, black Americans are last to receive the benefits. It is truly a mystery why blacks have not been provided opportunities to use anger and stress management techniques to help manage problems. Given the excessive stress, anger, and hypertension that we experience and the links between hypertension and anger, one would think that the first group to be offered such interventions would be blacks. This has not been the case. There currently exists some research indicating that anger causes an increase in blood pressure. Consequently, learning to manage anger and calmly talk about anger should help to lower blood pressure. Why this is the case is illustrated in the following examples taken from several of my interviews with black men.

"I might have a problem with how I manage my stress, but I don't have a problem with anger or expressing myself. If anything, I am overly expressive because I don't hold back from telling a person how I feel and what I'm thinking."

Herman, a twenty-nine-year-old, single college graduate in business administration, appears to be the prototype of good health, and yet he was recently diagnosed with hypertension. He says that he watches his weight, does not smoke, eats right, and makes it a habit to play basketball with the fellahs at least twice a week. Furthermore, there is no history of hypertension or heart disease anywhere in his family.

Herman is a handsome, well-dressed, healthy brother who works as a manager for a large company. Herman is also very "loud" and appears to have confused the word *talk* with the word *shout* because he expresses himself in a constantly loud and aggressive tone. On first examination, most of us would probably agree that he does not have a problem expressing himself. However, the problem that Herman has is *how* he expresses himself.

While there are a host of possible biological reasons for his hypertension, it is probable that his loud and aggressive manner contributes to his blood pressure problem. Studies conducted by me and other psychologists show that the verbal behavior—that is, volume, intensity, increased speech rate—of a person has a strong effect on blood pressure. As you would have guessed, the results show that blood pressure is higher for people when these verbal behaviors are elevated compared to when a person speaks slowly and softly. Some of my research also shows that these same verbal behaviors are a bit elevated when people are angry, even in the case where anger is repressed. When angry feelings

147

are repressed, we don't recognize that we are angry because we can't or won't allow ourselves to feel anger even when we look and sound the part.

Herman is a prime example. Of all of the black men that I interviewed, Herman was one of the angriest, and yet he does not believe that he has a problem with anger. His blood pressure problem, in my opinion, was caused or made worse by the manner in which he expresses himself. Herman's style of coping with anger was the opposite of the calm anger-control style that is related to the peaceful resolution of conflicts.

It is quite common for black men, and probably all men, to view ourselves in a fragmented fashion. Nowhere is the impact greater than during interpersonal conflicts. When we communicate and interact with other people, it is important to consider whether we are communicating as the man we really are, the man other people see, or the man whom we wish to become. In Herman's case, there was a large gap between how he viewed himself and how other people perceived him. For example, while denying his problem with anger, Herman admitted other people quite often perceive him as an "angry man."

Although it took some probing, Herman conceded that the disparity of views may be a result of the way he expresses himself when he is angry. To deal with this possibility, Herman was advised to deliberately take a few deep breaths before he said anything once he was upset. He was also advised to take breaths in between sentences and to speak slower as a way of developing a greater awareness of his speaking style when he is angry or upset. He is enrolled in a course on stress management and has learned to meditate (see chapter 11 on this topic) as a means of creating a calmer bodily response to frustration.

Does Talking Out Anger Make You More or Less Angry?

One of the dangerous myths that people have about anger is that it is best to talk it out. However, people who spend time talking out anger tend to experience an increase in the intensity of anger, and they increase the possibility of provoking anger in the person who received their anger. Instead of feeling good after expressing anger, most of us feel miserable, sad, irritated, depressed, guilty, ashamed. Some people are in physical pain or covered with black-and-blue marks as a result of physical assaults linked with the open expression of anger. However, it is the manner in which we talk about anger that can lead to a smooth resolution of conflict, to a heated debate that may escalate to violence, or to elevated blood pressure.

Earl, thirty-eight, has been married for five years and works as a restaurant manager. He admits that he is not too happy about his life and his work. He also admits that he takes out much of his frustration by assaulting his wife. "It seems that once we get into an argument, it is hard for me to be rational about what I say and what I do. I try to talk to her and express myself, but I tend to get angrier and more frustrated the more we talk. Sometimes things have gotten so bad and out of hand that I have hit my wife and called her some pretty bad names." Earl and his wife are victims of the idea that it is best to talk out anger. Rather than using his feelings to guide him to a more fulfilling solution to their conflicts, he allows himself to fall into the trap of continuing to talk about a troubling event even though he is already angry and ready to explode.

Earl is both hypertensive and diabetic. He also has a significant weight problem that probably contributes to his bad health. It's difficult for Earl to control himself once he is angry, and one of the major sources of stress for Earl is his relationship with his wife. "I think that the problems with my diabetes and hypertension get worse when my wife and

149

I are having problems. I also eat more when our problems get bad. It's like I can't stop eating when I'm angry and worked up about the difficulties in my life. I also know that I tend to blame my wife for some of my difficulties, but I know that she is not the cause," explains Earl. He seems to use both his wife and food as a means of expressing anger and hostile feelings.

Clearly Earl needs to learn how to better control and express his anger without suppressing his feelings. Unexpressed anger can cripple people emotionally, especially men with cardiovascular problems. When feelings of anger are not expressed, depression, anxiety, and guilt can result, sometimes contributing to alcoholism and drug abuse. A man like Earl can learn how to cope with stress using any of the techniques described in chapter 11. If you see yourself in Earl, review the steps that are offered in chapter 4 to help nuture a healthy relationship with black women. This information will help you develop better communication styles and create a positive atmosphere for talking about problems.

The tendency to have a short temper, much like the tendency to suppress anger, is learned automatically by children as they observe their parents. We further develop our habitual way of coping with anger once we begin to model our parents' behavior. Unfortunately, when either the expression (anger-out) or suppression (anger-in) of anger is rigidly learned and used to the extreme, bad habits are formed, and both coping methods can be psychologically and physically damaging.

So it appears that one of the keys to the effective management of anger is to express these feelings in ways that address what is triggering the emotion. Discussing your anger can lead to practical solutions to the things that are wrong in your life, but your perception of the causes of anger and your state of physiological arousal can be strongly affected by how you talk about your anger.

In cases like Earl's, talking out anger is ineffective because it is associated with yelling, screaming, threats, bodily tensions, and hostile facial expressions. Presumably, an individual like Earl who spends time talking out anger—caused by personal problems—is not getting rid of anger, but is "practicing it" or going through a rehearsal of how angry and furious he really is about the situation that triggered the emotion. Because behavioral responses such as yelling, threats, and hostile facial expressions are associated with anger, they can evoke angry reactions in subsequent interactions where there is no cause for anger. Anger occurs during subsequent interactions as a result of the same psychological conditioning principles that cause people to be cautious around a hot stovetop after they have been burned. People cope with being burned by paying close attention to whether the stove is turned on, and they test the stovetop to determine whether it is warm before carrying out their tasks. In the case of anger, the chain of angry and aversive communication can be broken by first becoming familiar with the situations that "trigger" angry feelings using the techniques in the "Prescriptions for Change" sections. Once you have identified the sources of your anger, you can use techniques, such as those in chapter 7, to learn how to stop anger before it escalates.

The Double Whammy: When Anger and Stress Are Combined

The stresses we encounter may vary, but stress affects us all in the same way, though some of us are more aware of the effects than others. The feeling of anguish and rage usually simmers in a man's bowels; it causes shortness of breath and tightness in the chest quite often during those times when our authority is challenged for no apparent reason or when someone cracks a joke at the expense of a black man. When these things happen to black men, as they often do, the physical side effects are damaging.

Scott, thirty-seven, is a physician who became a casualty of this type of thing. He eventually developed an ulcer and suffers from angina (chest pains). He saw his dreams of a fast-track career stunted at every turn by a racist supervisor who repeatedly questioned his skills and his intelligence. "Things got so frustrating, so out of hand, that at one point I was so low that I didn't go to work for a month. I was so depressed and agitated that my career progress was being hindered by a man who is a racist."

In addition to his stressful, hectic life as a physician, Scott has a "temper problem." It does not take much for him to lose his cool, and he admits that he is particularly angered by the actions of white people who put him down. In short, Scott is suffering from what I call *double-barreled danger;* that is, he feels trapped in a situation that is extremely frustrating and he knows that this is precisely the thing that ignites his anger and rage. "It seems that the only way that I could cope with the situation was to not go to work. I knew that I would have gone off on somebody and possibly destroyed my career. But at the same time, I know that my primary supervisor, who is racist, wants to push me out of the mainstream so that I will get frustrated and go take some other job. I am so pissed off about all of this, and I know that the problems with my health are a direct result from the pressure that I am under."

Whereas it is not possible to determine whether Scott's temper or career frustrations caused his health problems, men who experience this type of stress are in a dangerous situation, especially if they have problems managing their tempers. This is more true for men who are competitive, aggressive, and who have problems managing their anger—particularly when manifested as chronic hostility. Research examining men with these characteristics, which will be discussed later, shows that they stand a good chance of developing heart disease, cancer, and substance abuse problems, and they have a shorter life span compared to men who don't have these characteristics.

Scott's situation is acute because he is caught in a double bind—convinced his career will suffer if he accuses his supervisor of being racist, yet remaining in a situation that is slowly killing him. To cope, Scott decided to take another job. "I knew the reason for my anger, and I didn't think that having a confrontation would do anything except put certain people on the defensive and possibly worsen my situation." Unfortunately, avoiding the stress in his life is not the best response for Scott because he has failed to learn how to cope with the stress. Rather than escaping the situation, Scott could have used the techniques described in chapter 9, "Coping With Angry People," or the procedures in the "Prescriptions for Change" section of chapter 5. If you see similarities between yourself and Scott, I suggest that you also pay close attention to the information in chapter 8, "Obstacles to Healing and Managing Anger," particularly the section entitled "Avoiding Hurt Feelings and Being Helpless."

Life Stress and Anger

It has been argued that intense angry reactions play a role in health problems because they play a crucial role in generating life stress. The information from the National Survey of Black Americans provided a rich source for examining this possibility. Life stress was measured by responses to such questions as "Over the past month, have you had family or marriage, money or job problems?" As you would expect, the experience of negative life events in the past month caused people to feel angry, and the ways that anger was expressed outwardly at people and objects in the environment predicted whether an individual had health problems. Interestingly enough, African-Americans who experienced the most negative life events also had the highest number of health problems.

The finding that anger conflict is related to a greater number of stressful life events is supportive of the perspective that argues that people who experience difficulty in handling their anger are more likely to destroy important supportive relationships. As a consequence, the individual is more apt to experience negative life events and health problems. Perhaps this was the sort of thing that was under the surface in Scott's case. That's not to say that dealing with racism is unimportant, but Scott admitted to having a temper problem, and it is quite possible that some of his difficulties were the result of his own actions and reactions.

Individuals like Scott who have problems managing anger also induce angry, hostile interactions with others, generating even more psychological distress for themselves. This hypersensitivity keeps them constantly on guard, setting up similar reactions in the body, which could increase the susceptibility to infectious diseases and health problems.

Regardless of how stress is defined, the stresses of modern living are endless, and one source tends to be intertwined with others. Lester, age forty-two, is another example of a brother who has let his angry attitude and stress get the most of him. For the past ten years Lester has been plagued by a series of health problems that include headaches, dizziness, high temperatures, chest pains, and high blood pressure. According to Lester, the problems started shortly before his divorce, and they have gotten worse over the years. "What gets me so upset is that I spend a lot of time at the doctors', but they can't seem to find the cause of the illness. They don't exactly say to me that it's all in my head, but I know that's the conclusion they have made about me." Prior to his divorce Lester claims that he was perfectly healthy. "I use to work out at the gym, play tennis, and I was on a bowling team. There was nothing wrong with me, except my marriage. We were always fighting, mostly because there wasn't much money."

Following his divorce, which left him bitter and financially drained, Lester developed a rash of health problems that appeared to have no specific cause, and yet it was curious that the problems started in conjunction with an event that is stressful for any man. According to Lester, the end of his marriage was a symptom of a deeper set of problems with himself and his destructive ways of dealing with people and relationships. "I never thought much about how I handled stress or about how I took my stress out on my wife. How I deal with frustration is the cause of my divorce and poor health." Lester deals with anger explosively, in that he tends to easily lose his temper, saying and doing things that he later regrets. "I've been this way most of my life, and I guess that some of my feelings are linked to abuse my father inflicted on me when I was a boy. He constantly beat me and was forever telling me that I would grow up and become a nobody."

In talking with Lester it was apparent that he was still upset about his divorce. He was also bitter about being abused by his father. Even though his style of dealing with stress and frustration was explosive, Lester never really learned how to work through his feelings. Instead of talking about his problems, he would sulk and keep to himself. Consequently, Lester also suffered from loneliness and depression because of his tendency to withdraw from people who could provide him the emotional support and reassurance that he needed to deal with his problems.

Lester's situation took on a new dimension during his last doctor's visit as he was informed that some test results showed that he had prostate cancer and some abnormal growths in his pancreas. "This took me by surprise because the only thing I thought I had was hypertension. I am upset about my health, and I don't think there is anything I can do except pray and hope for the best."

Interestingly enough, Lester's personality profile fits the description of the type in whom cancers occur most and where the prognosis for recovery is poor. For example, several studies have revealed that the typical cancer patient has difficulty forming close relationships and generally has lost either a parent or sibling early in childhood. A majority of these patients had also lost an important relationship before their cancers appeared. For unknown reasons, the cancer patients blame themselves and feel quite abandoned and lonely over the loss of these close primary relationships, and they tend to repress these feelings and deny their importance.

Other studies have found that cancer patients were submissive and not aggressive and experience many difficulties in their relationships with family members, particularly their fathers, early in their lives. Even in the face of cancer many people maintained an even temperament, almost never venting their anger, sadness, depression, or fear.

One of the things that men with cancer need to be aware of is that several studies have shown that cancer patients who expressed emotions more openly are often found to have less aggressive tumor growth, stronger immunologic responses, and are less likely to relapse than patients who have difficulties expressing their emotions. Therefore, to deal with the ill effects of his problem, Lester needs to learn how to better express his feelings. Many of the techniques offered throughout this book would be of benefit to Lester because they would help him identify the real sources of his anger. Lester would also benefit from learning how to better manage stress (see chapter 11) so that he could develop his inner peace and tranquillity. The meditation and relaxation techniques are particularly useful in relieving tension and provide the body and mind with rest that is deeper than sleep. As a consequence of the deeper rest, the body is more apt to heal. While the exercises that are offered throughout the book can help you cope with anger and stress, the prescriptions are no substitute for professional advice.

Anger and Mortality: Is Anger Killing You?

One of the sad truths about the impact of chronic anger on the body is that in time it can lead to high cholesterol, heart attacks, and even a premature death. The impact of constantly boiling over in anger appears to be as bad as smoking and drinking. Several studies have now shown that chronically angry people, even those who suppress their anger, are more likely to suffer from a number of major health problems and not live as long as someone who does not harbor angry and hostile feelings. The situation is nearly twice as bad for chronically angry individuals who also have hypertension.

Lee, forty-four, works as a supervisor for a large furniture company, and even though he looks healthy, he suffered a heart attack nearly two years ago. "I never thought of myself as the kind of person that would have a heart attack because I always seemed healthy regardless of my blood pressure problem." As it turns out, Lee has been taking medication off and on for the past ten years to help him control his hypertension. "At work I like to get things done. There are always orders that need to be filled and lots of paperwork. Most men like to let things stack up on them, but I like to keep my team of men going full speed. Sometimes my style causes some friction and arguments, but we always tend to get the work done on time."

Lee is the prototype of the hostile, aggressive, hard-driving, and time-pressured type A person who is prone to heart problems. Early in the 1960s, Myer Friedman and Ray Rosenman, two San Francisco cardiologists, were trying to determine what put individuals at risk for coronary heart disease and who was likely to have blocked arteries, heart attacks, and angina. They found that people who had heart attacks had some things in common, such as high blood cholesterol, hypertension, and some bad habits such as smoking, drinking, and a sedentary lifestyle (e.g., sitting around watching a lot of television). But Friedman and Rosenman hit the jackpot when they examined their patients' personality patterns. They found a cluster of personality traits that appeared to be linked to heart disease.

In the infamous book *Type A Behavior and Your Heart* (1974), Friedman and Rosenman made the claim that the risks of having a heart attack and coronary heart disease were as high for people with a type A personality as they were for people with bad health habits. They identified the type A as having personality traits of time urgency, competitiveness, high ambition, hyperaggressiveness, and free-floating anger/hostility.

Research conducted over the past twenty years has shown that men with type A behavior are more prone to have heart attacks and coronary heart disease. Interestingly enough, it is the anger/hostility component of the type A behavior that has stood up over time as being the most significant predictor of heart disease.

In addition to the heavy demands at work, Lee admits to keeping his schedule at home full, and most times he finds himself overcommitted. "I just like to stay busy, and before my heart attack I used to have several things scheduled at the same time. I would juggle the situations so that I could spend a little time at each meeting and still do other things. What was so frustrating about this is that everybody would tell me to slow down, but then I would lose my temper at them for telling me how to live my life."

According to Lee, he lost his temper quite a bit as a means of keeping the pressure on his men to stay on schedule. "I never thought that I had a problem with my temper until I started having chest pains. But even the pain didn't prevent me from pushing myself to keep things on schedule."

Lee is a fortunate man in that his heart attack was not massive enough to cripple him for life. He says that the rehabilitation program he went through has caused him to change his life and has taught him how to deal with his anger. In addition to changing the way that he copes with stress and anger, Lee also learned to change his diet, start an exercise program, and watch his sleeping habits.

Prescriptions for Change

Good health is the natural state for most people, but there is such a preoccupation with illness and continual pill-taking that some people will never learn this. Most of us have put physicians in the position of being gods rather than recognizing that each of us is the authority and bears responsibility for his own body. In thinking about illness, you must first understand that your body is a system that responds to signals that you create.

Many illnesses occur as a result of imbalances that we cause. The stresses that we suffer are a consequence of the various imbalances we have in our relationships and the disruptions in our bodies that have been brought about because of strong feelings of rage and depression. Most of us have varying degrees of stress in our lives, but most of the stress and emotional trauma we experience results when we feel separated from the knowledge that we have the power to create and control our own life. Stress is a response we suffer when we are not comfortable in our various relationships and feel threatened. As indicated in the earlier sections of this chapter, medical researchers are beginning to discover a causal relationship between stress and physical aliments, such as cancer, arthritis, heart disease, and various stomach ailments. There is fairly good scientific evidence that many of the ailments are often preceded by emotional trauma that causes individuals to feel that they don't control their own life.

Take a moment and look at the times when you feel really alive and healthy. Usually it's a day when you don't feel any pressure or obligations, when you are among fun-loving people and don't feel threatened in any way. Unfortunately, such days are too rare for many of us. We tend to experience them only when we are away from home, work, school, or any environment where we feel a suppressive influence. Take a moment and recall how your body feels when you're full of joy and happiness. Contrast this with when you're angry, upset, or depressed. You can bet that your body is trying to tell you something. One simple experiment is to listen to your body when you are deciding what to eat. As you tune in to yourself, your body will say yes or no to certain items on the menu because the body is a wonderful feedback machine that lets you know that you have destroyed or are about to destroy its natural balance. For example, when you get a headache, your body is trying to tell you something, usually about the tension and stress you are feeling. When you experience an upset stomach after a meal, your body is talking to you about either the quality of the food you consumed or the circumstances under which you consumed the food.

All of your aches and pains, mild and severe, are your body's method of communicating with you. When your blood pressure is elevated, this is a signal that the things (i.e., foods, negative emotions, stress, etc.) you are putting into the body are in excess of what the body can handle. Developing an illness is the body's final warning sign. If a man observes the initial alarm, he can often address the illness in time. We ignore these warning signs at our own risk.

For some brothers, becoming sick is an unconscious way to try to solve problems, a means of shunning confrontation, and avoiding the truth about who we really are. Unfortunately, a man may lie to himself, but his body does not lie. You have only to look at a man's body to see how much he loves or hates himself and how much he deceives himself. Many men are simply not conscious of their bodies until they get sick or someone tells them they don't look too good. On the other hand, many black men take better care of their cars than their own bodies. The reasons for this may have something to do with the need to have some external validation or status symbol as a reflection of one's worth. Or maybe it's just because having a nice-looking and well-tuned car has been linked to a richer source of pleasure and fulfillment than being healthy. Some brothers have that polished and well-preserved outward physical look of healthiness, but they suffer from some of the silent killers such as hypertension, prostate cancer, and colon cancer that tend not to have any obvious symptoms. However, it is not impossible or difficult for black men to feel younger and stronger, and to live healthier and happier lives. In fact, the typical brother can accomplish these things without driving himself nuts with rules and exhausting himself with exercise. The experts say that driving your body hard is not what's going to make you strong and healthy. On the contrary: moderate amounts of exercise deliver the greatest benefits.

Every man has total responsibility for the good care of his body, but this is not so much a matter of medicine as of avoiding excesses in what we eat and drink, using nutritional common sense, providing our bodies with needed physical exercise, and raising our consciousness to recognize that good health is natural. Of course, there are germs and viruses, but scientists and doctors have verified that each of us has an immune system and that we get sick when there is a breakdown in this system. Our bodies are the alarm system that tells us when the natural protective process is not working. And it is our consciousness that controls the system.

Unfortunately, many men are so caught up in thinking about the things they want to achieve in the future or feeling guilty and upset about past events that they rarely take time to really reflect on the notion that everything they have going on in their life, including their health, is a reflection of their consciousness. How does a man reach the consciousness that assures him good health? He first must accept the fact that he began life healthy and that good health is natural. Also, he must learn to ask himself questions that will reveal the truth about his circumstances.

To get a better idea of what I am talking about, try answering the following questions:

- What have I accomplished with my life?
- What are my attitudes?
- What are the situations that ultimately created disease or the lack of harmony in my body and relationships?

Look back at the times when you were ill and examine your emotional state at the time.

- What kind of changes were going on in your life?
- How did you react to these changes?
- Were you angry and upset during these times?
- What was your level of stress like?
- How were your bonds with family members and friends?
- Was there any stress in these relationships?
- Was there a lot of stress at work?
- How did you express your feelings?
- Did you keep angry feelings to yourself or did you talk out your feelings?

If your responses to the questions indicate much stress and change happening in your life that caused feelings of anger and strained family relationships, then you have experienced the right blend of psychological trauma that can contribute to illness. You can begin to reduce your stress by learning the progressive muscle relaxation or meditation techniques that are described in chapter 11. It would be a good idea for you to practice the techniques daily for the next month. If you are concerned that the stress in your life is related to a health problem, then you should consider having an examination by a physician. Another thing that you can do is complete the questions in the next section so that you will have some idea of your relative risk for health problems. The major reason for these suggestions is because the occurrence of a new illness or the aggravation of an existing problem for most men follows changes that are stressful and frustrating. Relationships with family members are often strained, and in some cases the level of family or marital stress is the event that triggered the physiological and psychological reactions that contributed to the onset of an illness or aggravated an existing medical condition.

Psychological studies confirm over and over that change, any kind of change, is a crisis time. Even though change is constant and eternal, we want to hang on to old relationships, cling to possessions. We put up a good fight against change because we think that tradition is the avenue to security, stability, and good health. This is obviously not so because the one thing that we undoubtedly accomplish when we resist change is to put stress on our bodies and thereby, create illness in our bodies and our relationships. We allow our fears of change to make us ill because we can't let go of the old to acquire the new.

Most of the health problems that plague black men are preventable because they are either caused or made worse by the way that a man lives and copes with stress in his life. When a man makes his security dependent on a person, a job, a place, or thing, he is setting himself up to become frustrated, angry, and to suffer an illness.

The stage for perfect health is set when a man becomes

aligned with the truth about himself and he is capable of fully forgiving and accepting himself. It is this fact that allows for many of the spontaneous remissions or "miracle" cures that can't be explained by modern medicine. These seemingly miraculous healings were not miracles but examples of what can happen when a person believes that being healthy is natural and within his power.

Living a Long and Healthy Life

Every man has the potential to live longer than the average age if only we would reverse or at least slow down the damage we do to our bodies through various choices and behaviors. Some researchers have calculated that by taking charge of key life-shortening behaviors, a man can boost his life expectancy by fifteen years. Please keep a tally of your responses to the quizzes. Give yourself a score of 1 for each yes answer.

Quiz Yourself: Take a Good Look at Your Health

Family History: Your greatest risk for health problems starts with your genes. All of the major health problems—heart disease, hypertension, prostate cancer, and colon cancer—are inheritable. Having a family history of any of them doubles your chances of developing them. However, a man who has a positive family history of diseases can reverse his risk by fighting the factors that contribute to the problems. Eating a diet rich in fruits and vegetables, for example, lowers your risk of colon cancer and cardiovascular disease. Regular doctor's exams for early detection vastly increase your chances of surviving prostate and other cancers.

1. Do any immediate family members (parent, sibling, grandparent) have or once have had cancer or a heart condition or diabetes since childhood?
2. Do any immediate family members have or once have had hypertension since childhood?

3. Has any immediate family member died of prostate cancer or colon cancer before age sixty?

4. Has your mother or father died of a heart attack or stroke before age fifty?

Record your score here _____

Exercise: Research shows that a man with high blood pressure and high cholesterol who's in great physical shape is actually less at risk of dying young than a man with a lower cholesterol reading who's inactive. Active older men have also been found to have fewer strokes than their inactive peers. Some research shows similar results for cancer, particularly colorectal cancer. If you don't exercise now, start. Even a twenty-minutes-a-day walking program can improve your overall fitness. People who walk also feel more energized and are better able to deal with stress and avoid feelings of anxiety, depression, and anger.

5. Do you avoid exercising aerobically for at least thirty minutes three or more times a week?

6. Do you avoid playing sports or doing light physical activities like yard work once or twice a week?

Record your score here _____

Cholesterol: High cholesterol is one of the critical reasons men have three to four times as many heart attacks as women. Some research has also suggested that high cholesterol is a risk factor for prostate cancer. Cholesterol can be lowered by reducing your intake of saturated fat and by staying physically active.

7. Is your total cholesterol above 240?

Record your score here _____

Alcohol: This is an addictive drug and is abused because it is so often used as part of socializing and celebrating important accomplishments. When it is abused, it ruins the liver. However, when used in moderation, a drink or so every other day, it may actually boost longevity. Some studies have shown that drinking red wine is associated with a reduction in cholesterol. However, if you don't drink, it's best not to start.

8. Do you drink heavily (more than two beers, two glasses of wine, two shots of whiskey, a day on average) or until you are intoxicated?

Record your score here _____

Diet and Fresh Water: What you eat is highly related to your chances of getting heart disease and certain types of cancer. Fatty foods, for example, can raise cholesterol, boost blood pressure, and contribute to cancer of the colon. Eating plenty of fruits and vegetables supplies life-extending nutrients, particularly vitamins C, E, and beta-carotene, which have been shown to reduce the risk of a wide variety of health problems including heart disease.

One piece of health advice that most men are aware of is that they should drink plenty of water, preferably six to eight glasses a day. However, most men are not aware of the reason. As it turns out, the body is about 70 percent water, and fresh water helps maintain the systems within the body. When we don't take in the right proportion of water, the buildup of waste within the body makes it difficult for the various systems to function correctly. The result is usually an illness or disease.

9. Do you eat fewer than five helpings of fruits and vegetables daily?
10. Do you eat a lot of high-fat foods such as red meat, fried foods, and snack items?
11. Do you drink fewer than six glasses of water a day?

Record your score here _____

Smoking: This is the one bad health habit that plays a role in just about every major health problem men face. Smoking is the leading cause of lung cancer and seems to play a role in prostate and colon cancer. Smoking is also associated with high blood pressure, and the death rate for smokers is roughly twice as high as for nonsmokers. However, the risk of health problems can be reduced if you quit. Within five to ten years of quitting, lung cancer risk reverts to near normal. If you can't quit, perhaps you can get your nicotine fix in other ways, such as using nicotine gum or the nicotine patch.

12. Do you smoke?
13. Do you smoke over a half pack of cigarettes a day?
   Record your score here _____

Hypertension: This is a silent killer because hypertension has no obvious symptoms. About one out of every three black men has high blood pressure. What this means is that the heart has to work harder to pump blood through the body. As a consequence the pressure throughout the body is high, and in the long run this causes damage to the organs in the body, strokes, heart disease, and kidney problems and contributes to blindness. The blood pressure reading is expressed as two numbers—anything close to 120/80 is considered normal, and consistent readings above 140/90 are considered high. (Some further information about blood pressure is located in an earlier section—"Is Anger Related to Ill Health Among Black Men?"—of this chapter.) Some physicians consider only the second number, diastolic blood pressure, as the primary yardstick for defining hypertension. While persistent high blood pressure often requires medication, studies show that regular exercise, lowering weight, reducing alcohol and salt intake, and learning how to manage stress can lower your blood pressure.

14. Do you avoid having your blood pressure checked at least once a year?
15. Is your diastolic blood pressure greater than 90?
   Record your score here _____

Obesity: Being more than a few pounds overweight can shave years off your life. Obesity is strongly related to high cholesterol, hypertension, and adult-onset diabetes. Some strong evidence suggests that being overweight increases a man's risk of developing certain types of cancer. The good news is that weight, like the other risk factors for disease, can be controlled. The best weight-loss plan combines a low-fat diet with modest exercise that results in gradual weight loss. Avoid crash diets because some studies show that losing weight rapidly and then gaining it back puts you at even higher risk for coronary artery disease than just being moderately overweight.

One way to determine whether you are overweight is to calculate your body mass index. This is a way of figuring out where you stand by using a single number so that those with different heights can be compared. This number, called the body-mass index, is your weight in kilograms divided by the square of your height in meters.

Here's how you figure it out: First, multiply your weight in pounds by 0.45 to get kilograms. Next convert your height to inches. Multiply this number by 0.0254 to get meters. Then multiply this number by itself. Then divide this into your weight in kilograms. Your answer will probably be a number in the 20s or 30s.

Example: Let's take my weight of 170 and height of five feet nine inches as an example.

Step one: 170 pounds times 0.45 = 76.5 kilograms
Step two: 5 feet 9 inches = 69 inches times 0.0254 = 1.7526 meters
Step three: 1.7526 times 1.7526 = 3.0716
Step four: 76.5 divided by 3.0716 = 24.9055

My body-mass index is 24.9055. Most research studies have found that the risk of health problems is lowest for people with a body-mass index below 30.

16. Has your weight fluctuated by more than ten pounds several times since high school?
17. Are you currently more than 20 percent overweight for your height and body frame?
    Record your score here _____

Stress: As indicated throughout the chapter, emotions such as anger and hostility, which are often associated with stress, are linked to a wide range of health problems, including hypertension and heart disease. Frustration associated with demanding work is one of the major reason for stress, as we have shown.

18. Is it difficult for you to be easygoing and relaxed?

19. Are you easily angered?

20. Do you have a demanding job and little say over how things are done?

Record your score here _____

Regular Doctor's Exams: Most of the health problems that black men develop can often be detected early during regular health examinations. The basic problem is that most black men don't routinely get annual physical examinations. As a consequence, health problems that could have been prevented or treated while they were in their earlier stages worsen and often lead to a massive breakdown. Annual examinations are extremely important for warding off premature death from either prostate or colon cancer. Testing is especially important after age forty, when these problems are most likely to develop.

21. Did you avoid having a physical examination within the past year?

Record your score here _____

Evaluate your score by adding the numbers you have recorded. Generally speaking, a score of 0 is perfect and means that you are at relatively low risk for health problems. A score between 1 and 5 means that you are taking care of yourself, while a score between 6 and 10 means that you need to take immediate actions to modify your risk factor. A score above 10 means that your risk for developing major health problems is high.

Self-Awareness Strategies and Exercises

Take Notice of Yourself

Take a moment and notice those times when you really felt healthy and alive. What were you doing? Whom were you with? What were your feelings about the situation? Reflect on how you really feel when you were healthy.

Now, take a few moments and notice those times when you felt sick. What was going on in your life? What problems had you had recently? What sort of stress and pressures had you been experiencing? How had you been coping with your anger? Does it make you angry to see yourself sick? Be honest with yourself. Take a moment and wonder about what you gain from being sick. What problems are you avoiding?

Notice how you feel around people who are health conscious and healthy. Do you feel better or worse? Does being around healthy people make you feel healthy? Now take a moment or so and think about how you feel when you are around someone who is sick. Do you tend to stay happy or does this pull you down? Take a few moments and look for differences in your behavior, attitudes, beliefs, and feelings as you interact with people who are healthy and people who are sick. Do you see any patterns in your attitudes and beliefs? Are you doing anything that hinders the development of your health or relationships with people? Why are you doing these things? What pain and hurt are you avoiding by doing these things? Are you sick to get attention?

Are you happy or unhappy with your health? Are you worried about your health? Are you angry and upset because you can't take charge of your health? If you are, ask yourself why.

Make Decisions About What You Want

Whatever your health situation at the moment, take full responsibility for what you have done. If you are sick, say, "I have done this to myself and I have chosen to be sick." Accept that you may have been using sickness to avoid problems or to avoid making difficult decisions or to get attention. Do you use sickness as a way of dealing with your anger? Has sickness been your way of getting other people to love you? Be honest with yourself and accept this if it is so. Accept that this is the way that you are because you have made a conscious choice to be this way.

Stop Blaming Yourself and Others

Don't blame yourself and make the situation worse. Just accept that you are responsible for your sickness and know that you don't have to stay sick. It is so easy to blame outside forces—weather, food, water, relationships, work—for our sickness. Stop blaming these things outside of yourself because they can cause you to lose sight of the fact that you are responsible for your own life. Just accept that you have choices about your health.

Create Your Own Destiny

Take a few moments and visualize yourself free from sickness. Imagine yourself being perfectly healthy. Form a clear mental picture of the way you would like your life to be if you are in perfect health. Visualize yourself with the various people in your life. What would you like to say to them? What would you do? How do you want to respond to them? What feelings do you have about these relationships? Now, make contrasts between the way you want your health to be with your current level of health. What are the differences in your behaviors, attitudes, feelings, and beliefs? You are responsible for creating your own health, and remember, it is up to you and not things outside of you. The picture of your health starts with the picture that you have of yourself. If you don't like the picture you have of yourself, then it is up to you to change. Real change occurs when you truly accept yourself with perfect health being your real destiny.

PART 2

OTHER STRATEGIES FOR MANAGING ANGER AND STRESS

7

Strategies
for Stopping Anger
Before It Escalates

Anatomy of a domestic explosion: A woman—Joanne—makes an offhand remark to her mate—Robert—as they are cleaning the dinner table. Robert is stung by her comment but doesn't respond. Later that evening, Robert makes a thinly veiled insult to Joanne—actually a delayed response to the perceived hurt after dinner.

Joanne, interpreting it as a dart from out of nowhere, fires back in classic "back-at-you" style.

And then Robert erupts with a volley of verbal put-downs that is so withering—coming as it does from someone Joanne loves—that she flings her favorite dish at Robert, narrowly missing him!

Robert's next move in this escalating chain of *aversive behavior* is likely to be physical abuse of Joanne.

Had they calmed down enough to discuss the incident, the couple would probably be shocked at how innocuously it began, and how long feelings had simmered before finally erupting. But a trivial action such as an unintendedly harsh comment can generate patterns of reaction and counterreaction that are the basic building blocks of family anger and violence.

Initial hurt and wounded pride can sometimes turn to murderous rage, especially if the aversive behavior occurs between people with approximately equal power—such as a husband and wife, coworkers, even a parent and child.

The first step toward stopping anger before it escalates into a confrontation is to observe the early-warning signs. Early-warning signs can be either verbal, as with Robert and Joanne, or nonverbal. The nonverbal signs include

- increased pulse rate
- heavy, rapid breathing
- increased body temperature
- sudden sweating

For some people, tension and tightness in the gut is a signal of growing anger. For others, the tension might be located in the neck, shoulders, or jaw. A particularly telling sign of tension occurs when the hands are balled up into fists. Robert might have prevented the episode with Joanne from escalating by observing any of the warning signs during the buildup of hostility and responding in a nonangry way. Since no one reacts aversively to the provocation, it lasts only a few seconds. Three-or-four-step sequences generally last less than a minute. But when aversive chains last longer than half a minute, yelling, screaming, threatening, or hitting may occur. As a rule, the longer the chain lasts, the more likely it is that violence will occur. Sequences lasting a minute or so are frequently observed in dysfunctional families.

The last link in the chain is called a trigger behavior, and this usually precedes and precipitates an angry and violent outburst. Triggers can be verbal or nonverbal and usually occur when a person feels threatened, rejected, or abandoned. Some of the typical verbal and nonverbal triggers used to build an aversive chain of communication are presented below:

Verbal Triggers

- criticism ("I don't like the way you talked to my mother. You are always putting her down.")
- blaming ("If it weren't for you, I would be finished with this project.")
- teasing ("I know that you are a smart man because of your degrees, but I need a man with brains to work with me.")
- put-downs ("Is this what you call a finished product? I could have gotten a better product from a garbageman.")
- sarcasm ("Sure you're going to finish the report. Like the last time I had to complete it for you.")
- ultimatums ("This is your last chance. If you don't change, I will divorce you.")
- stonewalling ("Don't say anything to me because there is nothing to talk about.")
- mind reading ("I know what you're really trying to do: blame me for everything that went wrong.")
- humiliating statements ("You used to take good care of yourself, but now I'm embarrassed to be seen with you.")
- profanity ("You son of a . . .")
- accusations ("I asked you not to do that and I know that you did it anyway.")
- global labeling ("People like you are all alike, now go and . . .")

Imagine that you are being confronted by someone who is criticizing, blaming, and teasing you using the verbal triggers described above. How does it make you feel? How likely are you to get angry as a result of someone's using these triggers? Would you feel more or less angry if the person was putting you down, using sarcasm or ultimatums?

Simply being aware of how verbal triggers stir your feelings is an important step in stopping anger before it escalates. However, at times your feelings of anger are stirred by a person's nonverbal behaviors or vice versa. Some of the typical nonverbal triggers that stir feelings of anger are presented below.

Nonverbal Triggers

- sighing ("I can't take this crap anymore")
- mocking, contemptuous tone
- mumbling under your breath
- snickering
- shaking a fist or pointing a finger to intimidate or accuse
- folded arms
- looking away or rolling eyes
- grimacing, sneering, or frowning
- hands on hips
- shrugging
- moving or leaning forward to intimidate
- pacing as a sign of increased irritability and agitation
- throwing or kicking objects
- pushing or grabbing

Nonverbal behaviors usually trigger a stress reaction, which provides the fuel for anger. Nonverbal triggers often contribute to a cycle of actions and verbal reactions that cause anger to escalate. An example of an aversive cycle is described below.

Aversive Cycle of Verbal and Nonverbal Communication Between Husband and Wife

1. Husband comes home, is unusually silent and looks sad.
2. Wife (frowns, sighs): "What's the matter now?"

3. Husband (with folded arms, complaining, tightening lips): "My boss is an asshole."

4. Wife (in a cold tone, giving advice and using guilt): "Well, you'll just have to stick it out. You know that the children and I can't afford for you to quit or be fired."

5. Husband (using an expletive and global labeling in a loud voice): "Dammit, you never give me support. I can't take you doing this to me!"

6. Wife (abrupt limit setting, guilt, flatness): "Stop shouting right now! The children can hear you."

7. Husband (in a constricted voice, using global labeling and threats, finger-pointing, and an expletive): "Yeah, all you think of is the children and telling me what to do. You don't give a damn about me, and if you really want to do something about the children, then get a job. Don't you ever raise your voice at me again. You know what I will do to you."

8. Wife (sneering, sarcasm, accusation): "Oh, yeah! I didn't know you had feelings. You haven't talked to me decently in weeks. All you do is threaten to beat me."

9. Husband (with tight lips and narrowing eyes, complaining and using profanity): "You never have time for me anyway. You're always on the phone to your goddamn mother. I wish she would keep the fuck out of our life. I've had it with you telling me what to do. If you don't like the situation, then leave, because this is the way it will always be."

10. Wife (loudly and harshly, with narrowing eyes, using profanity and a dismissing comment, leaning forward): "Shut up, asshole! You need to get out of my life."

11. Husband (loudly and harshly, using profanity, threatening): "All right, bitch, I've had it from you. I'll leave, but I'm going to make sure that you don't get a damn thing from me, and I don't care about what you have to say about the situation." (He makes a threatening gesture with his fist.)

This aversive cycle could be altered using many different techniques. Some of the quick methods to stop anger before it escalates are presented below. The key to using these or any other methods for dealing with anger-provoking situations is consistency.

When you feel the first symptom of anger, it is best to decide which of the strategies will work best for your situation. Try different techniques and find the one that's most effective for you. Once you find the best strategy for reducing anger, use it consistently and take notice of the differences in how you and other people respond. As a rule of thumb, earlier interventions are best. It's a lot easier to stop a car that has just started to roll than one that is speeding downhill, out of control.

Some Quick Methods to Defuse Anger

1. Take ten slow and deep breaths.
2. Change your posture and stretch.
3. Get up and walk around the area you are located in.
4. Rotate your shoulders forward and then backward for a few moments.
5. Listen without talking for a few moments.
6. Talk more slowly and in a softer voice.
7. Modify your personal thoughts: remind yourself that what's going on is not more important than your health.
8. Ask the other person to explain why he or she is upset.
9. Call for a "time-out."

Of all of the strategies on the list above, time-out is perhaps the single most useful in controlling the escalation of anger. Part of its effectiveness undoubtedly stems from the fact that *time-out* is a familiar and acceptable metaphor in sports. It is also a guaranteed method for stopping anger before it escalates to violence. Time-out is a particularly useful method for situations where there is stress or frustration between a husband and wife, strained relationships between coworkers, or conflicted interactions between a parent and child.

Time-out works in defusing anger because either person in an interaction who notices the early-warning signs of tension and irritability can decide that a time-out is needed. This need for time-out is communicated simply by holding the left palm over the right hand in a T sign—the same gesture referees use. Nothing need be said at this point except perhaps "Time-out!" The other person is then obligated to return the gesture and stop talking. It is permissible to say "Okay, I'm beginning to feel angry and I need (or want) to take a time-out." However, there is some evidence that merely using the word *angry* will trigger an automatic anger reaction in other people. Therefore, it is recommended that you stick with the neutral term *time-out*.

The T is a signal that it is time to separate for a while. Ideally, the person who is "beginning to get angry" will take the cue and leave for an agreed period of time. Agreeing on the rules ahead of time will prevent any misconception that this necessary separation is a form of running away or a means of punishing the other person. A good rule of thumb is to separate for one hour. It is important to allow yourself an adequate amount of time to cool off. Although it may seem hard and painful to do, it is even more important to return when the time is up. It takes real courage to return to an emotionally painful situation without the protective shield of anger.

Anger is not something that happens in a flash. Even people who are hot tempered or have a short fuse go through progressive stages. Beginning with tension and irritation, anger is kindled, and then destructive self-statements fan the flames that then trigger behaviors and actions that ignite the explosive rage. Just imagine how the situation between the husband and wife that is described above could have turned out if either the husband or wife had called a time-out.

While you are away from the stressful situation, practice some of the techniques that have previously been described.

Taking a long walk or going for a run are two of the best methods for reducing tension in your body. Practicing one of the breathing, relaxation, or meditation techniques described in chapter 11 can also help you relax. Above all, don't hang on to your angry thoughts or waste time building a case. Basically, the more you focus on proving how wrong and awful the offender is, the angrier you will become. Instead, use the problem-solving approach to generate possible solutions. When you are away from the stressful situation, it is best that you don't drink or use drugs, and please don't drive, because angry drivers are a real danger to themselves and others.

When you return from a time-out, it is best to "check in," because this will help to establish trust in the relationship. The check-in involves a willingness on both sides to communicate about the issue in a way that will help you both reduce the possibility of escalating anger in the future.

Proactive Problem Solving

It has been said that an ounce of prevention is worth a pound of cure, but for some of us there are few words to describe situations that cause chronic emotional reactions in our lives. For some people anger can best be prevented by developing a greater sense of awareness of the situations and problems that cause stress in their lives. Once the problems have been identified, it's much easier to find the possible solutions. Unfortunately, many of us don't perceive the solutions because of the increased anger, anxiety, and despair that we have experienced related to the problem or because we have attempted to cope in usual ways that have often failed. Many of our problems might appear to be insolvable, but the solutions are always inherent in the conflict if we don't allow ourselves to become prisoners of our own emotions.

Step #1: Identifying Problems That Cause
Stress and Anger

One way to determine the problem areas for stress in your life is to make a checklist, category by category. Once the list is formed, pay particular attention to problems that seem associated with anger, anxiety, emotional distress, and tension. Listed below are common problems that often result in chronic emotional pain, expressed as anger. For each problem, indicate whether you have experienced it within the past month, and if you have, then indicate whether the problem has caused a 1, mild, 2, moderate, or 3, extreme, amount of distress in your life.

Within the past thirty days have you experienced . . .

		Amount of Distress		
Financial or money problems	yes or no	1	2	3
Increasing debt or difficulty making ends meet	yes or no	1	2	3
Unexpected expenses	yes or no	1	2	3
Work-related problems	yes or no	1	2	3
Boring working conditions	yes or no	1	2	3
Trouble with a boss or coworker	yes or no	1	2	3
Fear of being fired	yes or no	1	2	3
Unemployment or underemployment	yes or no	1	2	3
A desire for a career change	yes or no	1	2	3
Feeling like you are in a dead-end job	yes or no	1	2	3
Racism on the job	yes or no	1	2	3
Family problems	yes or no	1	2	3
Fighting and arguing all of the time	yes or no	1	2	3
Recurring hurt and criticism from your spouse	yes or no	1	2	3
Troubles with your parents or children	yes or no	1	2	3
Children having problems at school	yes or no	1	2	3
Feeling rejected by your spouse or family	yes or no	1	2	3
Sickness in your family	yes or no	1	2	3

Death of a family member	yes or no	1	2	3
A marriage breaking up	yes or no	1	2	3

Health problems
Health problems	yes or no	1	2	3
Insomnia	yes or no	1	2	3
Feeling constantly tired or run down	yes or no	1	2	3

Unsatisfactory living situations
Unsatisfactory living situations	yes or no	1	2	3

Interpersonal relationship problems
Interpersonal relationship problems	yes or no	1	2	3
Being unable to get along with people	yes or no	1	2	3
Ending a romantic relationship	yes or no	1	2	3
Feeling like you can't find the right partner	yes or no	1	2	3

Psychological problems
Psychological problems	yes or no	1	2	3
Feeling nervous or depressed or worried	yes or no	1	2	3
Feeling blocked from attaining goals	yes or no	1	2	3
A lack of motivation, like you can't get going	yes or no	1	2	3

Not having enough fun
Not having enough fun	yes or no	1	2	3

Problems with the law
Problems with the law	yes or no	1	2	3

Evaluate Yourself: Add up the points (1 for each yes response) for each item to determine the number of changes you have experienced in your lifestyle. Record your score here _____. The next step is to determine the level of distress associated with the changes you have experienced. You do this by adding the numbers (the amount of distress) you have assigned to each situation you have experienced. Record your score here _____. If you have experienced fifteen or more changes in your lifestyle (examine your first score), then there is enough stress going on in your life to take a toll on your health and emotional well-being. This is more likely to be the case if your level of distress (examine your second score) associated with these changes is a score above 30.

If you scored in the high or problem zone, then learning the relaxation and meditation techniques in chapter 11 can help relieve much of the tension and distress you are experiencing. However, it is important for you to pay particularly close attention to those situations that have caused you the most distress. If you are more distressed by work-related problems, then it is a good idea for you to review chapter 5, which deals with handling rage in the workplace. If family or relationship problems are the source of your distress, then review chapter 3, "Stretching the Family Roots," and chapter 4, which provided some suggestions for coping with family and relationship stress. Finally, if you are mostly troubled by feelings of depression and lack of energy, then evaluate the things you are doing to have fun. A few suggestion are located in "Relaxing Things to Do," which is located in chapter 11. I also suggest that you review "Maintaining a Meaningful and Purposeful Life," also located in chapter 11. If you follow the advice, your chances of learning how to lower your stress and reduce the occurrence of anger are great. However, your might consider seeking a professional counselor or therapist if the way that you are coping with your anger is interfering with your work, family life, or your health.

Step #2: Clarify the Source of the Problem

The second step in problem solving is to describe the problem in as much detail as possible. Begin by examining who is involved; what happens; where it happens; how it happens; and why it happens. Then it is important to examine your response by summarizing what you do or don't do. Describe where you do it; when you do it; how you feel; why you do it; and what you gain or lose by doing it. If a person takes this approach, he often discovers that the real difficulty is not the problem, but his response to the situation. Because of this it is often useful to create a statement along these lines:

In reality, the problem isn't _____, *the real problem is* _____.

For example, "In reality, the problem isn't *the stress in my relationship*, the real problem is *how I'm responding to my spouse.*" One of the most self-empowering things that happens when statements like this are created is that you can better pinpoint what needs changing. In most cases, the thing that needs changing is not the problem, but your approach to coping with the problem.

One of the frequent consequences of using a statement like the one above is that the intensity of angry feelings is lowered. This probably occurs because once you have identified the problem, your emotions settle a bit and you are better able to start searching for solutions to the problem.

Step #3: Generating Alternative Coping Strategies

The strategy that I recommend for creating possible solutions to problems is what I refer to as "the one-minute problem solver." After the problem has been identified and I have examined my responses, I then spend a minute writing down, one after another, whatever ideas come to my head without considering whether they are good or bad. To use this method, it is a good idea not to let your pen stop moving during the minute and to be as creative and as wild and crazy as you can.

The basic idea is that people often limit themselves because they don't spend time generating solutions. For some odd reason, it seems that most people think of problem solving as worrying about their problems rather than as a way to generate creative and fun-filled solutions.

Step #4: Analyze the Consequences of Your Choices

Now that you have developed a list of strategies for dealing with the problem, the next step is to consider the most promising approaches. Go over your list and rule out the bad ideas by either thinking out or writing out both the positive and negative consequences of each strategy. In considering the consequences, think about how the action will affect you personally; how it would affect other people in your life; how it would affect your life now versus a month from now or a year from now. Some people can do these evaluations automatically, while some of us need to take time to figure it out, step by step. Sometimes it is helpful to rank the choices from one, the best all-round possibility, to five, the last choice. Regardless of the approach you take, one of the final things you have to do is choose a few good alternatives. Whatever your approach, it is best to be thorough when you analyze the consequences of your choices. Now that you have figured out a few good approaches, it's time to take action.

Step #5: Taking the First Step

In considering how you should best put your decisions into action, spend time mentally rehearsing the concrete steps. It is best to do this after practicing one of the relaxation or meditation exercises that are described in chapter 11. As you mentally rehearse, it is a good idea to think of the smallest possible step you can take that will get you started on the road to solving your problem. Sometimes it is important to remember a time when you experienced a similar situation and to realize that you've successfully handled the situation before. Since you have handled it in the past, surely you can handle it again today. The truth is that if you have successfully coped with a similar situation, you already have a strategy of how to handle the situation while controlling your anger.

What I want you to do now is to take a look at the situations that can cause stress and anger that are presented with step one. Choose a situation that you have experienced and where you felt good about how you handled your anger. Take a moment to think about the emotions you experienced. Stop right now and think about the time when you

185

felt angry or upset because of this situation and how you dealt with it in a positive way. Use this as the role model or checklist for what you can do to control your anger while you solve the problems in your life. What did you do back then? Did you change what you were focusing on, the questions you asked yourself, your perceptions? Or did you take some kind of new action? Decide to do the same thing to handle this situation, with the confidence that things will work just as they did before. Taking the first step is perhaps the hardest part of the process and the most important one, but it is necessary. Now take a deep breath and do it.

Making a Personal Inquiry

This approach assumes that anger is a response to personal pain that is often not apparent. It follows that when someone is beginning to get angry, it makes sense to ask, "What is causing this pain?" You can also say, "Tell me what's really bugging you." Sometimes it is possible to avert a hopelessly escalating argument by choosing to comment on how the discussion is progressing. This can be accomplished by one of the people involved saying something like "I'm getting pretty heated up and I want us to talk about this more quietly" or "Let's stop talking now and talk some more when we've both cooled off." Comments like these can effectively alter the chain of angry-aversive communication by changing what a person is focused on and giving the people involved time to cool off. As with all of the intervention strategies, the sooner in the sequence this personal inquiry is made, the more effective, because once an angry confrontation escalates, it is more difficult to stop.

Modifying Your Personal Thoughts About Anger

There aren't too many things that happen to us where thoughts are not involved. Our thoughts are what intensify feelings of anger in most instances or cause us to cope poorly with the situation. Your thoughts, however, can be modified so that they remind you how to respond effectively at the moment of provocation. Some of the messages that I recommend you say to yourself are presented below. I suggest that you read through the list and think about which of the coping statements could be of use for you. However, it is best not to limit yourself at this time because it usually takes two or more coping statements to defuse anger.

Some people find it helpful to create their own coping statements. This may be true for you because the thoughts you develop will probably be more effective for you than anything from a list. To develop your own coping statements, all you need to do is consider that coping with anger has three parts: (1) preparation, (2) coping with confrontation, and (3) coping in retrospect.

Anger-Coping Statements

- This may upset me, but I know how to deal with it.
- I can make a plan to cope with this.
- I can find a way to say what I want.
- I can manage the situation.
- I know how to handle my anger.
- Take a deep breath and relax.
- I can relax and reduce this tension I feel.
- If I find myself feeling tense and getting upset, I'll know what to do.
- There's no need for an argument.
- I can handle the conflict without escalating it.
- I believe in myself and I can handle this without losing my cool.
- If I feel tense and upset, all I need to do is take a deep breath and relax.

Try over several days to systematically use the different coping statements as you deal with conflicts that you en-

counter. It is not necessary for you to use each of the statements, but it is important that you find one or two anger-
coping statements that work for you. Doing this requires a
fifteen-to-twenty-minute relaxation and meditation session
in the morning and evening. (See "Progressive Muscle Relaxation" and "Meditation" in chapter 1 for some techniques.) Following the morning meditation session you will
use what is called imagery to imagine yourself dealing with
a provocation by using one or two coping statements. Conjure a clear picture of a situation where you often find yourself feeling angry and upset. Try to create in your mind the
things you hear, who is with you, and what is being said.
Try to re-create anything else that's important about the
scene—the location, time of day, and so on. Hold on to the
image for half a minute or so and notice how your body
reacts. For most people there is a readily noticeable change
in heart rate, respiration, and muscle tension as they imagine
situations that cause them to feel angry and upset. At this
point begin using your coping statements.

It is important for you to continue doing your relaxation
procedure throughout the scene. After holding the clear
image of the scene for half a minute or so, shut it off. Focus
on relaxation for a few minutes, then repeat the imagery
procedures several more times. It is important for you to
really try to believe what you are telling yourself.

Sometimes these procedures are too stressful for an individual to complete. In this case, you need to develop a hierarchy of anger-provoking situations that starts with the least
upsetting provocations and goes all the way up to the angriest you can get. By doing this you can begin modifying your
angry thoughts about situations that are less stressful and
then work your way up to the situations that cause you to
feel the most upset.

To start this process, list the specific situations in your life
where you typically become angry. Try to include at least
twenty items on your list, and rank them in order, from the
least to the most upsetting. This can be accomplished by
rating each item from one (mild anger) to five (extremely
angry, the angriest you can get). After you have created the

hierarchy, it is best that you spend some time doing a situational analysis of each item. Determine what you are doing and saying to yourself to turn on your anger. For each item on the hierarchy, write down the thoughts that trigger anger and describe the behavior of other people involved or anything else that can help you understand why you become angry in the situation.

After you have completed your analysis for each of the situations, practice the imagery techniques again. Start with the first scene (the least anger-provoking situation) and construct it in your imagination. Conjure up a clear image of the situation with as much detail as possible about where you are and what you're doing. See who is with you and try to hear the sound of his or her voice. As before, you need to notice how you feel and how your body is reacting because these are the early-warning signals of anger. Now hold on to the scene for a half minute or so. While it is clear in your mind, use the anger-coping statement(s) that seem appropriate to help you relieve the stress and irritability of this scene. As before, you need to focus on relaxing and staying calm.

After holding the clear image of the scene for half a minute or so, shut it off and relax. Repeat this procedure several more times until you have imagined the scene without feeling any tension or anger. Once you have mastered the first scene on your hierarchy, it is time to move to the next situation. Don't try to rush the practice periods. Most people need to spend several days slowly moving up the hierarchy. If you have problems dealing with a particular scene, defer the item till later. Another problem may be that you need to try other anger-coping statements to help build a defense against the behaviors that are triggering your anger.

As you work with the hierarchy during your morning and evening practice periods, you will develop many of the necessary skills to stop anger from escalating. In between practice periods, throughout the day, I recommend that you spend a few minutes at the beginning of every hour reflecting on the coping statements. This should ideally be done with the eyes closed so that you can imagine yourself coping with provocations by using the coping statements. At the end of the day you have another relaxation and meditation session. Following the evening meditation session, repeat the imagery exercise and spend some time thinking about the situations where you could have used the coping statements to avert anger. These exercises should be repeated over several days using one or two different coping statements each day.

For some people, their angry conflicts seem endless. They continue to think about them. They remember what was said and what they should have said or done. As a consequence of this constant judging and grading, many people will find themselves feeling angry all over again. One of the most important parts of coping with anger is knowing how to cool off and leave the situation alone. This may be difficult for situations where the problems are unresolved. However, it is still a good idea to develop some coping statements that you can use for these situations because of the difficulty that most people have detaching themselves from their angry feelings. Some recommended statements are presented below.

- That wasn't as hard as I thought.
- Thinking about this situation only causes me to feel more upset.
- I actually got through that without getting angry.
- I'm doing better at this all the time because I can get my needs met without getting angry.

Thought Stopping

Perhaps the single most useful tool for dealing with anger is thought stopping. This technique is used to stop your train of angry thoughts and images before they get out of control. Thought stopping is a kind of deterrent that lessens the chances that angry thoughts and images will do much damage.

The first step in using this technique is to schedule time

for the exercises—all you need is a few minutes a day. Now sit in a comfortable chair and allow yourself to think about situations that cause you to get angry and upset. It is important that you try to recall the images as clearly as you can. After you entertain these negative images for a few minutes, suddenly shout, "Stop!" As a way of reinforcing the experience, either snap your fingers or stand up. Most people find that the images stop and are replaced with neutral thoughts. If the angry fantasies return, shout "Stop!" again. To strengthen its effectiveness it is a good idea to use the thought-stopping technique as you go through the hierarchy of anger-provoking situations that are troubling you. Remember to start with the situations that are less stressful and work your way to those that cause you to feel most angry.

After you have successfully interrupted a chain of angry images by shouting, you can start lowering your voice to a normal tone. When your normal tones proves effective, you can continue to lower your volume until you reach a whisper. The last step in this process is to "subvocalize," or to imagine hearing the shouted word *Stop!* By using the thought-stopping technique you can effectively stop intrusive angry images or fantasies anywhere or anytime.

If this technique is not completely successful, you can also combine thought stopping with an imagery technique. This requires you to create some vivid images of yourself coping with the situation in a positive way after you have shouted the word *Stop!* Another option is to create some positive images that depict you being relaxed and totally enjoying nature. One good example that is often used is to imagine yourself taking a walk through a wooded area on a beautiful sunny day. Birds are singing and the sky is totally blue.

Another option is to create images that help you see the angry, provocative person from a different and humorous point of view. For example, a useful technique to de-escalate anger is to imagine the person as a cartoon character. For this to work you really need to imagine this person looking and acting like a cartoon character. For example, if one of the situations that is troubling you involves your spouse, it is best to imagine her looking like Donald Duck, waddling when she walks, and sounding like Donald Duck as she talks. If you do this successfully, you will find your angry reactions replaced with humor and laughter.

The thought-stopping technique can be an effective means of altering the chain of aversive communications that often leads to the escalation of anger and violence. Recall the example of the husband and wife that was described earlier in this chapter. In this case, either person could have changed the outcome of the interaction by using thought stopping.

Creating a Problem-Solving Attitude About Dealing With Anger

One of the keys to the healthy management of anger is your attitude. How you act when you're angry has as much to do with your attitude about conflict as the conflict itself. Some people respond to conflict by becoming avengers. They want to injure and punish the offender to the same degree that they've been hurt. Pain must be paid back because they believe in retribution: an eye for an eye. Avengers make their point. They're loud. They're mean. They're cutting. What they do the most is damage relationships and provide more fuel for the continuation of anger and conflict.

To really get at the cause of anger and nip it in the bud takes some good problem-solving skills. The problem-solving attitude assumes that conflict has no moral dimensions. Instead, conflict is a matter of opposing needs. Disagreements are more easily resolved when each person's needs are legitimate and important. In this way, arguments about whose needs are more important are avoided. In fact, nagging, shouting, being angry or coldly rational, usually won't get other people to change their views. Negotiating to solve problems allows two people with conflicting needs to find a middle ground where they both can get some of what they want.

To develop this attitude requires that you learn three responses to provocations that are designed to de-escalate conflict and create an atmosphere for problems to be solved. It is best that the responses be memorized because the less you have to think about when you're angry, the better. When one response doesn't work, you simply choose another. Eventually you will find a response that breaks the tension and gives you the emotional safety to start searching for solutions to the real problems.

The key to using this method is to remember that no single response is likely to avert anger in yourself or other people. In some cases your first, second, and third response may not have much impact. But taken together, a series of adaptive responses is likely to cool you down and de-escalate anger in the other person.

The problem-solving approach to managing anger requires you to use your anger as a signal to start using the three responses to avert provocations. Anger is a signal that something is wrong and that you are not getting your needs met. Anger is also a signal for pain and that your method of coping isn't solving the problem.

De-escalating Responses

First Response to Avert Anger:
State Your Specific Need

Be specific and ask for something that is behavioral rather than attitudinal. Asking for someone to be more sensitive, loving, or more responsible sets you up because this implies that she or he is generally nonsensitive, uncaring, or irresponsible. It is important to ask for one specific behavior. The more you ask for, the less likely you are to reach agreement or negotiate a compromise. The response to memorize is *"I'm feeling angry (upset or whatever is bothering you) and what I think I want (or need, or would like to have) in this situation is _____."* To learn how to use this opening line, we will use the example (from chapter 5) of the white coworker who changed a few key decisions you made on a project without letting you know and then took credit for your work.

This is likely to be an inflammatory situation where most black men would believe that it was caused by the racist attitudes of the white coworker. Let's suppose that your response to this situation is rather primitive and involves a messy confrontation with you calling the man a racist and then using a few derogatory words to describe his attitude. You accuse him of sabotaging your work because he is too stupid to do things on his own. He openly denies your allegations and says that you are crazy. You respond with a threat with other employees looking on.

What do you think will be gained from this interaction? Did your actions solve the problem? Did your actions make you feel better?

For most men the situation will continue to escalate until the accusations, threats, and loud language cause a fight. You will gain a bad reputation from this and you could lose your job. Essentially, nothing positive was gained from the interaction. By contrast, if you had used the opening line from above ("I'm feeling angry and upset because you changed my decisions and took credit for my work, and what I think I want you to do is tell the boss the truth about this situation") to initiate the confrontation, you might have averted some of your anger and the reactions of the other person.

In some cases you can get the other person involved in problem solving by asking him to state his specific needs. This can be achieved by asking, "What is bothering you about this situation and what do you need?"

Second Response to Avert Anger:
Negotiate and Engage the Other Person in Solving the Problem

Getting the other person to propose a solution, no matter how inadequate or self-serving, is the first step toward reaching a negotiated agreement. The response to memorize is *"How would you propose to solve this problem?"* In some instances the other person will open up the channels for a negotiation and your role will be to acknowledge the negotiation. This can be accomplished by using the following statement: *"So what worries and concerns you is* _____*."*

Using the example from above, the opening line *"How would you propose to solve this problem with our boss?"* would serve to get the person involved in the problem and offer the person an opportunity to generate a dignified approach to a solution. Using opening lines like the ones above can allow you to gain a more complete understanding of the problem. Opening lines are questions, and remember that our questions are important because they do three things: (1) they instantly change what we are focusing on; (2) they change what we are deleting from a situation; and (3) they help us get access to the resources that are needed to solve problems (see the section "The Power of Our Questions" in chapter 3 for further discussion).

Sometimes your first solution will be opposed and you will need to make a counterproposal. If this is the case, then it is a good idea to encourage the other person to come up with another solution that you can both live with.

It is important to remember that each person's needs must be taken into consideration for a negotiation to result in a mutually satisfactory agreement or compromise. Deal with one area at a time and be specific about what you want and what you will give. People often hesitate to negotiate when they have conflicting needs because it requires that they listen and understand the other person's position. Sometimes people have an easier time being assertive if they see the other person as wrong, stupid, selfish, inconsiderate, or unfair. Instead of negotiating, they may try to convince the other person of the rightness and fairness of their own position. In other words, they expect others to do all of the changing.

Third Response to Avert Anger:
Taking Care of Yourself

For most of us, this is a difficult thing to do because it generally involves giving an ultimatum. What this means is that you simply let the other person know you plan to take care of your own needs even if she or he fails to cooperate. This is usually accomplished by using the line *"If (specify the problem) continues, I will have to (specify what you will do) in order to take care of myself."*

By framing the ultimatum this way you are letting the other person know the penalty for ignoring you, rather than attacking the person for not participating in problem solving. This approach to de-escalating anger emphasizes your commitment to meeting your own needs and finding alternative solutions. If you take care of yourself and your needs in this fashion, you will be less likely to trigger an angry reaction from the other person.

8

Obstacles to Healing and Managing Anger

The materials that you have covered thus far have provided you with a wide range of techniques useful in changing or eliminating unhealthy angry reactions. However, some common obstacles can interrupt your progress and bring your personal development program to a halt. The following sections explore these obstacles and offer solutions so that you can heal yourself.

Coping with Criticism

Of all of the obstacles that can hinder the development of different and effective ways of managing anger, dealing with criticism is the most difficult to overcome. Criticism is painful regardless of its source. It doesn't matter if the issue is minor or if the critic is not someone whose opinion you value. It doesn't even matter if the criticism is inaccurate. Being criticized is usually enough to make most of us feel guilty, judged, wronged, and fearful.

Sometimes we overreact to the criticism because we perceive the critic is a racist. The feelings can set off a chain reaction that weakens self-esteem, diminishes confidence, and causes us to defensively consider counterattacking with anger and rage. If the criticism is launched at you in a public arena such as the workplace or a social gathering, the reactions can be especially acute.

During an end-of-the-year evaluation, Earl, a third-year medical resident, received mostly praise for his work and ability to handle difficult patients. But there was one negative observation: "When Earl gets behind in his work, he sometimes becomes rushed and careless. He desperately needs to learn how to be a better doctor and develop his time management skills," one of the supervisors wrote.

First, Earl disregarded the majority of the evaluations, which were positive and praised his skills and strengths. He read the one negative line over and over, allowing it to feed his self-doubts.

After few minutes of this self-deprecation, Earl turned angry, blaming his supervisors for "routinely scheduling too many patients as a way of making him [the black doctor] fall behind." Earl accused his supervisor of doing the same thing to other black doctors and called him a racist in front of other staff and patients.

Rather than being overwhelmed, Earl could have coped with the criticism by allowing himself to better assess it, evaluating whether he could benefit from the feedback, and then deciding how he would handle the situation.

To effectively deal with criticism, first, limit the damage of the criticism by focusing on what the critic is saying. Go back over the situation and pay attention to what you are saying to yourself. Identify exactly how the critic is putting you down. In Earl's case, he could have limited the damage from the situation by using these three rules:

1. Make the criticizing statement accurate rather than exaggerated.
2. Make it specific rather than general.
3. Use nonpejorative language.

Even if the criticism is wrong and the supervisor is a racist, Earl did not have to fall into the trap of focusing on circumstances that are not directly related to the written comments. He could have limited damage by taking a time-out, or by refusing to continue the discussion with his supervisor. Simply walking away from the discussion would have brought a halt to the criticism.

Second, remind yourself that the criticism is only one person's opinion, about one specific aspect of your *behavior*. It is not about *who you are*. Damage can also be limited by accepting the idea that perfection is impossible and mistakes, therefore, are inevitable.

You can also distance yourself from criticism if you change the way that you talk to yourself when faced with an angry attack. Rather than buying into the attack with your own self-defeating statement, repeat the statement "There is nothing wrong with me. I am doing the best I can and there isn't any problem I can't handle."

Probe whether the feedback can be used constructively. In some cases, criticism will enable you to grow in your relationships or your work. But in the face of discomfort, most people avoid questioning the critic to understand exactly what the critic is conveying. Without probing, it is terribly easy for people to misinterpret criticism and then react defensively in rage. Take the following case as an example. John, a recent dental school graduate, had just started a new job. His supervisor approached him and said, "You need to improve your attitude if you're going to get along." Puzzled, John asked what the supervisor meant, and he elaborated, "The receptionist and all of us notice when you come and go. You are usually fifteen minutes late. It makes all of us look bad, and the other dentists and staff resent it when you are late." In a few minutes John learned that, in this office, coming to work late was interpreted as a "bad attitude."

By taking time to probe and understand the full meaning of the criticism, John recognized that the complaints were inaccurate. As it happened, John's tardiness did not constitute an "attitude problem," but an unexpected new-highway construction project that had thrown him off schedule. "My supervisor took three days where I was late and made a complete generalization about my attitude. I knew he was wrong, but I needed to know why he felt that way," explains John.

Rather than starting an argument, John effectively deflected the criticism by remaining calm as he dealt with the reasons behind it. For individuals who have not yet mastered the art of staying calm under critical attack, I recommend a delayed-response technique. The simple act of taking a time-out, even for a few minutes, will allow you to relax and activate coping strategies, consult with others to gather information, and so on.

The delay technique can be brought into play simply by saying, "I understand what you are saying about my behavior. I need some time to think before I respond to you. I will talk to you later today or tomorrow." In this way you minimize your chances of getting angry and protect yourself by setting limits. In some cases it is best to completely stop talking about the issue and shift the focus to a discussion about your sense of being attacked. This particular method is useful when the discussion is escalating into a stormy argument, when you feel the critic is over- or underreacting to something, or when you suspect that the critic is not saying what's really bothering him or her.

By shifting the focus you can get to the underlying issue of the conflict. One way is to use the following statement: "I'm feeling frustrated and I think you are, too. What's going on between us that causes us to end up feeling angry like this?" Assertively communicating in this manner will eliminate many anger-generating situations and improve the quality of your relationships.

Using Anger as a Defense Against Your Inner Feelings

For most of us, anger is often used to obscure or cover something that is perceived as being too difficult to confront. Rather than deal directly with the issue, our anger allows us to temporarily shift the focus. But the real issue will ultimately surface. If you have trouble getting in touch with how you really feel about a particular problem, use your visualization skills to fully experience the sights, sounds, and sensations of your anger. Then ask yourself this question: Without anger, what is it that I truly feel?

To face fear head-on, I suggest that you restate your concerns using the following guidelines:

- Focus on the accurate details of the situations rather than exaggerated expectations.
- Be specific.
- Develop a fallback plan for the worst-case scenario, but execute your plans to prevent the worst from happening.

Avoiding Hurt Feelings and Being Helpless

Wounded pride, feeling hurt, is one of the major inner emotional states that men use anger to avoid. An angry man rarely talks about the hurt feelings that triggered the anger. When the spot of vulnerability in his masculinity is pricked, he will talk about the faults of others, but no one knows how silently wounded he becomes at a sharp remark or gesture, or his inability to find a solution to a vexing problem. While the short-term effect of anger is to block feelings of hurt, the long-term consequences are that no one ever learns to recognize or accommodate vulnerabilities. Take Dennis, for example, a construction worker who feels hurt each time his wife mentions a recent six-month period of unemployment he suffered through. He counters by criticizing her spending habits or inability to lose weight. Dennis would rather lash out than allow his wife to know how deeply affected he still is by the long, fruitless search for work, and the helplessness and rage it engendered.

To face helplessness a man must give up the crutch of blaming other people for his misfortunes. Anger is a signal that something about a situation or relationship is not quite right. However, anger won't change anything because people will keep doing what they need to do, not what you want them to do. Facing helplessness requires action. The first step is to take full responsibility for being stuck. Look at the specific choices you made that led to the current situation. To accept responsibility, you must face that you are the one in pain, the one whose needs are unmet. One effective way this can be done is to imagine the deep sense of disappointment and embarrassment that you have experienced because the ways you chose to cope fell short of the mark. As you imagine this, consider all of the losses (your self-respect, relationships, economic, health, etc.) that you will incur if you continue on the same path year in and year out.

The second step for dealing with helplessness is to generate a new set of coping strategies by developing clearly stated, specific goals. Sometimes it is useful to ask yourself some direct questions, such as "What must I achieve to be rid of this feeling of helplessness?" After establishing concrete goals it is time to brainstorm for alternative solutions. I like the one-minute problem-solving method discussed earlier. The goal is to write as many alternatives to an action as you can think of in one minute.

The final step in coping with helplessness is to take action and monitor the outcome. If none of your solutions seem to offer much improvement over the current situation, brainstorm for new alternatives. I use the one-minute problem-solver technique to generate at least ten solutions every day for five days and then deal with the challenge.

Overcoming Guilt

Guilt, regret, and remorse are among the emotions that most of us do the most to avoid. For most people, guilt results from a conflict between needs and values. Guilt is a signal that you have violated one of your own highest values, and that you must do something immediately to ensure that you do not make the same mistake in the future. Some people try to deal with their guilt by denying and suppressing it. Unfortunately, this rarely works and the guilt intensifies. Some people use their anger to prevent themselves from honestly evaluating the values and standards that have been or will be compromised to get their needs met. Rather than acknowledge they have violated a critical standard they hold for themselves, they use anger to deflect the blame to other people or circumstances beyond their control. Other people surrender and wallow in their guilt and allow themselves to feel helplessly inferior for the rest of their lives.

Much like anger, guilt is an emotion designed to help you understand that something is wrong about your behavior or a situation. It is a signal to make sure that you either avoid behaving a particular way out of your certainty that your behavior will lead to guilt, or, if you've already violated your standard, it's a signal to induce enough pain to get you to recommit to your higher standard once again.

To deal with guilt you must identify the rules that stand in opposition to some important need. Once you've identified the values and standards that generate guilt, your next step is to examine and evaluate these values. Evaluating a rule simply requires you to ask yourself some questions that will permit you to understand your values. Some questions that I suggest are, Does the rule come from your own experience? Or is it the rule of a parent or some authority figure that you've accepted without question? Is the rule flexible?

Does it allow for unusual or mitigating circumstances? Is it realistic? Is the rule based on strict, unbending concepts of right and wrong? Does the rule support taking care of yourself in a way that's healthy for you and those you love?

Only you can evaluate the values and rules you live by. If you feel good about your standards, if your values make sense to you, then guilt is a healthy response to your behavior. If you decide that your rules are okay and that your guilt is appropriate, then it is your behavior that has to change. To deal effectively with guilt you must acknowledge that you have violated a critical value you hold for yourself. After this you must absolutely commit yourself to making sure that your behavior will never happen again. Rehearse in your mind how, if you could experience the situation again, you could handle the situation in a way that is consistent with your highest standards. To maximize the effectiveness of this rehearsal, consistently practice visualizing the situation you want to change. It might take several sessions for you to feel comfortable believing that can change your old behavior.

Guilt expresses the ultimate disappointment when a man constantly fails to meet standards that he holds for himself. As indicated earlier in the introduction, some men are unable to recognize anger in their lives, but they admit to feeling "stressed-out" because of the hard time they face in their lives. For these men it was recommended that they substitute the word *stressed-out* every time the word *anger* appears in this book to make things more applicable to themselves. If what you are suffering from is guilt, perhaps it would be helpful for you to substitute the word *guilt* every time the word *anger* appears in this book. Guilt, like anger, is an emotion that should be utilized and not avoided. The techniques that are discussed throughout the book for dealing with anger can also be used to learn how to cope with guilt.

9

Coping with Angry
People

Being the recipient of another person's anger can cause
you to question your self-worth, your values, and the relationship you have with the person. It is easy to fall into the
trap of coping with this situation by becoming defensive and
letting anger fly. But this will only make the situation worse
and slow your progress toward inner peace.

The best way to cope with an angry person is to emotionally
distance yourself. This can be accomplished by changing the
way that you usually talk to yourself when you cope with
such a situation. This kind of distancing will enable you to see
the other person as fallible and momentarily out of control. It
will also let you understand how distorted the person's opin-
ions and judgments are because of anger. Anger is a frightening emotion and clearly sends out a strong signal that
something is wrong. Regardless of the real problem, you can
distance yourself from the other person's anger.

The art to distancing is to use statements that empower
you to see yourself being calm and under control. Some of
my favorites are:

- I won't be manipulated into losing my cool.
- Getting angry will only give them what they want.
- I'm not going to let this person push my buttons.
- It's really a shame that he (or she) has to act like this.

To receive the full effect of the distancing method it is best to practice it in conjunction with your meditation and stress-management exercises. First imagine a situation where you are on the receiving end of another person's anger. During this exercise you will need to see yourself using one or more of the distancing statements to alter your response to the provocation. Once you have sufficiently practiced the technique, put it in effect.

As with most things, there are likely stumbling blocks. One of the most notorious problems is what are called trigger thoughts. They fall into two categories, *shoulds* and *blamers,* and create a distorted, anger-inciting picture of reality that will often leave you feeling victimized and controlled by other people.

Over any given day, each of us makes a number of judgments about the behavior of other people. Our judgments are based on a set of rules about how people should or should not act. When people break the rules, they are wrong because they should have known better. They should have acted according to the rules.

People tend to react with anger when someone violates an established rule. However, people at whom you feel angry because of a rule violation seldom agree with you. In most cases their perception of the situation will leave them feeling blameless and justified in their actions. It's as if their rules and beliefs make them exempt from the judgments you think they deserve. Also, the more you attempt to convince them that they are wrong, the more indignant and defensive they become.

In most cases others will not agree with your rules and values. People seldom do what they "should" do. They only do what is reinforcing and rewarding for them to do or what brings pleasure or avoids pain. Consider the case of a driver who waits until the last minute to cut in front of you in heavy traffic. Most people will feel some irritation because this driver should know better. Any driver in this situation should wait his turn, and those who don't should be punished because what they are doing is unsafe. This all sounds good, but the driver's motivation to cut in front and save time has been reinforced by his previous successes in doing the same thing. Thus, he is not afraid of disapproval or reprisals from other drivers. He is not fearful of getting a traffic ticket, and he has no guilt about his behavior. By all measures this driver is motivated simply by the pleasure that he gains from cutting in front of people to save time. Judging the behavior of the driver by our rules of right and wrong misses the point. However, as I said previously, most of us would feel some irritation because the driver has violated our rules.

Try using the following exercises to deal with the angry trigger thoughts that arise when rules and values that people "should" follow are violated.

Coping with Shoulds

Look at the problem from the other person's point of view. This requires you to imagine being in his or her situation. This can be accomplished by answering these questions about the person. Answer the questions as completely as possible.

1. What pleasures is he or she gaining from these actions?
2. What pains or burdens is he or she avoiding by this behavior?
3. What values or beliefs influence him or her to act this way?

After you have answered the questions, you will then need to imagine yourself having a discussion with this person you are angry at. It's best to start by accusing the person of acting wrongly, of violating a basic rule of conduct. Really imagine yourself telling this person how he should have acted. Now imagine yourself as the other person, trying to respond to your attack. Imagine this person explaining why he acted the way he did. Do your best to imagine that you are this individual so that you can see the problem from his or her perspective. After you've answered as the other person, go back to your original feeling of anger and expand on your accusations. Imagine yourself being as persuasive as you can be as you explain why the behavior was wrong. Keep the attack going. Now go back again and respond to the situation as the other person. Now shuttle back and forth between your accusing tone and the other person's defensive reaction a few times. My bet is that your feelings have started to change and that you have a better understanding of the person with whom you feel angry.

One of the behaviors that often makes it difficult to see the other person's point of view is blaming. Blaming helps to trigger angry reactions because it places the responsibility for your pain and emotional anguish on someone else. Upon doing this, you begin to develop a negative cognitive set (e.g., this person is always insensitive) in which you label and interpret the person's behavior in consistently negative ways. As this negative cognitive set develops, so do your assumptions about the other person. After a while this negative cognitive set is brought into play when dealing with neutral and ambiguous situations. The more the cognitive set hardens, the more the relationship is tainted by the negative way the other person is evaluated. A kind of tunnel vision develops that blocks out every behavior that doesn't fit your assumption of bad behavior. As a consequence, you don't see the things that are positive, caring, loving, and devoid of angry reactions.

By constantly blaming other people for your behavior (and feelings) you begin to create a worldview in which people are always deliberately doing bad things and not behaving as they "should" behave. The major problem with blaming is that it assumes that someone else is responsible for your anger because they "should" have known how to behave. Blaming doesn't make sense because people seldom do what they "should" do. People choose the actions that seem most likely to meet their need, which is to avoid pain and create pleasure. Blaming makes no sense because it labels people and behavior as bad when in fact the person is making what he or she perceives to be the best choice available at the moment.

Dealing with blaming requires you to become more aware of the other person's point of view. The exercise for enhancing how you cope with blaming is similar to the exercise used to cope with shoulds.

Enhancing Your Empathy

This exercise is best practiced as part of the relaxation and meditation procedures that are described in chapter 11. Following the relaxation and meditation procedures, you will need to think of someone you have blamed on several occasions.

Think of a decision that the person made that angered you. Really imagine the scene where this happened. Imagine what was said or done and your reactions. Now, try to reconstruct the decision from that person's point of view. To help you with this, it is best to consider what you know about the person's values, beliefs, needs, emotional state, competencies, and limitations. Imagine how each of these factors influences the person's decisions. Imagine being this person as he explains why he acted the way he did, so that you can see the problem from his perspective. Imagine being this person and responding to strong judgmental statements about the way he or she should have acted. Now go back and imagine yourself confronting the person about his behavior without being judgmental. Imagine making no assumptions about the motivations of this person without checking out your assumptions with the other person. Imagine that you know nothing about this person and that you have to ask him questions to understand his behavior and motivations. Now imagine yourself as the other person, responding to your confrontation and questioning. Really imagine how open and honest this person would be with you if your tone was one of understanding rather than blaming. Now shuttle back and forth between this last way of responding and the other person's reactions a few times. My bet is that your feelings of anger have subsided a bit because of the empathy you have established with the person.

Thoughts of Retribution

Most people have fantasized about revenge against someone for some misconduct. Fantasies of retribution often provide some short-term relief from stress. However, the poetic justice that is derived during these thoughts can, in the long run, cause you to feel helpless and a greater intensity of anger. It seems that each replay causes a new surge of rage and hurt. Worse yet, repeated revenge fantasies tend to increase the chance that you will act them out in ways that destroy chances for solving the real problem.

Thoughts of retribution are problematic because replaying painful scenes is a form of self-torture that often hinders the development of new ways to manage anger. In fact, the replay will often contribute to a greater sense of failure because of the ineffective ways in which a person deals with the situation. This happened to Sam, a dental assistant for a large dental service. On several occasions one of the dentists has criticized his work and commented on his competence. The last time this happened, all that Sam could do was listen as the dentist constantly criticized him in front of others. As unflattering comments flowed, Sam could feel his body becoming tense. A gnawing sensation started in his stomach and chest and slowly expanded throughout his entire body until he was tense all over.

That evening as Sam reflected on the event, he imagined telling the dentist to be quiet. He heard himself telling the dentist that none of the other assistants wanted to work with him. Sam imagined himself exacting a terrible revenge, with the dentist being a patient undergoing dental work without painkiller. He imagined that all of the dentist's teeth were extracted, causing much agony. If the dentist tried to escape, he was painfully prodded back into the chair.

As usually happens, this fantasy did not succeed in diverting Sam's anger but actually sustained it. Each time Sam worked with this dentist or overheard people talking about him, it brought back the scene where the dentist was receiving care without painkiller. Rather than feeling some relief, Sam felt angry. The more he imagined the scene, the angrier he became. His fantasy of retaliation grew more cruel. Even though he felt right about getting back at the dentist, he felt angry because he thought he "should" have responded differently when he was confronted by the dentist.

On one particular day Sam was assisting the dentist and he "accidentally" tripped and damaged some bridgework a patient had been waiting to receive. On another occasion Sam "forgot" to inform the dentist that Sam would not be available to assist him with a patient. On another day Sam "accidentally" spilled mouthwash on the dentist.

Now, Sam is in trouble, and there is a good chance that he will lose his job. Rather than directly dealing with his anger, he let it seep out in destructive ways. It seems that over time, the anger images loosened Sam's impulse control. Instead of directly acting out the fantasy, Sam got back at the dentist in other ways. In the end the way that Sam acted out his anger tarnished his record at work.

Replaying angry scenes causes most people to feel frustrated, hopeless, and intensely angry. In most cases the fantasies of retribution don't include healthy problem-solving methods. Instead we often see ourselves acting in revenge to either hurt or hinder the work of another person. However, we don't have to be at the mercy of our fantasies. Each of us has a choice about whether we want to take control or give in to our fantasies.

Chapter 7 reviews several methods for changing your thoughts, but the single best method for dealing with anger imagery is "thought stopping." You can use this technique to derail the train of angry thoughts and images before they escalate into an explosion. Negative and vengeful fantasies are replaced with images where you see yourself responding in ways that diminish your anger and produce positive results. The thought-stopping technique can be enhanced by substituting positive images for the offending scene. However, the real secret to using any of these techniques is to mentally practice them before you encounter a potentially explosive situation. The major aim in using them is to prevent and alter your usual ways of letting your anger rule your thinking and your actions.

One of the favorite healing images is that of a sunny beach. Regardless of the location of this beach, the effect is the same. The warm sun relaxes your whole body. You smell the ocean and hear the sound of the waves as they come in and go out. You hear the sound of seagulls and the faint sound of people laughing and having fun. Lying there, totally at peace with the universe, you imagine all your troubles washing out to sea. You imagine your problems being carried farther and farther out by the waves. All of the sounds become fainter and fainter, until there is nothing left but the surf, the sea, and the cry of an occasional seagull.

As you try this image-substitution technique, you will find that it is terribly difficult to remain angry while imagining the scene. Once you have relaxed your problems away, imagine dealing with the offending situation. If you find that you continue to feel angry and upset, continue with the imagery of the beach scene. Alternate until you can comfortably deal with the offending situation without allowing your anger to rule your actions.

10

Changing Your Thinking Is Not As Difficult As You Think

Quite often we are told that "change takes hard work and discipline." While this may be true for some people, it does not have to be true in your case. Changing long-standing patterns of thinking can be an easy task if the behavior you want to change is linked to enough pain and suffering. If you are going to effectively deal with anger, you first have to change your internal dialogue.

If you can't find ways to change the way that you talk to yourself when you are angry and upset, then angry feelings will continue to plague you. But if you link enough emotional anguish to the faulty patterns of thinking and behaving that got you in trouble, you will avoid indulging in them at all costs. Please keep in mind that this pain and suffering does not have to be real.

For most of us, the pain and suffering that we avoid is triggered by the "possibility" of its occurrence. For example, people who drive cars automatically stop at red lights, and most of us feel a bit uneasy and upset when we witness a motorist who fails to stop at a red light. Why do you think

213

we stop at red lights? It surely has nothing to do with anything that we inherited from our parents, or where we were
born. We stop at red lights because we have become conditioned, with practice, to associate the red light with a particular action, and that action is to stop the car. What made
the conditioning of this behavior possible is that if we don't
stop the car, we could have an accident and seriously injure
ourselves or other people. What I am saying is that the
avoidance of pain and suffering is the motive that stirs us
to stop at red lights, even though most of us have never
experienced an accident. The possibility of pain and suffering linked to running a red light causes us to stop. You can
use this simple idea to help yourself develop ways to avoid
the faulty pattern of thinking we turn on when we feel angry
and upset.

One of the secrets to getting yourself to avoid angry and
hostile interactions with other people is to teach yourself
how to consistently link intense, massive amounts of emotional pain to everything that is associated with the particular provocation. Once you have done this, you will then
avoid being angry in the situation. I realize that all of this
may sound a bit simplistic, but all of us will do everything
we can to avoid pain and to seek pleasure. Why? Because
it is instinctive to enhance our survival. It is part of our
social makeup, how life, happiness, and the pursuit of
dreams are sustained.

Take a moment and really ask yourself a few questions
such as:

- Who is your best friend?
- Why do you like certain clothes?
- What's your favorite song or group?
- Why do you work at the job that you have?
- Why do you wear jewelry or a particular hairstyle?
- Why do you like certain people or things and not
  others?
- Why do some relationships last while others fail?
- Why don't you really give your boss a piece of your
  mind when you feel put down?

- Why did you buy your best friend that particular birthday gift?
- Why did you decide to go to work (or school) today?
- Why did you send flowers to your "honey" after the fight?
- Why do you like Christmas or parties?
- Why do you stop at red lights?

My guess is that some of you gave two rather distinct sets of answers to these questions. The first probably had something to do with making yourself feel good, happy, comfortable, or attractive, while the second had something to do with avoiding discomfort and tragedies or distress. The first set of answers clearly focus on the desire to seek pleasure, while the second have to do with the avoidance of pain and discomfort. As stated previously, this force has more to do with the shaping of human behavior than anything else. In the following section I will show you how to use this force and other laws of learning so that you can develop better strategies to help anger from destroying your life.

Developing an Avoidance Response to Angry Encounters

Psychologists have used what is called the law of reinforcement to create avoidance patterns like those cited. Reinforcement means simply responding to behavior immediately after it occurs. Any pattern of behavior or emotion that is continually reinforced will become an automatic and conditioned response. In contrast, any behavior pattern or emotion that we fail to reinforce will eventually dissipate. You can use this information to teach yourself how to avoid anger-related behaviors and emotions and to develop alternatives that are pleasurable, fun, and safe. The secret is using the following five steps:

1. Decide on the specific behaviors or emotions that are to be changed.
2. Link massive amounts of pain and suffering to the behavior and emotional reaction patterns.
3. Create alternatives that are pleasurable, fun, and safe.
4. Rehearse the alternatives until the new behavioral or emotional reaction pattern is consistent and occurs automatically.
5. Reinforce the new behaviors in positive and pleasurable ways to ensure their long-term presence.

There is nothing difficult about this or any of the techniques that have been described in the preceding chapters. You simply need to mentally practice the procedures. One effective technique for developing an avoidance response is what I call "a mind trip into a better reality." Bringing a halt to the way you think you "should" act when you are angry requires you to ask yourself some powerful questions. These questions will help you associate pain and emotional anguish with your angry reactions. You can use this technique to deal with thoughts of retribution or any other thoughts that you have about how you "should" act when you are angry and upset. Some questions that I suggest are:

- What will it cost me emotionally if I lose my temper?
- What will I lose if I continue to do these things?
- How will my relationships with those I love be affected?
- How will all of this affect my job and my earning potential?
- Who are the people that I will hurt if I don't change how I act?
- Who will suffer if I don't change how I act when I'm angry?

You need to reflect on what you feel, your bodily sensations and the thoughts that you have when you think about the pain and suffering that will be there if you don't change your behavior. It is essential that you use the questions to get yourself to feel the pain and suffering as if it were real. To link even more pain and suffering to your angry thinking, focus on how your emotions and actions affect people who love and care about you. Practice asking yourself these questions and other ones that will trigger the deep emotional pain that will motivate you to immediately cease any angry thoughts.

Picture in graphic detail how much sadness and misery you will create for the people who love you if you don't change how you think and react when you are angry and upset. Visualize the misery and sadness, in graphic detail, that would be present if you lost your job and your family and became deathly ill because of how you handled anger and stress in your life. Imagine how miserable your life will be two, five, ten, and twenty years from now if you continue along the path of self-destruction. Don't be surprised by the intensity of the emotional reactions that these questions will generate, and by all means let yourself experience these feelings.

From a practical standpoint, you will need to devote about fifteen to twenty minutes a day for as many days as it takes to really experience the type of pain and suffering that motivates you to adopt new behavioral practices. It could take a few days for you to develop the desired response, or it might take a few minutes. The secret ingredient is the intensity of the emotional experience that you are teaching yourself to experience.

As children, many of us learned the pain associated with fire in one simple lesson that usually lasted for only a few moments. During those moments we either directly experienced the pain or we witnessed someone else flinch from the pain of fire. All that I want you to do is to imagine how your life will be if you don't change how you deal with anger.

Once you have linked all that pain and suffering to the behaviors and emotional response patterns that you want to eliminate, a natural avoidance-response pattern will become conditioned. The stronger the linkage between the pain and suffering and the behaviors, the stronger will be the conditioned avoidance response.

Basically, the same laws of conditioning are being used that Ivan Pavlov, a Russian scientist, employed in the late nineteenth century to conduct conditioning experiments. In his most famous experiment, he rang a bell as he offered food to a dog, thereby stimulating the dog to salivate and pairing the dog's sensations with the sound of the bell. After repeating the conditioning enough times, Pavlov found that merely ringing the bell would cause the dog to salivate—even when food was no longer being given. You can create a conditioned response to angry situations by linking intense emotional pain and suffering to angry behaviors. When you pair enough pain and suffering with your angry reactions, you will eventually do everything possible to avoid acting out your anger inappropriately.

Please remember that an individual does not have to experience physical harm to learn to avoid particular situations. The goal of linking pain and suffering to your angry reactions is to correct for the "mixed messages" that society has projected about anger. To illustrate this point, take for example a traffic light that is turning red as you approach. The red light is a signal or cue that certain consequences (e.g., physical harm from an accident) are likely to occur if you don't stop at the red light. What do you think would be the consequences if some new rule says that beginning at 9 A.M. tomorrow morning motorists don't really have to stop at red lights. People would panic. There would be accidents like we have never witnessed. People would argue, fight, and kill each other. The consequences of creating such a "mixed message" about the meaning of the red light would be difficult to fully comprehend. Believe it or not, this is essentially what our society has done to the meaning of angry feelings and having confrontations—the messages are all messed up. Being angry is not the problem, it's how people think they should act when they feel angry.

Creating Alternatives to Anger

In some cases the linkage of massive amounts of emotional pain and suffering to the undesired behavior is enough to develop the desired response. However, most of us need some type of pleasurable and useful alternatives that we can do instead of engaging in the behaviors that are problematic.

The replacement behaviors can be anything you choose that is pleasurable, pain free, and not related to angry and hostile emotional reaction patterns. It also needs to be something that produces the same feelings that you had originally sought, or perhaps something that makes you feel even better. The replacement behavior could be some structured activity at home with family members, or it might be reading a interesting book about people who overcame bad situations to become successful.

A practical approach to establishing alternatives is to generate a list of things that you consider to be fun and pleasurable. Be creative and don't place any boundaries on the things that you put on the list. It is important that this task be approached in a friendly, warm, and caring manner. Basically, have some fun, let your guard down, and enjoy discovering new ways of dealing with problems.

Some of the things on the list can be used immediately while others can be used as a future reward for engaging in nonviolent ways of coping with stress and conflict.

Conditioning the New Alternatives to Angry Reactions

Once you have discovered the alternatives, the next step is to condition the new behaviors or emotional reaction patterns until they are consistently part of your life. The simplest way to condition something new is to rehearse it again and again, much like driving a car or tying your shoes, until your brain forms a pattern of this habit.

Once you have started the program you might find few opportunities to really reinforce the new nonangry behaviors and emotional reactions. However, once you find the positive and pleasurable alternatives to angry and negative emotions, you must imagine engaging in these behaviors until you can see that the alternative gets you quickly out of trouble situations, away from pain and into pleasure. You need to practice this mental imaging technique with great emotional intensity daily for as long as it takes for the new behaviors to become the rule rather than the exception.

Role-playing exercises can also be used to aid development of the new alternatives. In these exercises you basically pretend that you are about to engage in the undesired behaviors so that you can get a better idea of how to deal effectively with the situation. Role-playing will require you to work with a trusting partner or friend who is noncritical and willing to help you. If you are not satisfied with the behavioral responses you see, practice again and again until you get it right. In this regard, anything that you can think and see clearly in your mind you can become and do.

Don't be afraid to experiment and try new things. Be serious, but have fun and remember that it is the intensity of the emotions that you stir up that will let you know whether you are effectively teaching yourself these new ways of approaching the prevention and management of anger.

Establishing a Reinforcement Schedule

The final step is to set up a schedule to reinforce the new behaviors and emotional reaction patterns. The real secret to reinforcement is to immediately reward yourself after engaging in the desired behaviors. When this happens, any behavior or emotional reaction pattern will become an automatic and conditioned response. The reward or reinforcement can be praise, a gift, a trip, or a new freedom or privilege.

Social reinforcers such as verbal praise, attention, physical contact (including affectionate or approving touches, pats, and hand-holding), and facial expressions (including smiles, eye contact, nods of approval, and winks) for loved ones can be used to strengthen desired behaviors. Numerous studies have shown that attention or praise from a wife, coworker, or friend can exert considerable control over behavior. For some people, these types of reinforcements work better to shape behaviors than material things such as gifts or money.

Social reinforcers have the advantage of being easily administered in a large number of situations because they are naturally occurring in everyday life. They take little time and there is no delay in praising a number of individuals at the same time.

Praise can also be given while the individual continues to engage in the desired behaviors. Praise is important as a positive reinforcement because it has often been paired with many positive circumstances such as good feelings, important social events, and people who love and care about us.

Positive reinforcement is not limited to reward, praise, money, or new freedoms. Sometimes allowing yourself to engage in certain behaviors can be used as a positive reinforcement. Basically, when an individual is given the opportunity to select among various possible things to do, behaviors performed with a relatively high frequency (e.g., watching television) can be used as positive reinforcement for behaviors that occur at a relatively low frequency (e.g., being nonargumentative). In psychology this is known as the Premack principle and it works by forming a contingent relationship between the performance of the more probable behaviors (watching television or some other pleasurable behavior) and the less probable behaviors (communicating without arguments). When the participation in the more probable behavior depends on the participation in the less probable behavior (no arguments or hostile communications), the frequency of the less probable behavior should increase. If this is not the case, then it means either that the more probable and pleasurable behavior is not as pleasurable as you thought or that the relationship between the two behaviors has not been fully explained.

Remember that the secret is to engage in the less probable behavior first. Don't talk yourself into a contractual arrangement where you have to engage in the less probable activities after you have had fun with the more probable behaviors. This is one of the errors that some people consistently encounter, and it teaches you to expect rewards before you have worked to earn them.

Psychological studies discovered long ago that any behavior or emotional reaction that has been reinforced every time (continuous reinforcement) rapidly extinguishes when the reinforcer is no longer provided. In contrast, a response that has been reinforced once in a while (intermittent reinforcement) extinguishes less rapidly when the reinforcer is not presented. Basically, the more intermittent the schedule (or the less frequent the reinforcement), the greater is the resistance of the behaviors to extinction.

During an intermittent reinforcement schedule the individual is never sure when the reward will be given—it may be given immediately after the first occurrence of the behavior or after the third or after the seventh time. Because the individual is uncertain when he will receive the reward, he tends to consistently engage in the desired behaviors. Therefore, if you wish the new behaviors to stand the test of time, it is important that you understand and use what is known as an intermittent or variable schedule of reinforcement.

The intermittent reinforcement schedule is the major reason why some people develop a gambling habit. Basically, once the individual has enjoyed the pleasures and excitement (reward) associated with winning a bet, he wants to continue to try to win again and again. The gambler is motivated by the possibility of winning. If the person were never to win at gambling, he would stop. However, winning now and then increases the anticipation of winning the "big one." The same is true here—you will perform wonderfully and put forth all kinds of extra efforts if there are occasional rewards that are not predictable. Each of us would do more than the minimum amount of work to earn our paychecks if there were unpredictable rewards such as bonuses, promotions, free trips, recognition, and other little goodies. The same is true in our relationships with others and ourselves.

11

The Psychology
of Staying Cool

Staying "cool"—managing anger in an emotionally mature way—requires work in the intervening hours or days when you aren't feeling angry. Contemplating how to respond to feelings of anger in the quiet periods when you're not provoked decreases the frequency, intensity, and inappropriateness of your anger. The common psychology associated with staying cool is usually constant, regardless of the circumstances that trigger anger and hurt feelings. No personality type is immune from responding to provocations with uncontrolled anger. Neither education, job, nor income level exempts you, as the case histories in this book show. While men raised in homes without fathers seem to encounter more stress in life, this, too, is not a predictor of how a man will cope with anger.

The first step in developing a plan for managing anger is reevaluating your attitudes in a few key areas.

Maintaining a Meaningful and Purposeful Life

Every man has a unique talent and way of expressing himself—something that he can do better than anyone else. Unfortunately, many men travel through life with no idea of their unique talents or their purpose in life.

If a young boy could begin life with the thought that discovering one's purpose is paramount, he would soon be too consumed with learning and growing to have time for problems. Remember situations where you were so consumed by your work on an exciting project that you seemed to be in a zone entirely your own, filled with zest and purpose? Men usually have these experiences when they are working on projects where they feel that the end product is useful and can serve humanity.

Maintaining an active life in general is essential to preventing anger. Men who have positive pursuits in their lives have less time and reason to be angry at people who are stuck in a rut. The man who is progressing toward personal and career goals is less likely to be jealous of another man's success, which is often the cause of anger. So if you have not found your purpose in life or your spiritual self, isn't it about time that you do?

Begin by making a commitment to find your unique talents. Make a list now of what you consider them to be. Then make a list of all the things that you enjoy doing while using your unique talents. These are the things that you do where you lose track of time. After you have made these two lists, ask yourself, "If I had all of the money I wanted, what would I do?" If you would still do what you currently do, then you have found your purpose and you are using your talents to serve humanity. If there is an incongruity between the two, then it's way past time to reevaluate your goals.

The process for discovering one's purpose in life can be enhanced through the daily practice of inward experiences.

Meditation, prayer, exercise, yoga, and other mental and physical practices that require self-discipline can be used.

During meditation the mind is set free from all constraints and preconceived notions about one's self, especially destructive ones that are not in your best interest. As the mind settles and relaxes during meditation, the body reacts in kind. Eventually the mind reaches a state of integration, transcending all constraints and moving to a higher level of consciousness. A deep state of relaxation and bliss is achieved, and yet the mind becomes more alert because it has awakened.

During the state of restful alertness, time seems to stand still, problems melt away, solutions to challenges become clear. The connectedness to the spiritual self is not diluted by concern over trivia. As the mind is unburdened, it tends to provide an abundance of energy to the body. It is believed that healing is taking place in a more integrated fashion because the mind is free to concentrate on this task.

The state of consciousness during deep meditation, for me, is quite different from prayer, where I tend to focus my attention on a particular desire. However, the connectedness that I experience with God seems more powerful as a result of my daily meditations.

Although stress accounts for a wide assortment of diseases ranging from peptic ulcers and high blood pressure to depression and nervous disorders, the stress response isn't all bad. The same stress hormones that prepare a person for an attack also produce the strength that enables a horrified mother to lift a car off her trapped child. Athletes, dancers, actors, and speakers all benefit from these hormones. Trouble arises when the stress alarm systems are turned on chronically. Serious damage to the body will occur, which often results in a chronic health problem.

Stress is the fuel of anger. If anger is a problem in your life, it's essential that you learn a method for reducing stress that works for you. Earlier sections dealt with specific applications for managing anger. The prescriptions presented in this chapter focus on general stress reduction techniques that will enable you to deal with stress without allowing it to produce anger. These techniques are useful in anger control because of the chain reaction between physical tension in the body and anger. Stress creates physical tension, which then predisposes a person to become angry. Becoming angry and upset causes additional body tension, which exacerbates the anger response.

The techniques described in this section induce relaxation by enabling an individual to attend to one thing at a time, to concentrate fully on a single action. Most of us spend our waking time thinking and engaging in some form of verbalization or inner dialogue about the important things in our lives. The techniques here serve to cleanse your attention of preconceptions and distracting thoughts, allowing you to perceive reality more clearly. The exercises should be practiced daily. You will also be introduced to some techniques that are designed to stop anger before it starts.

Scanning Your Body for Stress

To better manage stress, you must first recognize how and when tension is affecting you. If you haven't learned this, you are probably unaware of those things that cause you to become angry and upset. By learning to scan your body for stress, you will also learn how to become more aware of those situations that trigger anger in you.

1. Begin by paying attention to your feet and legs. Start by wiggling your toes, then rotate your feet and relax them. Note any tension in your calves. Relax.
2. Now focus on your lower torso. Become aware of any tension or pain in your lower back. Relax as fully as you can. Notice any tension in your hips, pelvic area, or buttocks. Relax these areas.
3. Move the focus to your diaphragm and stomach. Take a couple of slow, deep breaths. Feel yourself relaxing, more and more deeply. Notice any tension that you are experiencing in this area.

4. Focus on your breathing and your chest area. Search for any tension here. Take a few slower breaths, then a few deep breaths, and let go of any tension.

5. Next, pay attention to your shoulders, neck, and throat. Swallow a couple of times and notice any tension or soreness in your throat and neck. Rotate your head clockwise a few times. Now reverse and roll your head the other way. Shrug your shoulders, noting any tension, and then relax.

6. Begin at the top of your head and scan for tension. Look for pain in your forehead. Perhaps there is a band of pain around the top of your head. Maybe there is pain or tension behind your eyes. Notice any tightness in your jaw. Check for locking or grinding of teeth and taut lips. Be aware of your ears. Go back over your head and relax each part.

7. Now re-scan your entire body for any remaining tension. Allow yourself to relax more and more deeply. I recommend doing this exercise every day for a few weeks until you have a good idea of where your body holds tension. It is a good idea to do these exercises at work, in between tasks, and when you return home at the end of the day. It is also a good idea to keep a diary each day of the location where the tension seems to concentrate and whether you experienced angry feelings or felt upset.

No one but you will be aware that you doing these exercises. For example, get up right now and gently walk around the room. Become aware of any tension in your body. Now really scan your body and let go of any tension. Now deliberately walk a bit slower and lighter. Let go of the tension in your feet and legs, relax your torso and stomach, slow your breathing, relax your shoulders and neck as you walk, and release any tension you feel in your head. This body-scanning technique can be used in any situation, including when you are eating.

The Breath of Life

Proper breathing is one of the most natural antidotes for stress, and yet most people take breathing for granted. To live a healthy life, you have to breathe. Deep breathing is one of the ways that the body stimulates the lymphatic system, which helps remove waste from the body. In fact, deep breathing is the only way the lymphatic system is turned on to perform the vital function of removing cellular waste from throughout the body.

1. Lie down on a blanket or rug on the floor. Bend your knees and place your feet about eight inches apart, with your toes turned slightly outward. Make sure that your spine is straight.
2. Scan your body for tension and release any that you note.
3. Place your left hand on your stomach and your right hand on your chest.
4. Inhale slowly and deeply through your nose, filling your abdomen. Push the air down to your belly. Notice your left hand being pushed up. Your chest should move only a little underneath your right hand and only with your abdomen.
5. Now inhale through your nose and exhale through your nose. Your mouth, tongue, and jaw will be relaxed. Take long, slow breaths and raise and lower your abdomen. Close your eyes and focus on your breathing as you become more and more relaxed.
6. Continue this breathing exercise for about five or ten minutes. Do this once or twice a day.
7. At the end of each deep-breathing session, take a moment or two to scan your body for tension. Compare the tension you feel at the end of the exercise with what you experienced when you began.

Even though you were instructed to do this exercise lying

down, the basic technique may be practiced in a sitting or standing position. The key point is to concentrate on your abdomen moving in and out, as the air moves in and out of your lungs. It is also important to learn to breathe with your mouth closed because it is the passageway from the nose that filters the air entering your lungs. Much like the first exercise, you can practice the breathing exercise anytime during the day that you feel stress.

Balanced Breathing

Another breathing exercise that I recommend is called *pranayama* or alternative nostril breathing.

1. Sit upright in a comfortable chair with your spine straight and both feet on the floor.
2. Close your eyes and let your mind rest. Scan your body for any tension and release whatever tension you find.
3. Take your right thumb and use it to close your right nostril by gently pushing down on it from the outside. Then breathe gently and deeply out of your left nostril. Now take a deep breath inward through your left nostril. After this close your left nostril with your index finger by gently pushing down on it from the outside. As you do this, breathe out of your right nostril, then take in a deep breath through your right nostril.

After you perfect the mechanics of this movement your goal is to repeat the process for five minutes with your eyes closed. As you do this breathing exercise, you might feel a deep sense of relaxation and some lightness in your head. This is a wonderful exercise for making sure that you have opened up the air passageway for both hemispheres of your brain to receive the vital oxygen that they need.

Progressive Muscle Relaxation

This is one of the most widely used methods to help people learn how to relax. It is a body-scanning technique where you tense and then relax the major muscle groups in your body. This exercise is to be practiced alone in private. It is particularly helpful to use it before dealing with potentially stressful situations. The best way to do this exercise is for you to make a tape recording of yourself reading the instructions. As you make the recording, read the instructions slowly, spending some time between the steps. Most people who practice the technique will find that the tape is not necessary after a short time.

1. First, find a comfortable position and relax. You can be sitting or lying down while you do this exercise. It is best to begin while you are sitting because relaxing while lying down tends to lead to sleep. Now clench your right and left fists, tighter and tighter, studying the tension as you do so. Keep them clenched and notice the tension in your fists, hands, and forearms. Now relax. Feel the tension fade away and notice the difference in how your hands and forearms feel now with how they felt when you made the fists. Repeat this procedure. Tighten your fists for about ten seconds. Always notice as you relax that this feeling is the opposite of tension. Relax and feel the difference. Spend a few moments simply paying attention to how your body is relaxing and reducing tension.

2. Now bend your elbows and tense your biceps. Tense your biceps as hard as you can for ten seconds and observe the feeling of tightness in your arms and shoulders. Relax and straighten out your arms. Let the relaxation develop. Observe the difference. Repeat this procedure and then relax and observe the differences.

3. Turn your attention to your head. Wrinkle your fore-

head as tight as you can for ten seconds. One way to do this is to frown and close your eyes as tightly as you can. Now allow your forehead to relax while you close your eyes. Squint tighter and take notice of any tension you feel and let it go. Relax your eyes. Now clench your jaw, bite hard, and notice the tension this creates. Relax your jaw. Now press your tongue against the roof of your mouth and feel the ache in the back of your mouth. Relax. Compress your lips now, pushing them into an O. Relax your lips and blow out forcefully. Repeat this procedure and then scan your head and relax any tension that you find.

4. Place your attention on your neck. Press your head back as far as it can comfortably go and observe the tension in your neck. Roll your head to the right and notice any tension. Roll your head to the left and notice any changes in tension. Now straighten your head and bring it forward, pressing your chin against your chest. Feel the tension that this creates in your throat and the back of your neck. Now shrug your shoulders. Hold the tension as you hunch your head down between your shoulders. Now relax your shoulders. Drop them back and feel the relaxation spread through your neck, throat, and shoulders. Repeat this procedure, then scan your neck and let go of any tension.

5. Turn your attention to your stomach and back. Breathe in and fill your lungs completely. Now breathe out and continue to breathe out until you pull your stomach inward until you can feel tension near the lower area of your rib cage. Hold this tension for a few seconds and then relax. Repeat this procedure several times, and as you relax, notice the difference between how this area feels when you are tense and when you are relaxed. Now arch your back, without straining. Keep the rest of your body as relaxed as possible. Focus on the tension in your lower back. Now relax. Repeat this entire procedure and let go of any tension that you feel.

6. Tighten your buttocks and thighs. Flex your thighs by

pressing down on your heels as hard as you can. Relax and feel the difference. Now curl your toes downward, making your calves tense. Take notice of the tension and then relax. Repeat this procedure, then let go of any tension you notice.

7. Now feel the heaviness throughout your lower body as you become more relaxed. Relax your feet, ankles, calves, shins, knees, thighs, and buttocks. Now let the relaxation spread to your stomach, lower back, and chest. Scan your shoulders, arms, and hands and notice how these areas feel. Let go of all of the tension in your neck, jaw, and all of your facial muscles. Now, continue to relax and let your mind wander. Continue relaxing for ten to fifteen minutes. If at any time you feel tension in any part of your body, simply tense and then relax the area.

Meditation

Meditation is another constructive way to cope with stress. Meditation has its origins in civilizations of ancient Africa, Japan, and India. In ancient Egypt it was traditionally used for calming and regeneration. This method of getting personally focused is enjoying increased popularity among people of all ages. A lingering aura of mysticism causes some people to shy away from meditation. It seems bound with elaborate rituals, strange language, clothing, and abstract philosophical and spiritual notions. But you don't have to wear exotic clothing, join a religion, go to some remote mountaintop in Tibet, or sit in a lotus position to meditate. Simply sitting quietly and letting your mind wander or looking within can be a simple form of meditation.

There are many forms of meditation. Some meditation techniques use a sound called a mantra as the object of focus during the meditation practice. Other meditation techniques offer little instruction except that the person is to be still and ignore all thoughts during the meditation. Some techniques require an elaborate initiation that is embedded in traditions from Africa, India, or the Far East. Whereas each of the meditation techniques is beneficial, meditating with a mantra is easier and offers the more predictable way of achieving the same quiet mental and physical state from one session to the next. However, no one meditation technique is suitable for all people. Each person must ultimately find the way that appeals to his or her consciousness. All methods require that you let go of worrisome thoughts so that your mind and body can relax. By all means, meditation is one of the most constructive ways to cope with stress and unglue yourself from being a prisoner of your own intellect.

During meditation there is a narrowing of the focus of attention, and yet there is an enlarged sense of being where individuals often feel as if the distinction between self and environment has been eliminated. As the mind settles down to a single focus, the body relaxes, respiration slows, along with the heartbeat. In general, all of the bodily actions slow down during meditation, allowing the individual to relax and reach inner peace and tranquillity. Research has shown that the level of restfulness achieved during meditation is equal to and in some instances greater than the rest attained from sleeping. As a consequence of this deeper rest, the body and mind are more likely to have the energy and stamina that are necessary to support healing and prevent illnesses.

Meditation creates a deep relaxation in a fairly short time. Its beneficial effects are numerous, and it has been shown to relieve anxiety, irritability, and stress-related health problems such as high blood pressure, high cholesterol, chest pains, and even cancer. People who consistently practice meditation show a substantial reduction in the frequency of stress-related symptoms. Some people have found that meditation, used in conjunction with medical treatment, helped them heal more rapidly from serious illness.

Four basic components make up a meditation practice. First, you should be in a quiet place with a minimum of external distractions. Second, it's vital that you choose a comfortable position that you can maintain for about twenty minutes without causing stress to your body. For example, it is important to avoid meditating within two hours after a heavy meal or a physical workout. Third, find an object or mantra (a repeated word or sound) to focus your attention on, and let thoughts simply pass by. It is important to concentrate on one thing only. Learn to eliminate internal and external mental distractions. When distracting thoughts enter your mind, you can let them come and go, returning to your chosen object of focus. The last, and most difficult, component is maintaining a passive attitude, which is characterized by a lack of concern about everything (including how well you are doing). It means freeing yourself of all evaluations and avoiding the usual thinking and planning. In the silence that comes from meditation a man learns how to be detached from how he think things "should" be. With the consistent practice of meditation a man can learn to avoid aggravating situations. This occurs as a result of learning to be attentive to what is happening in the "present moment" rather than continuing to be drawn into arguments about how things should be. By becoming more attentive and detached from how things should be, a man is more capable of finding solutions to the problems at hand.

Many excellent books can help you learn to meditate effectively, but discipline and consistent practice are required. Some people find it easier to learn how to meditate by taking a class from a meditation instructor. A class offers group support and an instructor is available to answer questions that might come up during the training sessions. Most meditation experts recommend twenty-minute sessions before breakfast and before dinner. It is best to do the meditation practice for about a month before you evaluate the results.

The breath-counting meditation described below is used throughout the world and is particularly useful for achieving deep relaxation and reducing stress.

1. Go to a quiet place and assume the posture of your choice. Scan your body for tension and relax. Close your eyes and become aware of your breathing. Breathe through your nose. Inhale, exhale, then pause. Allow yourself to breathe in an easy and natural way.

2. As you inhale, say the word *so* to yourself. Continue to breathe out and say the word *hum* to yourself. Continue breathing in and out, repeating *so* as you inhale and *hum* as you exhale.

3. When thoughts or perceptions threaten to take your attention away from your breathing, let go of them quickly and return to saying *so* as you inhale and *hum* as you exhale. Continue this for twenty minutes.

4. After you complete the exercise, spend a few minutes resting with your eyes closed. Allow yourself to experience your thoughts and feelings. Take time to appreciate the calming effects of the meditation before returning to your activities.

Setting an alarm clock to keep track of time is not a good idea because it will cause too much of a startling response as you come out of your meditation. Most people find that setting an alarm is not necessary because they naturally know when twenty to twenty-five minutes have gone by. The words *so* and *hum* are Sanskrit and are translated to mean "everything that I am is perfect."

Relaxation and Time-Out

In our complex world we often encounter many obstacles that prevent us from fully relaxing and taking time out. It is so easy to blame things in our environment for not having time to relax. However, the real cause of the lack of relaxation resides in the attitudes that some of us have about taking care of ourselves. If we genuinely learn to relax and take care of ourselves in positive and nurturing ways, the benefits will enhance our lives and those of the people who live with us.

Before you continue reading, take a few moments to "relax" and think about how you relax. Do you engage in certain forms of relaxation regularly? What do you consider relaxing? Look over the following list, and decide which forms of relaxation are best for you. Consider the quality of each form of relaxation and how often you use it.

Relaxing Things to Do

- sitting in a quiet place for a few minutes before and/or after work and just letting your mind wander
- listening to music, fully hearing and feeling it (without making it the background of another activity)
- sleeping deeply and restfully
- having a hobby that gives you pleasure
- engaging in sports that calm you
- asking for and receiving a massage
- taking longer than usual in lovemaking
- walking in the woods or on the beach
- closing your eyes and listening to the sounds of nature
- practicing some form of meditation each day
- sitting in a hot tub
- allowing yourself to have fun with friends
- regularly practicing muscle-relaxation exercises

Rest and recreation may be the best everyday methods for controlling stress and anger in your life. If you don't take time out for yourself, you can be assured that nobody else will do this for you. It is vital that you allow some space in your life for doing things that are fun. It is these experiences that tend to buffer the effects of stress and frustration on our health and emotional well-being.

If you are having difficulty figuring out what to do to relax, I strongly suggest that you start off doing nothing. It might sound like an easy thing to do, but this is most difficult, and yet it is the most rewarding thing to do. As we are busy working, being productive, accomplishing, and achieving, we rarely allow ourselves the ultimate luxury of simply doing "nothing." After you have mastered doing nothing, you are ready for the big leagues. I recommend that you spend a little time each day listening to your favorite kind of music. Your stress will automatically decrease. The best way to achieve this is to listen while sitting comfortably with your eyes closed, giving the music your full attention. If you practice this daily, you will enjoy increasing waves of happiness.

Aerobic Exercise

Some years ago a famous stress research study was conducted with a mouse in a cage placed within another cage occupied by a hungry cat. The cages were constructed so that the mouse was in full view of the cat and yet the cat could not reach it. In the study, some mice were provided with a running wheel while the others had nothing to do as they were being terrified by the hungry cat. Just imagine being in a situation where the stress is potentially life threatening (e.g., under the watchful eye of a hungry lion).

At the end of the experiment all of the mice were examined, and surprisingly, the mice that were provided with a running wheel had few symptoms from the prolonged exposure to stress. On the other hand, the mice that faced the hungry cat day after day without any means to relieve stress developed heart problems, ulcers, cancers, and a host of other health problems as a result of their ordeal. The results of this study clearly suggest that vigorous physical activity provides a natural outlet for your body to reduce stress.

Exercise releases special chemicals in your brain called endorphins, which act as natural tranquilizers and have tremendous stress-reducing properties. When you experience stress, exercising can return your body to its normal state of equilibrium, leaving you feeling relaxed and refreshed. Aerobic exercise increases your body's need for oxygen. To meet the increased demand, the heart rate is increased, breathing increases, and small blood vessels relax to allow more oxygen-carrying blood to reach the muscles.

The best advice before starting a strenuous exercise program is to get a physical checkup from your doctor. No matter what form of exercise you choose, start slowly by walking or doing easy calisthenics. Once you have started your exercise program, it is also a good idea to monitor yourself. If you develop heart palpitations, dizziness, or chest pain, see your doctor as soon as possible.

Aerobic exercise provides a good release from stresses, and some evidence suggests that stress is managed better by people who regularly exercise. To benefit from aerobic exercise, your heart must beat at 70 percent of its maximum rate for at least twenty minutes. The exercise must be repeated at least three times per week. By following this procedure you will improve the efficiency of your heart and reduce your risk of developing a number of health problems.

Laughter Can Reduce Angry Reactions and Save Your Life

Throughout history there have been reports that a positive attitude and laughter have improved the health of individuals with chronic illnesses. However, no case has received as much attention as that of Norman Cousins, who recounted his recovery from a crippling disease in his book *Anatomy of an Illness As Perceived by the Patient: Reflections on Healing and Regeneration* (New York: W. W. Norton, 1979). After returning from a tiring European trip, Cousins fell ill with a serious disease of the connective tissue and was told by physicians he had one chance in five hundred for a full recovery.

Cousins carefully analyzed the events leading up to his illness and concluded that it was a result of exhaustion, emotional tension, frustration, and repressed anger. As he thought about the cause of his illness, he began to wonder if positive emotions such as love, hope, confidence, faith, and laughter could reverse the chemical changes that had been produced by stress. After consulting with his doctors, he decided to put his plan into effect. He was also motivated to use laughter as a means of coping with his illness because he was concerned about the toxic effects of the drugs that had been prescribed for him as painkillers.

Armed with a movie projector, a collection of old Marx Brothers films, and *Candid Camera* television shows, Cousins discovered that his idea worked. "Ten minutes of genuine belly laughter had an anesthetic effect and would give me at least two hours of pain-free sleep," he wrote. After a few months Cousins returned to his work as editor of *Saturday Review*, and his illness continued to improve year after year.

After leaving *Saturday Review* to accept a faculty position at the UCLA Medical School, Cousins carried out several laughter experiments with groups of cancer patients, and it was routinely noted that after ten or more minutes of laughter, many of the patients said that their pain had receded—mirroring Cousins's experience. Medical research, much of it sparked by Cousins's efforts, has continued to reveal that pleasurable emotions actually cause the brain to release its own painkilling secretions.

While Cousins's therapeutic use of humor—deliberately induced laughter from watching comic films or reading humorous essays—was solitary, for most of us the experience of laughter is usually a social event. In fact, it's often contagious. While we might laugh aloud while watching a humorous movie alone, we would almost certainly do so if watching the same movie in a room where several other people were laughing.

A well-developed sense of humor that allows us to see the sunny side of things is an undisputed social asset as well as good medicine. Just think for a moment about your own mood after being with a friend with whom you shared some laughter, compared with the way you were feeling after listening to someone's problems for an afternoon. My own mood is depressed and agitated after spending an hour with a chronic complainer who keeps repeating the same mistakes.

Unhappy feelings do have to be expressed, and I am not suggesting that you deny this need, but I urge you to interject touches of humor into your relationships with others as often as you see fit. These bits and pieces of levity can effectively be used to interrupt the chain of events that turn anger into rage and despair by tactfully introducing a more cheerful topic. It may seem contrived at first if it represents a dramatic change in behavior, but if you are determined to begin every conversation with a joke or good news, you can do so. You'll feel better as a consequence, and so will the people you encounter.

For many years the *Reader's Digest* has published a piece called "Laughter Is the Best Medicine." This is a wonderful, continuing source of amusing stories that will help to raise your spirits each time you repeat one. If you can learn to look at the funny side of life, stress will automatically diminish.

12

The Role of Spirituality in Managing Anger

When more than 1 million African-American men gathered on the Mall in Washington, D.C., on October 16, 1995, the event was remarkable not only because of the sheer size of the turnout for Nation of Islam leader Louis Farrakhan's call for a "Day of Atonement and Reconciliation." Just as stunning in the dramatic TV images was the serious demeanor and deportment of the black fathers, sons, grandfathers, from all walks of life. In short, a spiritual aura permeated the march from beginning to end.

March organizers tapped into a spiritual yearning among African-American men that must be harnessed and made a part of our lifestyle, especially if we are to overcome the negative emotions that can lead to angry outbursts.

Part of what was so fascinating about the march was that most of the men were not followers of Farrakhan's or members of the Nation of Islam. Apparently a large portion of the black men assembled at the march were there because of what they felt in their heart about the struggle of black men rather than a desire to become followers of Farrakhan.

This was confirmed by a survey of men conducted by the Wellington Group and Howard University. The results of this survey showed that 88 percent of the respondents at the Million Man March said it was "very important" to attend the march because of concerns they have about improving and affirming moral values in the black community.

The march invigorated the black community and is believed to be the cause of the record number of African-Americans signing up as volunteers in local organizations and churches across the country. Leaders of local organizations and churches continue to report that the spirit of the march is still alive around the country as black men adopt principles of love and peace rather than violence. It is the collective power of black men that could cause a shift in the values of African America that lasts long after the march.

As we prepare to enter the next century, it is important to remind ourselves that we have defined ourselves and others with cynical mistrust. This has probably resulted from our reliance less on societal and cultural norms and more on personal needs, wishes for immediate satisfactions, and desires for material goods. For black men to move forward will require a collective effort and the removal of fears that we have about ourselves. Each of us was born to manifest the glory of God within us, and the pledge of the Million Man March (see the appendix) is one way to let your own light shine forth. As you let your light shine in your life, you will unconsciously give other people permission to do the same. As you are liberated from your anger and fears, your presence automatically liberates others.

Living with Righteous Principles

The ultimate goal should be to handle anger-producing situations in an extremely mature way—in the way that Jesus Christ would have handled the situation. A man must be emotionally and spiritually mature to benefit from using the various techniques described in this book. By all means, a man must feel good about himself and understand his purpose for living. He must genuinely care about his relationships. He must feel secure and loved by God, and he understands that his deepest aim is to please God.

For a man to live life using righteous principles, he must excel in four areas: (1) his relationship with God; (2) his ability to ignore inconsequential issues; (3) his ability to forgive and forget past injustices; (4) his ability to live by loving everyone and everything, despite what was done against him.

Having a Holy Relationship with God

Having a holy relationship with God does not simply mean going to church on Sunday morning, singing in the choir, or memorizing Bible verses. It is personal and yet it is impersonal because through this relationship you can discover that nothing separates you from any other person or object in the entire universe. All of us is as God created us, and all of us were created in the image of God. This realization alone is enough for some people to understand that any angry or hostile actions against another person are in essence an act of violence against one's own self. Incorporating this notion is enough for some men to resolve their anger over hurts inflicted on them.

When the relationship with God is compromised, a man's purpose and reason for living can feel diminished. With his own self-criticism heightened, his tendency to feel jealous and then angry at other men who seem to be living a life of abundance and affluence also grows.

A holy relationship with God is a tremendous aid in giving a man a proper perspective on the issues that he will face throughout his life. Unfortunately, many men and women have fallen into the trap of seeking God only when they encounter a problem that they just can't seem to handle. Many of us get so caught up in acquiring material possessions that our self-image and self-respect are tarnished when we fail to do so. Ironically, we have been conditioned to see only one solution for each problem and thus give up if it fails to provide the answer.

Every man is truly blessed that God provided him with a wonderful and magnificent mind, a brain, whose sole purpose is to seek solutions to whatever questions we bring forth. Unfortunately, many of the questions that we ask ourselves when we encounter a challenge are weak and presuppose negative outcomes. By this I mean that it is often the case that a man, when faced with a problem, will ask God, "Why did this problem have to happen to me?" As discussed in previous sections, these "why" questions presuppose negatives, and whatever answers a man receives won't have much to do with workable solutions to the problem. As a consequence, some men become angry with God because from their standpoint, God has let them down and left them to suffer from the mistreatment they receive from other people. The problem with this is that it is not true.

While God hears all our questions, if a man has not forgiven himself, or if he has put weak, limiting questions out there for God to deal with, weak, limiting solutions will result. Some of us miss hearing the answers to our questions because we get so caught up in trying to figure out why God has not solved the problem.

The bottom line is that each of us has the power to focus on the positives rather than the negatives. If you focus on questions that presuppose negativity, then you are going to get negativity. If you focus on love and peace, then you are going to get love and peace.

What we focus on is determined by our beliefs and how we have learned to evaluate things. All of us make evaluations. But, how do we evaluate things? Well, you already know the secret to how we evaluate what's going on—we ask ourselves questions.

Just as questions help us to seek solutions to problems, they also provide us with the opportunity to get to know who we are. Rather than describing ourselves in great detail, most of us provide other people with as little information as possible about ourselves. This vague way of describing ourselves also applies to how we relate to our own stories about ourselves. Take a few moments and ponder your answers to the question "Who are you?" Really stop reading and think about your answers. Did you really answer the question or did you describe yourself according to what you do?

Regardless of the answers that came across your mind, everything about your answers started first as a thought that was put into motion by the question "Who are you?" Our thoughts are what we are, and if you really examine the truth about yourself, if you really answer the question about who you are, you would never see yourself in the same way twice. You would not see yourself as a body because 98 percent of the atoms in your body were not there a year ago. You would not see yourself as a solid substance because structures such as your skeleton, as solid as it appears, were not there three months ago. Sure, the configuration of the bones remains somewhat constant, but atoms of all kinds pass freely back and forth through the cell walls, and through all of this you obtain a new skeleton every three months. Your skin is new every month. You have a new stomach lining every four days, with the cells actually in contact with the food being renewed every five minutes. Every six weeks you have a new liver. Even the content of carbon, nitrogen, oxygen, in your brain cells is totally different today from a year ago. Even though the rates of change are different from one organ to the next, change is always happening in every organ in the body.

While you might look the same as you looked when you started reading this book, you are now different. So if you are not the solid stuff that makes up the body, then, "Who are you?"

Everything about yourself is consciousness. A consciousness that is so powerful that it manifests itself in such forms as stars, planets, whole galaxies, and human beings. In appearance you are made up of skin, bones, flesh, and cells. Your cells are made up of atoms, and these atoms comprise subatomic particles that are essentially energy in nature. The truth is, at every breath you take in millions of atoms, and every time you exhale, you breathe out millions of atoms. We are literally breathing in the life of all humanity, and we are freely giving life every time we exhale. What's so fascinating about all of this is that an intelligence is always at work, re-creating the divine order that makes us up. This intelligence is *spirit*, it is consciousness. It is alive, it never sleeps, it never runs out of energy, it never gets a cold or gets old; it is eternal and immortal.

In essence each of us is energy that is put in motion by spirit. We exist as one with spirit, living in a universe where everything is connected to everything else, where any action or thought has an effect on everything else in the universe. No boundaries separate us from each other. We are constantly in a divinely intimate relationship with everyone. There is a constant give-and-take relationship between everything and everyone in the universe. As you take in a breath, the universe has to exhale. As you give, so shall you receive.

God only knows what atoms are occupying and contributing to your human appearance at this very moment. Sure, we physically die and move on, but spirit is immortal. Much like water—which is chemically called H_2O and can be frozen as ice, thawed out as liquid (water) again, and then boiled away into invisibility as steam—spirit also changes form.

Having a holy relationship with God means that we have accepted the truth that we are divine spirits. It means that we have truly accepted our inheritance as a son of God that is only limited by our intellect. When a man knows who he is, then there is nothing that he can't do because he understands that everything in this world is consciousness. He also knows that he contacts this consciousness through the power of his questions. It's like the statement "Nature does not reveal its secrets . . . it only responds to a method of questioning" that many philosophers have made. In a similar way, a man's questions provide him with the power to release himself from bondage, from being imprisoned by his own mind.

Being Aware of Your Expectations About God

Most people have some expectation of God, a creator or some higher-order intelligence that orchestrates the actions of the universe, regardless of their belief about the existence of God. Although the expectations are seldom verbalized, they are at work in our daily life. All that you have to do to see this is to observe the emotional reactions of a person who has experienced a loss (e.g., becoming unemployed, going through a divorce, being confronted with a serious illness, etc.). In most cases the reaction is anger, resentment, and depression. Few people assume full responsibility for their actions, and some people even believe that God is responsible for letting them down. As a consequence, they become angry and bitter at God. When we react this way, we are doing so because our expectations were unmet.

The way in which the expectations are expressed is one of the reasons expectations are unmet. Some of us tend to only turn to God for guidance when we are in the midst of a problem. In these cases, the questions that are being put to God tend to deal with the removal of symptoms and not focus on the real cause of the problems. We expect and demand immediate relief from our suffering, and if we don't receive it, then we feel frustrated, disappointed, misunderstood, and angry at God.

I can't argue that it is right or wrong for a person to base his or her relationship with God on a crisis-to-crisis basis. However, as you look around and see those men who are suffering because of losses and disappointment, you will surely see people who have attempted to separate themselves from God. You will see men who have not learned that they create what they focus their attention on, and men who have a consciousness of lack and poverty.

As you reflect on these brothers, you will see them as people who have attempted to place God in the role of a servant whose only role is to come forward in times of trouble. Just imagine for a moment how empty and shallow your relationship with your best fried would be if the only time he or she had anything to do with you was when he or she needed help. For some men this is the way they have attempted to maintain their relationship with God. There is nothing holy about the relationship these men have with God, and yet they expect God to remove all frustrations from their life. Men with these expectations have not learned that it is the time in silence (e.g., in meditation, prayer) with God, in between the problems, that is used to conceive plans that move you toward your goals and away from problems.

Many people, including me, believe that anything is possible, particularly if you have faith in God. But, relationships that are built on selfishness and greed rather than mature faith will only generate negatives. By this I mean that a person will generally receive what he or she gives to others. The one thing that is so difficult in these situations is that the man who has a one-sided relationship with God, where he only expects to receive gifts from God, generally perceives himself as being entitled to his expectations. While it is unrealistic to live as though we have no expectations and rights, we must continually be aware of what our expectations are and evaluate whether they are appropriate.

In many cases men hold themselves so tightly accountable to their expectations and get so caught up in feeling worried, fearful, and angry that they often overlook other possible solutions to problems. These other solutions are often considered inappropriate because they have nothing to do with what the man expected. Some men are so rigidly fixed on having things their way that they don't even perceive solutions when they are actually happening. It's like the man who is shipwrecked on an island and refuses to be rescued by a passing ship, airplane, or a helicopter because he is waiting for God to reach down from heaven and save him.

The more a man honestly questions himself about his expectations, the more honest he will be with God. In being honest with ourselves and God we become more capable of sorting out the appropriate expectations from the inappropriate ones. As a man questions his expectations and rights, he becomes aware of the excessive expectations he is placing on himself and others. In doing so he is beginning to change angry and hurt feelings because, as he changes his expectations and rights, his feelings are automatically changed.

Minimize and Ignore Inconsequential Issues

One of the most important characteristics of an emotionally and spiritually mature man is that he can pass over issues that would normally anger and hurt most men's pride. When a man is not spiritually mature, most personal attacks have major emotional consequences. For the immature man, being attacked means a potential loss of something that is valuable (e.g., rights, personal objects, relationships). This loss implies that there is not enough of whatever is being lost so that everyone can have a piece. One of the consequences that flows along with this mentality of loss is that there needs to be competition and a battle to prevent the loss of the valued possessions.

Loss implies a consciousness of lack, a consciousness built on a foundation where interactions with other people are judged according to whether one's rights are being violated or whether there are potential losses. All problems or conflicts with other people, whatever their source, are perceived as leading to losses. As a consequence, it is nearly impossible for the man to distance himself from the problems or to grow toward that which he desires.

When a man is not mature, any attack is perceived as a major event, and he defends himself. However, as a man feels better about himself, both emotionally and spiritually, there is less need to defend himself because the event is now being perceived as it really is—not important. Issues that were thought to be important because of the perceived losses related to them are passed over. As a man is able to deal more constructively with anger in his life, his self-esteem will improve so that he can minimize inconsequential issues and focus on those things that he desires to achieve.

When a man feels good about himself and genuinely secure and loved by God, he has more to give to all of his relationships. He is more apt to pass over seemingly stressful but unimportant issues, forgive all people for whatever wrongs they have committed, and to genuinely love. He understands and accepts that his deepest aim for living is to please the God within himself. This attitude is developed as a man spends time in silence with himself.

In silence a man comes to understand that the more he becomes detached from things, the more he can fulfill all of his desires. *It is through detachment that a man truly learns to avoid aggravating situations.* Because when a man is detached, he is free to choose how he will respond at every moment rather than responding because of past conditioning. By detaching his actions from egotistic demands, angry and hurt feelings are avoided because there are no expectations guiding the response to challenges other than the complete belief in himself.

To be truly detached means to be comfortable dealing with uncertainty and having the wisdom and faith in yourself to deal with whatever challenges come your way. When a man functions from this level of maturity, he has more excitement and adventure in his life. Rather than being rigidly tied to ideas and plans about exactly how things "should" be, he lives in the present moment and tends to seize opportunities as they arise. This is in sharp contrast to the man who forces solutions on problems and has trouble seizing opportunities because he is so focused on what he should do rather than being fully attentive to what is actually happening.

To minimize inconsequential issues is to realize that the best possible solution to a problem, both for yourself and for the other person, is to simply drop the issue. It means that you hold no grudges and that you have decided to forgive and forget. It means that you have no time for senseless arguments and fights because these will only generate an emotional bondage that will keep you tied to negative attitudes and bad memories.

As a man matures spiritually to understand that there is nothing that he can't have or do, then his consciousness of lack and limitation will be shattered. When a man knows himself as the son of the king of all kings, as being one with the king, and as possessing the same attributes as the king, then concerns about lack are forever wiped away from a man's mind. What really makes this possible is the acceptance of one's real relationship with God, and the more sure a man is about his position with God, the more inconsequential the issues a man faces will be.

Forgiving the Offenders

To be free from anger, despair, illness, and to live a balanced life, a man must truly forgive himself and other people who have caused hurt and anger in the past and present. A man must forgive these injuries and hurts—not for the other person's sake, but for his own. Anger, resentment, condemnation, the desire to "get even" or to see someone punished or hurt, are things that can rot a man's soul. In many instances, not forgiving others for their wrongs keeps a man tightly bonded to many problems that have nothing to do with the original grievances. It's as if there is a cosmic link being maintained when a man holds resentment against another person. The one thing that is difficult for some men to learn is that this link to resentment and anger is broken by forgiving the one person whom they hold accountable for their rage.

Forgiveness means giving up a right or expectation. It is like canceling a debt that someone owes you. If a man does not forgive, he is adamantly holding on to his "rights" and "expectations," and he is continuing to demand payment from the other person, even though it may be impossible for the other person to undo the wrong that was committed. If a man is harboring angry and hurt feelings, he is retaining his right or at least his wish for vengeance. Also, when a man does not forgive others, he is often laboring under a great deal of guilt and low self-esteem probably because he has not fully forgiven himself.

Any man will suffer greatly because of the weight of the grudges that he holds. This tends to be true even if we haven't consciously thought about the issue for a long time. Sometime we bury problems deeply in our subconscious or unconscious, so that we aren't even aware of them, but they still affect us emotionally. Somehow we have the distorted notion that the other person suffers emotionally as we hold grudges against him. However, this is usually not the case. In fact, what usually happens is that the other person doesn't even know about the grudge, and even if he does, he probably doesn't care.

No matter how many steps a man has taken to deal with anger, if he doesn't forgive the person and try to forget about the situation, he is going to suffer from repercussions. Forgiveness is an important type of release and an important type of love. When a man is attached to his anger and resentment, he is in bondage to himself, other people, their attitudes, their behavior, and their way of life. He is also attached to negative attitudes and memories that have limited him to be less than the highest and best in his life experience. To acquire happiness and peace of mind, a man must allow himself to live in the present moment where he is free to choose to do the right thing. To be free means to live life without attachments that are based on fear, insecurity, and a consciousness of lack and limitations.

When a man lives without attachments, he is free to know his true self, which is the source of creativity, wealth, and abundance. A free man, much like the slaves who ran for freedom, is uncertain about the details of the journey, and yet he has faith that everything will be okay. To be free a man has detached himself from the known, which in essence is his past. A past that for many brothers, regardless of whether they admit it or not, is grounded in negativity, stereotypes, helplessness, anger, and a constant struggle to either fit into the mainstream of society or discover a means of rejecting it.

To be free means to live a life of uncertainty where you place all of your belief in yourself to create anything you want and to deal with any challenge that happens to pop up. Without becoming detached from the end products, a man will always be a prisoner of his past, which is the known. When a man is living life without attachments to the past, he discovers the excitement and adventure of living. He realizes that if he becomes rigidly attached to what's going to happen in his life, then he has shut himself off from the real source of his existence, which is to accept himself as the best at whatever he desires to do.

To become the master instead of the slave of circumstances, a man must practice forgiving. Through forgiving, nothing is lost because it opens the way for a freer, more satisfying type of love to develop, where everyone involved is able to give and receive love in a more harmonious way. If through the act of forgiving you feel you have lost something, then you have not truly forgiven the person or you don't intend to forget about the situation.

Here is a forgiveness technique that you can use to help transform your life: Spend half an hour every day mentally forgiving everyone you are out of harmony with or are concerned about. If you have accused yourself of failure or mistakes, forgive yourself, too.

To get started, the first thing that you should do is to make a list of the people, organizations, situations, or experiences in the past or present that you want to forgive. After you have made this list, offer your forgiveness by repeating this verse: *"I fully and freely forgive you. I detach you from all of the past hurts and pains and release you to our higher good with peace, love, and happiness in my heart. All is cleared up between us now and forever."*

After you have offered your forgiveness, it's time for you to ask to be forgiven by people, organizations, situations, or experiences of the past or present that you desire to forgive you. Again make a list and then ask for forgiveness by repeating this verse: *"You fully and freely forgive me. You have detached me from all of the past hurts and pains and released me to my higher good with the peace, love, and happiness in your heart. All is cleared up between us now and forever."*

When a man practices forgiving, he sets others free as he sets himself free. This in essence is one of the most divine forms of giving and loving. The more you love and give to others, the more you will receive. Anything that is of value in a man's life will multiply when it is given with love. To free another man from the bondage of the past and interact with him as if he were yourself, the son of God, is a true blessing. Regardless of the challenges that lie between you and any other person, it is important to remember who you are and who the other person is. I am not a Ph.D., psychologist, or a professor. I am that which I am, and that is a divine manifestation of the spiritual son of the entire universe. In other words, I am the son of God. I am the same as any other man because each of us is an expression of our father's love. I am no different from you.

Live Life by Giving Love to Everyone

Jesus is the example of a man who was willing to love even the people who wronged him, hurt him, betrayed him, deserted him, beat him, and even killed him. Jesus is the brother to all brothers and the example of the man whom all of us need to follow. His ability to give love unconditionally and from the heart is no different from our own. The major difference between us and Jesus is that some of us don't fully believe there is life-sustaining energy in giving love.

Instead of giving, some men have adopted the belief that it is better to receive because their identities are dependent on the objects they possess. These men have failed to understand the life-sustaining principle of giving love. In essence, whatever you want, you must first give it to others. If you want happiness, give happiness to others; if you want appreciation, show others how much you appreciate them; if you want love, learn to give love; if you want material wealth, learn to help others become wealthy. If you want all of the good things in life, then you must learn to pray for everyone to have all of the good things in life.

Every relationship that you are involved in is one of give-and-take. Giving engenders receiving, and receiving engenders giving. For your body to take in the life-supporting oxygen it needs to survive, you must exhale. What goes in must come out; what goes up must come down. In reality, giving is the same thing as receiving because giving and receiving are different aspects of the flow of energy in the universe. To keep the energy coming to us, we have to keep the energy circulating. Like a river, love or money or anything else we desire must keep flowing; otherwise it begins to stagnate, suffocate, and die. If a man holds on to his love and never shares it with others, then love will stop circulating back into his life. Circulating love will keep it alive and a vital part of your life. In reality, the more love you give, the more you will receive, because you will keep the love abundantly flowing in the universe.

To live a life of giving love is one of the most precious principles a man can live by. Embedded in this notion is the idea that all men are forgiven for whatever pain, hurt, or anguish they cause. It is analogous to Luke 23:34, where Jesus was able to pray for those who crucified him. On the cross, he prayed, "Father, forgive them; for they know not what they do." Jesus also tells us in Mathew 5:43–44, "Ye have heard that it hath been said, Thou shall love thy neighbor, and hate thine enemy. But I say unto you, Love your enemies, bless them that curse you, do good to them that hate you, and pray for them which despitefully use you, and persecute you."

Each of us must make every effort to communicate with love and clarity, without bitterness or anger. The challenge is to maintain a loving center no matter how someone else behaves. Regardless of the anger or hurt you are experiencing, you must love one another as God loves you, with a Divine Love. God's love is unconditional and unchanging.

It supports a man regardless of whether he is right or wrong, and regardless of whether he has behaved lovingly or badly. When a man is loving, he feels his inner peace and the harmony he is striving for. He knows that love is the reason he was created. If a man is fortunate, he will discover and live this truth before his time on this earth ends.

Appendix

The Million Man March Pledge

I pledge that from this day forward I will strive to love my brothers as I love myself. I, from this day forward, will strive to improve myself spiritually, morally, mentally, socially, politically, and economically for the benefit of myself, my family, and my people. I pledge that I will strive to build businesses, build houses, build hospitals, build factories, and enter into international trade for the good of myself, my family, and my people.

I pledge that from this day forward I will never raise my hand with a knife or a gun to beat, cut, or shoot any member of my family or any human being, except in self-defense. I pledge from this day forward I will never abuse my wife by striking her, disrespecting her, for she is the mother of my children and the producer of my future. I pledge that from this day forward I will never engage in the abuse of children, little boys or little girls, for sexual gratification. For I will let them grow in peace to be strong men and women for the future of our people.

I will never again use the "B word" to describe any female. But particularly my own Black sister. I pledge from this day forward that I will not poison my body with drugs or that which is destructive to my health and my well-being.

I pledge from this day forward I will support Black newspapers, Black radio, Black television. I will support Black artists who clean up their acts to show respect for themselves and respect for their people and respect for the bearers of the human family. I do all of this, so help me God.

Index

Index

Index